TIMELINES FOR WESTERN CHRISTIANITY

(2) GEOGRAPHIC HISTORY

Companion Volume
(1) CHRONOLOGICAL THEOLOGY

Thomas P. Johnston

Evangelism Unlimited, Inc.
Liberty, Missouri
2016

Copyright © 2008, 2009, 2010, 2011, 2012, 2014, 2015. 2016
by Thomas P. Johnston

All rights reserved

Printed in the United States of America

Thirteen-Digit ISBN: 9780983152699

Published by Evangelism Unlimited, Inc.
Liberty, Missouri

Dewey Decimal Classification: 270
Subject Heading: CHRISTIAN CHURCH HISTORY

Cover artwork by Stephan J. Albin

INTRODUCTION TO COMBINED VOLUMES

The complexity of writing on these subjects is related to seeking a balance between being wise as a serpent and gentle as a dove (Matt 10:16). Christ, when He walked on earth, was able to bridge these difficult approaches: "For the Law was given through Moses; grace and truth were realized through Jesus Christ" (John 1:17). This difficult balance is the challenge of this subject.

Furthermore, there are two very different purposes or reasons for selecting such a topic. One reason might be to convince a Catholic audience to turn toward Evangelical Christianity. This writing does not share this purpose. The second reason is to train Evangelicals and Baptists the historical points of deviation between the Church of Rome and Historic Evangelicalism. This second purpose is the goal of the present work. The first reason relates to evangelizing, while the second focuses on training believers in the faith.

Likewise, evangelism relates to the beginning of the Great Commission in Matthew, "Go, win disciples of all nations." It must be done with humility and gentleness, focusing on the gospel of salvation. Training believers in the faith relates to discipleship or the second part of Matthew's Great Commission, "teaching them to observe all that I have commanded you" (Matt 28:19-20). Training persons about Western Christianity or Roman Catholicism within the context of a Baptist institution ascribes to the latter purpose. The content and issues addressed in these books are neither intended as an evangelism tool nor as a conciliatory tool. Rather, these historical notes are intended to inform Baptists about points of differentiation between the *Baptist Faith and Message* (2000)* and the theology of the Church of Rome as described in their writings.

The acute reader will notice that primary writings have often been cited, and secondary sources have been referenced as such. Therefore it is left up to the reader to decide if the sources are trustworthy or if the concept being expressed is cogently argued. The purpose for these pages is to examine what may often be censored in select Histories of the Churches.

While grace is needed in the communication of any topic, it must not be exercized at the expense of truth. Both need to be maintained simultaneously. Perhaps it has been the case that mainstream U.S. histories of the churches in the past 50-100 years have tended to gloss over certain glaring aspects of the history of Christianity, even those that led to the forming of the United States as a nation. Furthermore, a misunderstanding of the history of the churches has tended towards theological naiveté and broadness of mind, and has often resulted in freethinking in the area of denominational and theological distinctives.

At stake is actually the Gospel itself, freedom to verbalize the Gospel, and even freedom of conscience.

Whereas Volume 1 focuses primarily on the larger chart, "Chronological Theology," it also includes eleven charts that have been in process for quite some time. Volume 2, "Chronological History," focuses on the years 1002 to 1572. It highlights evangelism and martyrdom, while providing a contextual timeline of simultaneous happenings within some of the language groups of Europe, as well as a pertinent primary source material. For further insights, I would guide the reader to the introductory comments to these other sections.

Maranatha. Even so come Lord Jesus!

Thomas P. Johnston, Ph.D.
March 2016.

*By the way, this author does not claim any authority to speak on behalf of Baptists or any Baptist group. The opinions here expressed a personally derived through study.

INTRODUCTION TO PART TWO

Teaching church history without looking at evangelism, and the response to evangelism, is like writing a history of the birth rate in the United States in the latter 20th Century and ignoring the impact of Roe versus Wade, and the ensuing millions of abortions. However, much like this analogy suggests, one's perspective on the issue does matter. Likewise, for the history of the churches, it matters how one feels about what is the true church and how one becomes a member of this church. Does salvation come through hearing the Scriptures, and particularly those related to redemption, and then receiving them by faith alone and through grace alone? If the esteemed reader accepts the concept of being "born again" in his theology, then the preaching of the same, and the ensuing martyrdoms of the 2nd Millennium will be important to his understanding of the history of the churches. If, however, a church, historian, professor, or reader does not consider the "new birth" relevant to the study of church history, then martyrdom and inquisition will likely be perceived as unimportant, irrelevant, superfluous, obscurantist, or even the "fallacy of the lonely fact."

A brief word about forgiving and forgetting the past. Some may consider the content of these pages objectionable because they: (1) unnecessarily dig up hurts from the past; (2) comprise of a "fishing expedition" exposing a sea of tertiary issues in the history of the churches, and/or (3) instill second-generation bitterness to unlearned readers. However, in their book on forgiveness John Nieder and Thomas Thompson made an important point:

> "The main reason some of us mistake forgiveness for excusing a wrongdoing is that we have the warped idea about what accompanies true forgiveness. We have the mistaken notion that when we forgive someone we must never mention what happened again, or we should act like it never happened" (*Forgive and Love Again* [Eugene, OR: Harvest House, 1991], 41).

In the history of the churches, as in the development of the U.S. constitution and the modern history of Western governments, the totalitarian control that led to a considerable amount of martyrs was not a secondary issue in history, but front and center to the Napoleonic Revolution and the Enlightenment era. Note for example John Locke's "A Letter Concerning Toleration" (1689) which promoted the need for religious toleration, and the subsequent impact of Locke's letter on the U.S. Constitution's terminology "life, liberty, and property [later: happiness]." The famous quote of Edmund Burke (1729-1797) is appropriate here: "Those who don't know history are destined to repeat it."

The reasons for beginning the compiling this chart are numerous: (1) to seek out New Testament evangelism prior to the "First Great Awakening" era (18th Century); (2) to open up the history of evangelism in the Medieval period; (3) to provide an understanding for why the Reformation was needed; (4) to provide a backdrop for the formation of the United States, and especially the first Ten Amendments of the U.S. Constitution; and (5) to provide an alternative source for the history of the churches.

May these charts provide an alternative view of the history of the churches, as well as a glimpse into the hidden world of evangelism and persecution during the later Medieval and early Reformation eras.

Thomas P. Johnston, Ph.D.
April 2016.

TIMELINES FOR WESTERN CHRISTIANITY

(2) GEOGRAPHIC HISTORY

Geographic History

Date	Germany-Austria-Scandinavia	Switzerland	France-Alsace	British Isles	Italy, Spain, Low Lands
993			**[Pope] John XV** wrote *Cum conventus esset*, to the bishops and abbots in France and Germany: "From a common opinion we have decreed that his memory—that of the Holy Saint Ulrich—be venerated with pious affection and faithful devotion: for when we venerate and venerate the relics of the martyrs and their confessors, so it is him for whom they are martyred and [unto whom] they confess that we venerate; we honor the servants, so		
993			that their honor overflows to the Lord who said: 'Who receives you, receives me' [Matt 10:40], and therefore we, who have no confidence in our own righteousness, by their prayers and their merits, always find help before our very merciful Father" (DS 675)		
1002			"First executions of Cathars in France, at Orléans and Toulouse. **Ten canons of the Collegiate Church of the Holy Cross sent to the stake.**"o		A teacher named **Vilgard** in Ravenne, Italy, is condemned by his bishop for having taught
1002			"In Champagne, a peasant named **Leutard** left his wife 'for the Gospel precept' to give himself entirely to chastity and to preaching, began		"much contrary to the holy faith" (Raoul Glaber)g
1002			either to destroy crucifixes and other holy images, either to hold that it was unnecessary to tithe: all founded upon passages of the holy Scriptures, and in particular the New Testament.		
1002			Being called in by the bishop, he was covered with ridicule because of His ignorance and they made him out as a fool. … the poor **Leutard** … killed himself by throwing himself into a well (Raoul Glaber)g		Birth of **Lanfranc** in Pavia, Lombardy [Italy], who became **Archbishop of Canterbury** under **William the Conqueror** of Englands3
1005			Cathars began to appear in the area of Limoges (Limousin)		
1012	**Antipope Gregory** sought favor of German court, but did not receive it (1012)				**Antipope Gregory** (1012)
1016				At the death of **King Egelred**, Civil War broke out between his son, **Edmund**, and **Canute**, the Dane ,son of **Swanus**f	
1017				At the death of **Edmund**, **Canute the Dane** became King of Englandf	

1018	In Aquitaine (Guyenne), a gathering of people to deny the baptism [of infants] and the cross, and to abstain from certain elements, led by two canons (Adémar de Chabannes)g					
1018						
1020		Death of the **Abbot Ælfric**, from Eynsham, Oxfordshire, who translated seven books of the Old Testament into Old Englishw2				
1022						
1022	**Fourteen Persons**, the chief of whom was called the "arch-heretic" Stephen, were burned alive in Orleans in 1022b; they were burned because they "had opinions different than those of the Church," notably that of spirit baptism by the laying on of handsg					
1025	**Synod of Arras** called by the **Bishop Gerard** to consider two groups of "heretics" from Arras and Liège: the Arras group were illiterate disciples of					A certain **Ramihed**n was preaching in the region of Cambray and Arras. He was seized by **Archbishop**
1025	an Italian named **Gandolfo**; they accepted only the New Testament and especially the epistles of Paul, the nutshell of their teaching was: "leave					**Gerhard II**, tried, and found innocent, until he refused to take the Eucharist from his captors in testimony of his innocence.
1025	the world, recklessly driven by lust, gather what is needed with one's own hands, not to hurt or kill anyone, and to be charitable toward all companions					**Ramihed** apparently said that he could not accept the Eucharist from them, being as they were all guilty of simony.
1025	in the faith"; their views included the full application of Gospel principles for salvation, devaluing every form of liturgy and ecclesiastical power, the					He was then placed in a cabin, and a torch was applied to the building, and he was consumed.n
1025	refusal to baptize infants who are incapable of understanding, and the condemnation of church buildings, the cross, every					

COLOR GUIDE: **YELLOW**=Roman Catholic areas; **TAN**=Bad years for Anabaptists; **GOLD**=Important events for Catholicism; **ORANGE**=Catholics "martyred"; **RED**=Evangelicals martyred; **GRAY**=Other martyred; Disclaimer: some dates may vary **PINK**=Marriage issues; **PURPLE**=Crusades or massacres; **TURQUOISE**=Martyrology info; **BLUE**=Part Protestant areas; **AQUA**=U.S. Const and Rel.; **LT GREEN**=Disputed areas; **LIME**=Bible issues; **GREEN**=Major dates. (Page 3)

Geographic History

Date	Germany-Austria-Scandinavia	Switzerland	France-Alsace	British Isles	Italy, Spain, Low Lands
1025			ceremony and rite, with the exception of the veneration of the apostles and martyrs.g		
1028					**Archbishop of Milan, Ariberto d'Intimiano**, found heretics at the chateau of Montfort in Piemont; he submitted their
1028					leader, Gerard, to prolonged interrogation: they had two levels of leadership: a pontifex and maiores, the latter charged
1028					to preach and restore virginity to those who lost it; they lived in community, had no sexual relations, did not eat meat, were
1028					hostile to the cross (Landolfo Seniore)g
1028					**Synod of Charroux** condemned Heretics
1032					**Benedict IX** became Pope for the first time (1032-1045)
1039			**Lanfranc** moved to Normandy [France] to found a school at Avranches3		
1040			**Berengarius of Tours** became director of the Cathedral school in Tours, it was not long until he denied the doctrine of transubstantiation as		
1040			taught by **Paschasius Radbertus** (~800-851), considering transubstatiation to be *inepta recordia vulgjs*3		

1044			Berengarius became more vocal on his beliefs against transubstantiation, leading to his disagreements with various scholars, and eventual condemnation and martyrdoms3			Antipope Sylvester III (1044)
1044						
1045						**4 Popes—5 Reigns—3 Years** Sylvester III Pope (1045)
1045			The **Rustici** were heretics found in Châlons-sur-Marne, Liège, and Goslar (↙), considered **pre-Cathars**; based on a letter of Roger II, Bishop of Châlons to Wason of Liège, they refused marriage, prohibited eating meat, and condemned the slaughter of animals, gave the Holy Spirit by the laying on of hands, etc.9			Benedict IX became Pope a second time? (1045)
1045						Gregory VI Pope (1045-1046)
1046		Lanfranc began dialoguing against Berengarius of Tours [France] on the doctrine of transubstantiation				Clement II Pope (1046-1047)
1046						[Clement II was presumably poisoned by **Brazutus**, who was said to have poisoned six popes within 13 years]f
1047	Foxe reported that there were up to three popes reigning at the same time: **Benedict IX, Sylvester III, and Gregory VI**f					Benedict IX became Pope for the third time? (1047-1048). Appears to have been poisoned
1048						Damasus II Pope (1048), poisoned after 23 days in officef
1149		Berengarius wrote **Lanfranc** on transubstantiation, which letter was used to accuse him of heresy in Rome ↗				Leo IX Pope (1049-1054), **Hildebrand of Sovona**, later Gregory VII, was Leo IX's secretary

COLOR GUIDE: YELLOW=Roman Catholic areas; TAN=Bad years for Anabaptists; GOLD=Important events for Catholicism; ORANGE=Catholics "martyred"; RED=Evangelicals martyred; GRAY=Other martyred; Disclaimer: some dates may vary PINK=Marriage issues; PURPLE= Crusades or massacres; TURQUOISE=Martyrology info; BLUE=Part Protestant areas; AQUA=U.S. Const and Rel.; LT GREEN=Disputed areas; LIME=Bible issues; GREEN=Major dates. (Page 5)

Geographic History

Date	Germany-Austria-Scandinavia	Switzerland	France-Alsace	British Isles	Italy, Spain, Low Lands
1049			**Council of Rheims** discussed the appearance of "new heresy" in France[o]		
1050					Without a hearing and without a summons, **Berengarius of Tours** was charged with
1050					"heresy" on the matter of transubstantiation at the Easter Synod in Rome
1050	It seems that the political authority of the Church of Rome, granted by **Valentinian III** in 445, was applied in the arrest of **Berengarius**		When **Berengarius** requested of **King Henry I** of France to travel to Vercelli, he was arrested by the King, and escaped because of some friends[s3]		**Berengarius** was again charged with heresy by the **Synod of Vercelli** (on Sept 1)
1051			**Council of Metz** decreed that priests should be utterly excluded and debarred from marriage"[f]		About 1050 the **Knights Hospitaller** were founded, currently called the **Sovereign Military Order of Malta**
1052	**Heretics** hanged in Goslar, Germany[ob] because they refused to kill a chicken[g]				An anti-clerical movement, called **Pataria** (later the **Patarini**), emerged from Milan,
1052					which was against simony and priestly concubines (from which movement came "Pope" **Alexander II** [1061-1073]
1052					among others); it had Donatist tendencies, and was influential in the **Gregorian Reform** later being considered heretical due t
1052					o its schismatic nature toward Rome[g]
1054 Great Schism			**Papal Legate Hildebrand**, later to become **Pope Gregory VII**, held a synod in Tours and was satisfied with the answers of **Berengarius**[s3]		The "**Great Schism**" **Pope** and **Archbishop of Constantinople** mutually excommunicated one another

Date									
1054 Great Schism									Leo IX showed humanity to those involved in 3 of 4
1054 Great Schism									positions of homosexual acts; threatened any opposers with loss of office (DS 688)
1058									Antipope Benedict X (1058-1060) elected by the Roman nobilityS3; **Nicholas II** by the Cardinals
1059					Lanfranc became Abbot of St. Stephen's in Caen, Normandy, France, having also attracted the attention of **William the Conqueror** who sought his adviceS3				→ The Cardinal Humbert de Silva Candida edited a statement of faith at the Council of Rome, in which Berengarius of Tours was to affirm his belief in transubstantiation (DS 690), which he did.
1059					Synod of Toulouse condemned Heretics				→
1059									→
1060									Antipope Benedict X gave up his claims to the papacy, and later was imprisoned by Hildebrand; he died in 1073 or 1080
1060					Lombards with Emperor Henry IV → ←**Pope Nicolas II** with Rome				
1061 Height of Investiture Contr.	Antipope Honorius II (1061-1072), Bishop Caladus of Parma, elected in Basel, Switzerland (by the Lombards)				Another Ecclesial War				Nicholas II died; Bishop Anselm of Lucca was chosen by Hildebrand and the Cardinals as **Alexander II**S3 It appears that Alexander II was kept under custody by Hildebrand for his 11 years as popef
1061									

COLOR GUIDE: YELLOW=Roman Catholic areas; TAN=Bad years for Anabaptists; GOLD=Important events for Catholicism; ORANGE=Catholics "martyred"; RED=Evangelicals martyred; GRAY=Other martyred; Disclaimer: some dates may vary PINK=Marriage issues; PURPLE=Crusades or massacres; TURQUOISE=Martyrology info; BLUE=Part Protestant areas; AQUA=U.S. Const and Rel.; LT GREEN=Disputed areas; LIME=Bible issues; GREEN=Major dates. (Page 7)

Thomas P. Johnston — Geographic History — Page 8

Date	Germany-Austria-Scandinavia	Switzerland		France-Alsace	British Isles	Italy, Spain, Low Lands
1066 Crusade against English Church			→	At the backing of Rome, and under the advice of **Lanfranc**, the French Norman, **William the Conqueror**, left the shores of Normandy, France, to conquer beleaguered England, weak and weary from the Danish Wars, to	The French Norman, **William the Conqueror**, conquered England; the church was centralized under **Archbishop Lanfranc**, where he applied the Continental "Reforming measures", among other things, there was curbed use of the Old English	
1066			→	be the "savior of the needy church in England"s3 ↑	Bibles, and restoring the use of Latin Biblesw2	
1067	**Henry**b beheaded in Sweden, and **Alfuard**b slain in Norway		→		At first, **Lanfranc** "refused the Archbishopric of Rouen," only to later become **Archbishop of Canterbury**	
1070			→		As 34th **Archbishop of Canterbury**, **Lanfranc** crushed the Anglo-Saxon desire for religious independence from Rome: "with diplomatic skill he	
1070			→		gradually displaced all the native prelates and abbots; **Lanfranc**'s chief work was on the doctrine of transubstantiation (*Liber de corpore et	
1070			→		*sanguine Domini*); he was loyally obedient to **Hildebrand, Pope Gregory VII**s3	
1072		Antipope Honorius II died in Parma [Italy]				
1073	Absolution of fealty [i.e. no need to honor an oath] to heretical princes or to any excommunicated person; for this reason, the Pope had precedent to rescind his vow of safe passage to John Hus in 1415				**Pope Gregory VII** (1073-1085), formerly **Hildebrand of Sovona**, published, *Extra, De Haereticis, cap. Ad abolendam*, "Holding to the institutions of our holy predecessors, we, by our apostolic authority, absolve from their oath those who through loyalty or through the sacred bond of an oath owe allegiance to excommunicated persons: and we absolutely forbid them to continue their allegiance to such persons, until these shall have made amends" (quoted in Aquinas, *Summa*, SS, Q[12], A[2])	
1073	**Gregory VII, "Dictatus Papae" excerpts** 1. That the Roman church was founded by God alone. (from Pullan, except as noted) 2. That only the Bishop of Rome is by law called universal.					

1075	3. That he alone may depose or reinstate bishops. 5. That the Pope may depose persons in their absence. 9. That the Pope is the only man whose feet shall be kissed by all princes. 10. That his name alone shall be spoken in the churches. (Henderson)					In 1075, **Gregory VII** published "Dictatus Papae," Canon 27 reads: "That he may absolve subjects from their fealty to wicked men."
1076	11. That this is the only name in the world. (Henderson) 12. That it may be permitted to him to depose emperors. 17. That no chapter or book may be recognized as canonical without his authority.				**Archbishop of Canterbury Lanfranc** began enforcing celibacy for the higher clergy and later for all clergy, at the **Synod of Winchester**s3	
1077	18. That no sentence of his may be retracted by anyone, and he is the only one who can retract it. 19. That he must not be judged by anyone. 22. That the Roman church has never erred; nor will it err to all eternity, the Scripture bearing witness. (Henderson) 27. That he may absolve subjects from their fealty to wicked men. (Henderson)					**Cathar heretic** condemned and burned alive in Cambraio
1079			**Synod of Versailles** condemned Heretics		**Berengarius of Tours** made to affirm transubstantiation at a **Council in Rome** under Pope **Gregory VII** (DS 700); two scenarios present themselves for the end of his life:	
1079			Condemned heretic **Bruno**,b bishop of Angiers, disappeared from history		(1) he retired to the Island of St. Cosme for the rest of his life;s3 (2) he was burned at the stake in 1088b	
1080	Antipope Clement III had friendly relations with the German court of **Emperor Henry IV**					**Antipope Guibert** (aka. **Clement III**) (1080-1100)
1084	→	*Chartreux* monastic order [English: Cartusian] founded by [St] Bruno near Grenoble				
1085	→		**Berengarius**b, deacon of Bruno, martyred on the day of Epiphany		**William the Conqueror** and his counselors conceived of a new taxation, it led to what was called the "**Doomsday Book**"; its two books were completed in 1086; "the judgments of the Doomsday assessors was final… there was no appeal. The text was written in Latin… highly abbreviated"	Death of **Pope Gregory VII** (1073-1085), who "canonized" the doctrine of transubstantiation
1088	→ **Pope Urban II** accepted or reconfirmed the invalid ordination of Dai[m]bert by the schismatic					**Pope Urban II** became Pope (1088-1099); he was known for organizing preaching missions for the crusades, [falsely] called "preaching the Cross"
1088	→ **Archbishop Wezelo of Mayence** (DS 701)					

COLOR GUIDE YELLOW=Roman Catholic areas; TAN=Bad years for Anabaptists; GOLD=Important events for Catholicism; ORANGE=Catholics "martyred"; RED=Evangelicals martyred; GRAY=Other martyred;   Disclaimer: some dates may vary
PINK=Marriage issues; PURPLE= Crusades or massacres; TURQUOISE=Martyrology info; BLUE=Part Protestant areas; AQUA=U.S. Const and Rel.; LT GREEN=Disputed areas; LIME=Bible issues; GREEN=Major dates.   (Page 9)

Geographic History

Date	Germany-Austria-Scandinavia	Switzerland	France-Alsace	British Isles	Italy, Spain, Low Lands
1089	→			Death of **Lanfranc, Archbishop of Canterbury**s3	
1091	→ Pope Urban II invalidated the schismatic ordination of **Poppo of Treves by Archbishop Egelbert of Treves**, who was of the party of **Antipope Clement III** and **Emperor Henry IV**, saying that the ordination was based on simony (DS 702)			So far there were 5 acknowledged regional "antipopes" since 1002 (as listed on the ewtn.com list of Popes) and the "Great Schism" (of 1054): • Was this not a major problem which **Urban II** had to address? • Was the problem of "antipopes" merely ecclesiastical authority or local rule (e.g. the autonomy of the local church), was it also theological (e.g. transubstantiation), or was it practical (e.g. forced celibacy)?	
1091	→				
1095	→		Hildebert became Bishop of Le Mans	• Differences in church government often signal differences in theology (consider, for example, the historic theological differences between the Episcopal Church and the Congregational Church).	
1098	→		**Benedictine** monastery founded in **Citeaux** (Burgundy) by Robert Molèsme		
1099	→				Jerusalem was taken by **Roman Catholic Crusaders**; The **Knights Hospitaller** became a military order
1100	Death of **Antipope Clement III**		**Peter the Lombard** born, future Archbishop of Paris, and author of the *Four Books of Sentences* (or 1105-1110) s3		Possible birth year of **Arnald of Brescia** [Italy], martyred founder of the **Poor Lombards**
1101			**Henry of Lausanne** [aka. the Italian] (of the Benedictine monastery at Cluny), Was expelled from the "Church", spent some time in Lausanne, Switzg ↓		Pope sent **Raoul Ardent** to Agenais and Toulousain areas to deal with Heretics
1102		**Henry** the Monk, spent some time in Lausanne, where his		**Pope Paschal II**, Vow of obedience to the Church: "I anathematize every heresy and especially those which disturb the present state of the Church, who teach and who affirm that one must neglect an anathema and distain the laws of the Church. And I promise obedience to the Pontif	
1102		preaching fomented discord against Rome; later at some		of the Apostolic Seat, the lord Paschal and his successors, taking as testifiers Christ and the Church, affirming what is affirmed by the Holy and universal Church, and condemning what she condemns" (DS 704)	

1105	Four persons, rejecting infant baptism and transubstantiation banished from the Bishopric of Treves[b]			unknown time, Henry returned to Southern France to preach the Gospel[g] →	Peter de Bruys (Bruys, France), former monk, began preaching in SE France (Dauphiné); his followers were known as Petrobusians	The Monk Henry returned to Southern France, as a "hermit" (solo) monk, preaching Justification by faith alone →			Antipope Sylvester IV (1105-1111) ruled for German kings from Tivoli and Osimo
1106	Disciples of Berengarius expelled from the Bishopric of Treves, they went on to the Lowlands, Liege and Antwerp, evangelizing as they went[b]							At the Council of Guastalla, Pope Paschal II made allowances for the reception of heretical Bishops (esp. from the Teutonic Empire) into the Church of Rome, as long as they did not act as intruders (DS 705)		→
1111					The monk Peter expulsed from his church, began	→				Death of Antipope Sylvester IV
1112					itinerant preaching, basing his teaching primarily on the	→				
1113					Gospels; Henry became the focal point of antithetical	Meanwhile, [St] Bernard took his vows at Citeaux				Pope Paschal II, on 15 Feb 1113, approved the Jerusalem Hospital as an Order (later the Order of Malta), under the
1114	The beliefs of the unlettered Heretics of Soissons [→] are described as typical Donatist issues: disagreed with "the Eucharist, of religious orders, [of the sacraments of] the baptism of infants, cemeteries, marriage, and the				writings, such as Peter the Venerable's Tractatus adversus Petrobusianos (see below in 1135) and Peter	"Several heretics[o] snatched from prison by a mob in Soissons				aegis of the Holy See Pope sent Robert de Arbrissel to Southern France do deal with so-called Heretics
1114	eating of meats. In addition, they professed a rudimentary form of Docetism, for which [the inquisitors] sought decisive proof of the Manichean beliefs; but – as is rightly noted by Manselli – the learned term phatasma,				Abelard's Introductio in Theologiam[g]	(northeast of Paris) and burnt[o]				
1115	placed in the mouth of [these] unlettered [men] to designate the human nature of Christ, must surely be attributed to the Benedictine author Guilbert of Nogent."[g]					Arnald studied under Irnerius in Bologne and		24 July 1115: death of Countess Mathilda. "Her enormous wealth she bequeathed to the papal chair. It formed part of the so-called 'Patrimonium	→	→
1115					→	Abelard in Paris, becoming a regular canon,		Petri'"s3 These enormous land holdings included Tuscany, parts of Lombardy, Mantua, Parma, Reggio, Piacenza,	→	In Anvers [Antwerp], Tanquelin[g] opposed a priest living with a concubine, leading a revolt against him; he was killed in 1115; his beliefs were said to be openly Donatist, preached against the tithe, the ineffectiveness of the
1115					→	returning to Brescia →		Ferrara, Umbria, Spoleto, etc. Furthermore, the reception of these land holdings necessitated the formation of "Canon Law"—the rules by which a	→	sacraments, rejection of church buildings; and according to an untrustworthy source, believed he was the Son of God, the

COLOR GUIDE: YELLOW=Roman Catholic areas; TAN=Bad years for Anabaptists; GOLD=Important events for Catholicism; ORANGE=Catholics "martyred"; RED=Evangelicals martyred; GRAY=Other martyred; Disclaimer: some dates may vary PINK=Marriage issues; PURPLE=Crusades or massacres; TURQUOISE=Martyrology info; BLUE=Part Protestant areas; AQUA=U.S. Const and Rel.; LT GREEN=Disputed areas; LIME=Bible issues; GREEN=Major dates. (Page 11)

Thomas P. Johnston
Geographic History
Page 12

Date	Germany-Austria-Scandinavia	Switzerland	France-Alsace	British Isles	Italy, Spain, Low Lands
1115			→	Catholic society ought to be administered.	spouse of the Virgin and filled with the Holy Spirit9
1115			→	Of **Gregory VII** (1073-1085), or **Hildebrand**, a contemporary of **Countess Mathilda**, it is said: "He exerted radical influence on the canon	**Arnald** returned to Brescia, his birthplace, and was a canon in the Catholic Church
1116	**Summary of the Beliefs of Henry of Lausanne** (from Gonnet and Molnar) "**Henry**, founding himself on passages of the New Testament, affirmed that he had received the order to preach directly from Christ, and to all who		←←→→ **The Monk Henry** preached at Le Mans, France, during the absence	law in its formative period, both by virtue of his own legislative activity and also through the digests that were compiled at his instigation"s3	Over time, **Norbert** was able to return the **Antwerp diocese** to Rome by following reforms
1116	dared to contest him he responded with a phrase that would later become celebrated in the mouth of **Vaudès** [Waldo] also, being, 'One must obey God rather than man.' He added that baptism ought to be refused to children, incapable of believing according to Mark 16:16; that original sin is		→ of its **Bishop Hildebert** of Lavardin; **Henry** led a revival in Le		associated with the order he founded, the Premonstrants9
1116	not transferable according to Galatians 6:5; and also, that the spiritual ["charismatic"] powers of the clergy are null and that the sacraments of the clergy are without value especially because they are administered by unworthy priests. In particular, marriage is not a sacrament but rather a		→ Mans, wherein prostitution was abolished; **Henry** retired when		
1116	judicial act, which consists of the free consent of the conjoined, which may be thereupon released in case of fornication. Finally, for **Henry** as already previously of **Peter de Bruis**, the Church exists only there were the faithful live according to the evangelical precepts by confessing their sins to one		→ **Bishop Hildebert** returned, who "humbled him" in a debate and ordered		
1116	another mutually: by consequence the ecclesiastical hierarchies, rendered useless by the love of riches, are superfluous with the same titles as cultural powers, [and are] places where pomp reigns more than prayer. It is necessary to add to all these the rejection of suffrages [or indulgences] for		→ him out of his diocese; thereupon he itinerated, a meeting with **Peter**		
1116	the dead as completely useless, for **Henry**, contrary to **Peter de Bruis**, believed that the person who dies is immediately saved or damned."g		→ **de Bruis** [←] is surmised, which may have accentuated		
1118			→ Henry's polemic against the Rome, since their critique was almost		**Antipope Burdin (Gregory VIII)** French Bishop of Coimbra (1098) and Metropolitan of
1118			→ identical, as can be noted belowg →		Braga (1111); excommunicated 1118; died 1137

Date					
1119				Council of Toulouse called, Canon 3 condemned those "who under false pretense of religion deny the sacrament of the body and blood of	
1119				Christ, the baptism of childen, the priesthood and all the other ecclesiastical orders, as well as the vows of legitimate marriage"g	
1123		Some issues in **First Lateran Council**: (Canon 2) Centralized power of Bishops to excommunicate heretics; (3, 5) disallowed anyone other than approved Roman Catholic bishops from electing a bishop; (4) only		Bishop **Hildebert** complained that his diocese had been infected by	**First Lateran Council**, focused authority in the church to duly authorized bishops approved by Rome only; removal of any lay
1123		approved clergy could receive prebends (or stipends) for the care of souls [thereby choking non-Roman priests from financial support]; (7, 21) forbade marriage of clergy; (8) lay persons were disallowed from any ecclesiastical business [contra congregational rule]; (10) granted remission of sins for		**Henricians**, who in 1209 were relabeled "**Albigensian**"	authority in the church; forced celibacy, including the voiding of existing marriage contracts
1126		participation in crusades; (12) removed all lay control of church/involvement in church government [contra congregational rule]; (16) no public worship allowed [e.g. no street preaching]; monks disallowed from visiting the sick, related to last rites [as the Albigenses were known to do]; (18) none but		(1209) by Roman Catholic holy crusade preacher **Jacques de Vitry**	
1126		bishops were to receive tithes [i.e. seeking to silence lay preachers or heretical preachers]		→	
1126				→	
1126				→	
1130		**Historiographic Problem Exemplified in Henry of Lausanne** Gonnet and Molnar wrote that the **Monk William** who debated **Henry of Lausanne** stated that he knew of a book containing his doctrines, as also		The **Monk William** told **Henry of Lausanne** in a debate: "You too are a leper, scarred by heresy, excluded	**Antipope Anacletus II** (1130-1138); came from a power struggle between two competing
1130		wrote **Peter the Venerable**.g However, all the writings of **Henry** have "dissapeared," with none remaining to the present day (as many others have been destroyed). Thus the accused cannot speak for himself. The only writings that remain are those of his antagonists, by whose hands he		from communion by a priest, according to the law, bare-headed [he had not kept his tonsure], with ragged clothing [he was not wearing his	Popes in Rome, that ended with his death in 1138

COLOR GUIDE: YELLOW=Roman Catholic areas; TAN=Bad years for Anabaptists; GOLD=Important events for Catholicism; ORANGE=Catholics "martyred"; RED=Evangelicals martyred; GRAY=Other martyred; Disclaimer: some dates may vary PINK=Marriage issues; PURPLE= Crusades or massacres; TURQUOISE=Martyrology info; BLUE=Part Protestant areas; AQUA=U.S. Const and Rel.; LT GREEN=Disputed areas; LIME=Bible issues; GREEN=Major dates. (Page 13)

Geographic History

Date	Germany-Austria-Scandinavia	Switzerland	France-Alsace	British Isles	Italy, Spain, Low Lands
1130	was imprisoned and died. What remains is only one side of the story (Prov 18:17), with an argument from silence for any other views.		monastic robes], your body covered by an infected and filthy garment. It befits you to shout unceasingly that you are a leper, a heretic and unclean, and		→
1130			you must live alone outside the camp, that is outside the church"m5		→
1134			Henry of Lausanne arrested and brought before Pope Innocent II at Council of Pisa, forced to abjure his position and imprisoned	Peter the Venerable (of Cluny) wrote a treatise against the teaching of the disciples of Henry of Lausanne, with their five heretical propositions:	→
1134			→	1. Refusal to baptize infants, under the pretext that it is faith that saves and that a young infant could not have sufficient conscience to believe. 2. Rejection of holy places; the Church of God does not	→
1135	Several persons [who presumably maintained the doctrine of Berengarius] were burned alive for heresy by Emperor Lotharius in Treves and Utrechtb		→	consist of an assemblage of stones but of a spiritual reality, the communion of the faithful. 3. The cross is not an object of adoration; it is on the contrary a detestable object, as the instrument of the	→
1135			→	torture and suffering of Christ. 4. Priests and bishops dispense a lying teaching as to the matter of the Eucharist. The body of Christ was consumed only one time and only by the disciples, during the	→
1135			→	communion that preceded the Passion. All other later consumption is only vain fiction. 5. The funeral liturgy in its whole (offerings, prayers, Masses, and alms) is useless; the dead can hope in	→
1135			→	nothing more than what they received when they were alive. (from D. Iogna-Prat)z	→
1138			→	End of Antipope Anacletus II's anti-pontificate (confirmed in Second Lateran Council)	
1139, Rome	Freedom of Conscience was taken away from the Roman Catholic countries of Medieval Europe which set the stage for the Albigensian crusades (1181, 1209-1227, 1240-1255). Issues in Second Lateran Council: (Canons 1, 2) rejected Simony [e.g.		→	Second Lateran Council, called by Innocent II, affirmed Peter the Venerable and condemned Henricians as Heretics and turned over to the secular powers, as was written in Section 23:	

Defined Heresy 1139	local church rule, such as congregational rule]; (3) disallowed bishops to accept anyone rejected by another bishop [later used against Waldenses]; (5) gave bishops complete control over the finances of their diocese; (6-8) disallowed clergy marriages; (9) disallowed clergy from earning a living by		→		"23. Those who, simulating a kind of religiosity, condemn: 1) The sacrament of the Lord's body and blood; 2) The baptism of children; 3) The priesthood and other ecclesiastical orders [hence,
1139	any other means (bivocational), learning another profession was "evil and detestable" [i.e. vow of poverty]; (10, 25) prohibited churches from hiring a priest or pastor [contra congregational rule]; (15) protected inquisitors from the reprisals of the locals; (22) dealt with "false penance"; (23) condemned		→		Sacrament of Holy Orders]; and 4) Legitimate marriages [marriage as a Sacrament, means of grace], "we expel from the church of God and condemn as heretics,
1139	four points of the **Henricians** [at right].		→		and prescribe that they be constrained by the secular powers. We also bind up their defenders in the fetter of the same condemnation."
1139			→		**Arnald**, a lector at Brescia (Italy), trained under **Abelard** (in France) taught against transubstantiation and infant baptism, was commanded to be silent by **Pope Innocent II**; he eventually fled to Germany and Switzerlandb, by way of
1139			→		France; Gonnet and Molnar add that Innocent II forced Arnald to leave Brescia as he opposed its Bishop Manfred, who had gained his office by simonyg ↓
1140		At the **Council of Sens**, Arnald defended **Abelard** who was under attack from [St] Bernardg			
1143	**Evervin** wrote a letter in 1143 to [St] Bernard, *Annales Brunsvilarenses*, describing heretics in Bonn and Cologne most of whom have abjured	[St] **Bernard** had Arnald expulsed from France by a decree of King Louis VII; Arnald fled to Switzerlandg ↙			
1143	when threatened with being burned at the stake; two, however, sought to defend their faith by the New Testament, not only preaching the	→		**Papal Legate** and **Cardinal, Bishop of Ostia Albéric** called on [St] **Bernard of Clairveaux** (of Citeaux) (founder of the Cistercians and preacher for the 2nd crusade) and **Geoffrey, Bishop of Chartres**, to stamp out Henricians from Southern France; **Bernard of Clairveaux** cursed their cities, assigning them the title of "heretic"	
1143	Gospel, but also living according to its truths, with apostolic poverty and no home; they were assured that their tradition was ancient	Arnald [and his followers]b was forced to flee to Bavaria, Germany, to the city of Passau ↙			[St] **Bernard** wrote of the so-called "heretics" in Southern France, "The sacraments are abused, and the Feasts of the Church are no longer celebrated. Men are dying with their sins still upon them. By refusing children the Grace of Baptism these people are depriving them of all life in Christ."o
1143	descending to the Greek times; among other things they did not eat meats or condone marriage; they recited the Lord's Prayer daily while		→		

COLOR GUIDE YELLOW=Roman Catholic areas; TAN=Bad years for Anabaptists; GOLD=Important events for Catholicism; ORANGE=Catholics "martyred"; RED=Evangelicals martyred; GRAY=Other martyred; Disclaimer: some dates may vary
PINK=Marriage issues; PURPLE= Crusades or massacres; TURQUOISE=Martyrology info; BLUE=Part Protestant areas; AQUA=U.S. Const and Rel.; LT GREEN=Disputed areas; LIME=Bible issues; GREEN=Major dates. (Page 15)

Thomas P. Johnston / Geographic History / Page 16

Date	Germany-Austria-Scandinavia	Switzerland	France-Alsace	British Isles	Italy, Spain, Low Lands
1143	breaking bread, believed in water baptism and the laying on of hands[b]				
1144	The Liege [Belgium] chapter wrote **Pope Lucius II** of a group of "heretics" who opposed infant		→		
1144	baptism, the Eucharist, marriage [as a sacrament], and vows; they had a hierarchy of listeners, believers, presbyters, and bishops; they		→		
1144	spread their teachings South and West.		→		
1144	**Arnald** stayed in Pasau until he sought to be reconciled to the **Pope Eugenius III** at his palace in Viterbe, Italy →		→	**Arnald** moved to Rome where he led a popular movement which called	
1145	**Arnald** fled to **Emperor Barbarossa**, who turned him over to the **Pope**[b] →	In Brittany, France, the **Cardinal Alberic** encouraged the	**Peter the Lombard** became a "magister" at the Cathedral school of Notre Dame	**Others** die in Paris for "true evangelical doctrine"[b]	for reforms in the Church [van Bracht wrote that the reforms included
1145		**Archbishop Hughes** to write a tract against the plenteous	Gonnet and Molnar placed the arrest of **Henry of Lausanne** in 1145, arrested by no less person than [St.] **Bernard of Clairveaux**, and placed in the prison of the **Bishop of Toulouse**[g]		being against infant baptism and transsubstatiation; Gonnet and Molnar →
1145		heretics in Brittany; those around Rouen interpreted the		→	**Peter Abelard** was confined to a dungeon in Rome for his views against transubstantiation and infant baptism[b] →
1145		Bible literally, opposing infant baptism, refusing the hierarchy and		→	stated that the reforms were populist dealing with evangelical poverty and the separation of Church and State][g] →
1145		rituals of Rome[g]		→	**Joachim of Floris** [Italy] was born →
1146				→	**Peter Abelard** died in dungeon wherein he was confined[b]

1147		Peter the Lombard began composing his "Four Books"s3	→	
1148		Others die in Paris for "true evangelical doctrine"b / Henry of Lausanne died in prison; [Ivan Bracht said that his fate was unknown, but that he was presumed to have died in 1147]b	Pope Eugenuis III called the Council of Rheims, among other things, against Gilbert de la Porrée, at which Peter "the Lombard" was a theological expert	
1148		→	Pope Eugenius III declared Arnald of Brescia a schismaticg	
1152		→	Pope Eugenius III declared Arnald of Brescia a heretic	
1155		Certain peasants, called Apostolics, against whom [St] Bernard railed, calling them Manicheans; they were put to death near Toulouseb	Arnald fled from Rome after Pope Eugenius IV placed a ban on the city, and went to Tuscanyg	
1155		Lombard was said to have completed his Four Books of Sentences" from 1147-1150, or as late as 1155s3. Two years of lectures on	Arnald was arrested in Tuscany by the Emperor Barbarossa, and turned over the the Prefect of Rome; Arnald was hung and burned, supposedly after an attempted escape; his ashes were thrown into the Tiberg	
1155		Lombard's Sentences were required of all doctoral students at least into the 16th Cent.c2		
1159		Peter the Lombard became a priest, deacon, archdeacon (by 1156), and finally Bishop of Paris	Roland of Sienna became Pope, and took the name Alexander III; he began the practice of writing letters to Princes, Kings, and rulers to enact inquisition against the "Waldenses" and any other Heretics that were against the Church of Rome	Octavian of Rome elected as second Pope / Roland of Sienna became Pope
1159	Octavian of Rome was elected as a rival Pope, becoming the German Emperor Barbarossa's Anti-Pope			
1159			Octavian of Rome was also elected Pope, taking the name Victor IV, ruled as antipope from Lucca in Central Italy (1159-1164)	

COLOR GUIDE: YELLOW=Roman Catholic areas; TAN=Bad years for Anabaptists; GOLD=Important events for Catholicism; ORANGE=Catholics "martyred"; RED=Evangelicals martyred; GRAY=Other martyred; Disclaimer: some dates may vary
PINK=Marriage issues; PURPLE= Crusades or massacres; TURQUOISE=Martyrology info; BLUE=Part Protestant areas; AQUA=U.S. Const and Rel.; LIME=Bible issues; GREEN=Major dates. (Page 17)

Thomas P. Johnston — Geographic History — Page 18

Date	Germany-Austria-Scandinavia	Switzerland	France-Alsace	British Isles	Italy, Spain, Low Lands		
1160 Waldensians appear 1160	**Bruno**, Bishop of Angiers, and his deacon, **Berengarius**, denounced infant baptism and transubstantiation[b]		**Peter Waldo** preached against the sins of popery in Lyons, France (others place this change at 1170 or 1173)[9]	**Durand d'Osca** [de Huesca] born some-where in Languedoc or Albigeois[9]		→ →	→ →
1161			Death of **Peter the Lombard**, archbishop of Paris, who authored "The Four Books of Sentences", the most commented on book aside from the Bible from 13th–16th Century		**Peter the Lombard's** *Sentences*, quoting **Augustine** and other ancient "Fathers", promoted philosophical theology and Rome's sacramental practices; they countered the "Evangelical" tendencies of the so-called heretical **Henricians** and **Petrobusians**	→	→
1161				At Oxford, **Gerard**, with about **30 persons**, called *publicans*, were accused of propagating their beliefs ("they aspersed baptism and thankoffering"); were branded and scourged out of the city, where they died from the cold[b]		→	→
1161						→	→
1163	Some from Flanders, **Arnold**, **Marsilius**, and **Theodoric**, with **5 men**, and **2 women**, found to be Heretics; burned alive in Cologne and Bonn[b]		**Council of Tours** denounced the "new heresy" (i.e. **Catharism**)[b2o]			→	→
1163						→	→
1164					**Guido of Crema** (aka. **Paschall III**) elected as the next "Anti-Pope"	→	→
1165			"The Council of Lombez pronounces against the *boni hommes* (*bons hommes*)"o [varia 1175]			→	→
1167	Herein was then founded a rival Eastern Rite Church West of Rome. The audacity in the founding of these churches rival to Rome's monopoly		Bulgarian **Bishop Nicétas** arrived from Constantinople to the chateau Saint-Félix-de-Caraman[o] to ordain six bishops in four bishoprics			→	→

Date						
1167	became the "Cause Célebre" for the crusades and inquisitions which would follow		for the independent church of Toulouse (Southern France). Information is preserved in the **Charter of Niquinta** (circa 1232)o2z2; these churches were later called "**Albigensian**" and			→ →
1167			"**Cathar**" and were considered **Manichean** (by using **Augustine's** *Contra Manichean*)			→ →
1167			Ecclesiastical conference held a **Vézelayx** condemns **seven Cathars** to the stakeº			→ →
1168					**Callistus III** elected as the next "Anti-Pope"	→ →
1170			**Peter Valdo** [Waldo] saw his need for salvation at the death of a guest at a great feast that he had givenb2d3			→ →
1172	"		Cleric accused of heresy burned in Arrasº			→ →
1173	Of the orthodoxy of the Waldenses, "Le Père Dondaine a retrouvé le manifeste, le 'propos de vie' de Valdès, qui atteste la parfaite orthodoxie du mouvement, plus ou moins approuvé par le Pape en 1179, mais condamné en 1184."d3 [trans "The Father Dondaine found the manifest, 'manner of life' of Waldo, that attests the perfect orthodoxy of the movement, more or less approved by the Pope in 1179, but condemned in 1184"]		**Peter Waldo** turned from his riches and began to evangelize on the streets in Lyon, founding the **Waldenses** as a group of lay evangelists			→ →
1173				**Archbishop Guichard de Pontigny** used **Valdo** and his followers in his struggle against the Cathedral chapter in Lyonz		→ →
1173						→ →
1177	Disciples of **Peter Waldo** were said to have preached in Frankfurt and Nuremberg		**Raymond V** of Toulouse reported to the Chapter-General of Citeaux monastery on the →			→ →

COLOR GUIDE: **YELLOW**=Roman Catholic areas; **TAN**=Bad years for Anabaptists; **GOLD**=Important events for Catholicism; **ORANGE**=Catholics "martyred"; **RED**=Evangelicals martyred; **GRAY**=Other martyred; Disclaimer: some dates may vary **PINK**=Marriage issues; **PURPLE**= Crusades or massacres; **TURQUOISE**=Martyrology info; **BLUE**=Part Protestant areas; **AQUA**=U.S. Const and Rel.; **LT GREEN**=Disputed areas; **LIME**=Bible issues; **GREEN**=Major dates. (Page 19)

Thomas P. Johnston
Geographic History
Page 20

Date	Germany-Austria-Scandinavia	Switzerland	France-Alsace	British Isles	Italy, Spain, Low Lands
1177	Due to the **Council of Nuremberg**, disciples of **Waldo** fled to Bohemia		"alarming development" of the Catharist heresy		→ →
1178			**Synod of Toulouse** condemned the Albigenses2		**Henry of Clairveaux** decried the growth of the Albigensian churches, affirming that they appointed leaders and had evangelists
1178	"This scourge [the growth and evangelism of the 'heretical' movements] has taken such an extension, wrote the Abbott Henry of Clairveaux about 1178, that the people have not only given themselves priests and pontiffs, but that they also have evangelists, who, corrupting and annulling the truth of the Gospel, shape for themselves new Gospels. They preach on the Gospels and the epistles and the other Holy Scriptures that they corrupt as they explain them, as doctors of error incapable of being disciples of the truth, because preaching and the explanation of the Scriptures is absolutely forbidden to lay people"¹		→		
1178			→		Death of "Anti-pope" **Callistus III**
1178			→		**Pope Alexander III** called **Third Lateran Council**

Third Lateran Council Convened by Pope Alexander III in Rome

Date	Germany-Austria-Scandinavia	Switzerland	France-Alsace	British Isles	Italy, Spain, Low Lands
1179 Third Lateran Council	**U.S. Constitution issues**: (1) Heretics had no right to defense; (2) they were to have their property seized under pain of excommunication; and (3) heretics were to be made into the slaves of princes (as later Reformation Huguenots received a life sentence to row for the ships of the King of France).	It dealt with schism by decreeing the need for a 2/3rds majority of Cardinals for election as Pope, and with schismatics by calling for the shedding of blood as a "salutary remedy": "26. **Jews and Saracens** are not to be allowed to have christian servants in their houses, either under pretence of nourishing their children or for service or any other reason. Let those be excommunicated who presume to live with them. We declare that the evidence of Christians is to be accepted against Jews in every case, since Jews employ their own witnesses against Christians, and that those who prefer Jews to Christians in this matter are to lie under anathema, since Jews ought to be subject to Christians and to be supported by them on grounds of humanity alone			
1179	Other issues in **Third Lateran Council**: (Canon 1) decreed on	"27. As St. Leo says, though the discipline of the church should be satisfied with the judgment of the priest and should not cause the shedding of blood, yet it is helped by the laws of catholic princes so that people often seek a salutary remedy when they fear that a corporal punishment will overtake them. For this reason, since in Gascony and the regions of Albi and Toulouse and in other places the loathsome heresy of those whom some call the **Cathars**, others the **Patarenes**, others the **Publicani**, and others by different names, has grown so strong that they no longer practise their wickedness in secret, as others do, but proclaim their error publicly and draw the simple and weak to join them, we declare that they and their defenders and those			
1179	2/3rds vote for Pope; (2) decreed against schismatics, especially regarding land taken from the Roman Church; (9, 14) denied churches not	who receive them are under anathema, and we forbid under pain of anathema that anyone should keep or support them in their houses or lands or should trade with them. If anyone dies in this sin, then neither under cover of our privileges granted to anyone, nor for any other reason, is mass to be offered for them or are they to receive burial among Christians. With regard to the **Brabanters, Aragonese, Navarrese, Basques, Coterelli and Triaverdini**, who practise such cruelty upon Christians that they respect neither churches nor monasteries, and spare neither widows, orphans, old or			
1179	related to Church of Rome from receiving tithes and offerings; (11) disallowed marriages of clergy; (16) disallowed any local input against	young nor any age or sex, but like pagans destroy and lay everything waste, we likewise decree that those who hire, keep or support them, in the districts where they rage around, should be denounced publicly on Sundays and other solemn days in the churches, that they should be subject in every way to the same sentence and penalty as the above-mentioned heretics and that they should not be received into the communion of the church, unless they abjure their pernicious society and heresy. As long as such people persist in their wickedness, let all who are bound to them by any pact			

1179	clerical appointments (contra congregational rule); (19) requested freedom from taxation of clergy and a stipend from the government; (26)	know that they are free from all obligations of loyalty, homage or any obedience. On these [or "Princes"] and on all the faithful we enjoin, for the remission of sins, that they oppose this scourge with all their might and **by arms protect the christian people** against them. Their goods are to be confiscated and princes free to subject them to slavery. Those who in true sorrow for their sins die in such a conflict should not doubt that they will receive forgiveness for their sins and the fruit of an eternal reward. We too trusting in the mercy of God and the authority of the blessed apostles Peter
1179	"We declare that the evidence of Christians who take up arms against them, and who on the advice of bishops or other prelates seek to drive them out, a remission for two years of penance imposed on them, or, if their service shall be longer, we entrust it to the discretion of the bishops, to whom this task has been committed, to grant greater indulgence, according to their judgment, in proportion to the degree of their toil. We command that those who refuse to obey the exhortation of the bishops in this matter should not be allowed to receive the body and blood of the Lord. Meanwhile we receive	and Paul, grant to faithful Christians who take up arms against them, and who on the advice of bishops or other prelates seek to drive them out, a remission for two years of penance imposed on them, or, if their service shall be longer, we entrust it to the discretion of the bishops, to whom this task has been committed, to grant greater indulgence, according to their judgment, in proportion to the degree of their toil. We command that those who refuse to obey the exhortation of the bishops in this matter should not be allowed to receive the body and blood of the Lord. Meanwhile we receive
1179	canon 27 against the "heretics" to the right: many rights taken from the "heretics", disallowing freedom of conscience]	under the protection of the church, as we do those who visit the Lord's sepulchre, those who fired by their faith have taken upon themselves the task of driving out these heretics, and we decree that they should remain undisturbed from all disquiet both in their property and persons. If any of you presumes to molest them, he shall incur the sentence of excommunication from the bishop of the place, and let the sentence be observed by all until what has been taken away has been restored and suitable satisfaction has been made for the loss inflicted. Bishops and priests who do not resist such wrongs are to be punished by loss of their office until they gain the pardon of the apostolic see" ("Fourth Lateran Council," Canon 27, From: http://www.dailycatholic.org/history/11ecume1.htm; accessed 28 June 2008).
1179		**Pope Alexander III** prohibited the preaching of the Waldenses, who quoted Bible portions in the vulgar tongues
1179		**English Monk Walter Map Interviewed Several Waldenses at the Council** "Walter Map, in his *De Nugis Curialium Distinctiones Quinque* composed before 1192, tells of having met at the council the Waldenses who came to present to the Pope a book written in Gallic which contained the text and comments on the Psalter, as well as a number of books of both Testaments. Because they requested with great insistence that they receive the authorization to preach, a type of jury was gathered to examine them. Walter was a part [of that jury], and he asked the questions of the two Waldenses who were present, simple and unlettered men, while "*sua videbantur in secta precipui.*" Questioned on the three persons of the Trinity, they quickly fell into the trap that only experts in theological subtleties would be able to avoid, and therefore had to retire confounded and baffled."g
1179		**Pope Alexander III** launched another preaching crusade against the loathsome "heretics" in Southern France
1179 Episcopal Inquisition 1179		**Establishment of Episcopal Inquisition** All Archbishops or Bishops, personally or by the intermediary of their Archdeacons or other persons who are honest and capable, must once or twice a year visit the parishes in their diocese, where it is said that their exist heretics. There they will necessitate three or more good witnesses, or where it is necessary the entire neighborhood, to swear that they will
1179		While the **Third Lateran Council** did not appear to pass judgment against **Waldo** and the preaching of the **Waldenses**, when **Jean de Bellesmains** became the new Archbishop of Lyons (1182), he excommunicated **Waldo** and his followers as heretics.z	denounce to the Bishop or Archdeacon those that they know as heretics, or whoever participates in secret conventicles and separates themselves from the life and morals common among the faithful. The Bishop, or in his presence the
1179		Hence with the disaffirmation of a Roman Bishop, **Waldo** and his preachers automatically became heretical everywhere (Vatican I, Canon 2); they then became known as "The Poor Men of Lyons", and their methodology of itinerant preaching (not their message) was later imitated by the Dominicans in 1214- 1215 with another	Archdeacon, will assemble the accused: if they do not purge themselves of the crimes of which they are being accused or if, after they have purged themselves, they slide back into their perversion, may they be punished according to the
1179		exception, that the Waldenses like their predecessors, the Albigenses, did not beg for food.d4	

COLOR GUIDE: YELLOW=Roman Catholic areas; TAN=Bad years for Anabaptists; GOLD=Important events for Catholicism; ORANGE=Catholics "martyred"; RED=Evangelicals martyred; GRAY=Other martyred; Disclaimer: some dates may vary
PINK=Marriage issues; PURPLE=Crusades or massacres; TURQUOISE=Martyrology info; BLUE=Part Protestant areas; AQUA=U.S. Const and Rel.; LIME=Bible issues; LT GREEN=Disputed areas; GREEN=Major dates. (Page 21)

Thomas P. Johnston — Geographic History — Page 22

Date	Germany-Austria-Scandinavia	Switzerland	France-Alsace	British Isles	Italy, Spain, Low Lands
1179					judgment of the Bishop. If anyone among them does not want to make a vow, judging it to be a blameworthy superstition, may he for this very reason be condemned as a heretic and submit to the prescribed punishment"g
1180	**Ten Point History of Waldo and the Waldenses**g (1) Conversion of the rich merchant of Lyons, who in 1170 (or 1160 or 1173) embraced the religious ideal of voluntary poverty and Evangelical perfection;		Peter Waldo gave himself completely to itinerant preachingb2	Near 1180 **Waldo** of the Waldensian movement signed a statement stating that he believed and confessed "Only one Church, catholic, holy, apostolic, and immaculate, outside of which no one is saved"g	
1180	(2) Translation and reading of the Scriptures, as well as maxims from the four Fathers of the Church (Augustine, Jerome, Ambrose, Gregory); (3) Preaching on the streets, in the public places, and even in the churches, done by simple lay people almost or completely illiterate, including women,		Pope sent Papal Legate Henry, Cardinal-Bishop of Albano to preach against Albigensian Hereticso		
1181 Crusade in South France 1181	which was immediately judged as prideful presumption (originally by Guichard); (4) Training and apostolic ministry of the first disciples, men and women: diffusion of error in Lyons and elsewhere; (5) Prohibition to preach [unless] approved by the ordinary (from pope, 1179); (6) Disobedience of the injunction justified either by the response of Peter (Acts 5:29), or by the mandate of Jesus (Mark 16:15);		Seige and capture of Lavaur, one of the main centers of heresy in Languedoc, by **Papal Legate Henry Abbott of Clairveaux** and his Catholic Knightso Bishop of Lyons, Guichard died (1165-1181); Jean Bellesmains replaced him (1182),	Chronicler Geoffroy de Vigeoisb2 provided historical information **Papal Legate Henry Abbott of Clairveaux** deposed the Archbishop of Narbonne (Languedoc), and gathered Catholic knights to lay siege on Lavauro	
1181	(7) Refusal, excommunication, and exile from Lyons (1182 or 1183) (8) Anathematized by a Council: condemnation as obstinate (impertinent) and schismatic (Verona, 1184); (9) Dispersion in the South of France and in Northern Italy, and mixture with		excommunicating **Waldo** and his followers, which excommunication must be observed by all other bishops (Vatican I, Canon 2)	Pope Alexander III died	
1182	the errors of other sects: heretical syncretism; (10) Definitive judgment [freedom of conscience] as being heretical.		**King Philip of France** rounded up those he called "Publicani" and burned them aliveb	**Count Philip of Alsace** condemned Heretics in his Realmb	**King Henry II of England** commanded that very many "Publicani" should every-where be burned aliveb
1182			**Papal Injunction for Humiliati**g (1) Forbidden to hold assemblies; and (2) Forbidden to preach in public.		
1183	**Views of the Humiliati**g (1) Stayed with their own families; (2) Followed a religious training;			**Philip, Count of Flanders** and papal legate, **William, Archbishop of Rheims** burned alive "over seven thousand Cottarelli" in the province of Bourgesb	
1184 Inquisitions	(3) Abstained from lying, taking an oath, and of going before secular judges; (4) Dressed modestly Also: Preached in public and heard confessions without authorization; disobeyed the papal injunction not to hold meetings or preach in public		**Waldenses** condemned as Heretics by Pope Lucius III; were given the name "**Poor Men of Lyons**"	Pope Lucius III's "**Ad Adolendam**" excommunicated Heretics (incl. **Catharists, Patarini—Humiliati or Poor Men of Lyons, Passaginians, Josephists, Arnoldists**); also	

Date	Event/Description
Begun 1184	**Lucius III, Council of Verona (end of October-early November, 1184)** (from DS760-761) "By this constitution, in virtue of apostolic authority, we condemn all heresy, whatever the name by which they may be designated: in the first place we decree that a **perpetual anathema** be imposed upon the cathars and patarins, and those who through lies call themselves *Humilié* or the **Poor of Lyons**, *Passagiens*, *Josephists* and **Arnoldists**.
1184	"And because certain ones under an appearance of piety … vindicate to themselves the authority to preach … all these, we bind by the same bond of anathema, who although they were prohibited or they were not sent, dare to preach in private or in public without having received the authority from the Apostolic Seat or a Bishop of God, and all those who do not fear to think or to teach otherwise on the subject of the Sacrament of the Body and the Blood of our Lord Jesus Christ, or of Baptism or of
1184	the Confession of sins, of Marriage or the other Sacraments of the Church, being that which the very Holy Roman Church preaches and observes, as well as, in a general fashion, all those whom this same Roman church or its diverse Bishops or in counsel with their clerks, or the clerks themselves when the Seat is vacant, have judged as heretics, if necessary, in counsel with neighboring Bishops."
	Concolati, Credentes, Perfecti), who "have assumed the authority to preach… all these we lay under an **everlasting curse**,"b organized searches for them, and charged bishops to make journeys of investigation
	During the **Council in Verona**, Lucius III, sustained by **Roman Emperor Frederick I**, condemned "heretics" who loved the Bible and who persisted in thinking or teaching something other than Catholic dogma would be excommunicated and handed over to the secular powers for punishment (normally to be burned alive)s
1187	Jerusalem's crusaders fell to **Saladin, Sultan of Egypt**
1190 Indulgences	Sale of indulgences establishedb3
1190	**Disputation in Narbonne**g President: Raymond of Daventrie, priest Catholic side: Archbishop Bernard Gaucelin and others Waldensian side: unknown Issue: The Waldenses were asked to defend their beliefs as to:
1190	(1) Rejection of the hierarchy, including: (a) disobedience to popes and other prelates, (b) refusal to accept the power of the keys,
1190	(c) his taking back the authority for all to preach, including women; (2) Negation of the effectiveness of efforts on behalf of the dead, and hence purgatory;
1190	(3) Lack of appreciation for consecrated holy places.
1192	**1192 Synod of Toul** (of Lorraine, near Metz, see 1199) condemned **Waldenses**, when found immediately	Bernard de Fontcaulde wrote *Contra Valdenses et Arianos*g

COLOR GUIDE: **YELLOW**=Roman Catholic areas; **TAN**=Bad years for Anabaptists; **GOLD**=Important events for Catholicism; **ORANGE**=Catholics "martyred"; **RED**=Evangelicals martyred; **GRAY**=Other martyred; Disclaimer: some dates may vary
PINK=Marriage issues; **PURPLE**= Crusades or massacres; **TURQUOISE**=Martyrology info; **BLUE**=Part Protestant areas; **AQUA**=U.S. Const and Rel.; **LT GREEN**=Disputed areas; **LIME**=Bible issues; **GREEN**=Major dates. (Page 23)

Thomas P. Johnston

Geographic History

Page 24

Date	Germany-Austria-Scandinavia	Switzerland	France-Alsace	British Isles	Italy, Spain, Low Lands
1192					Alain de Lille wrote *summa quadripartita adversus haereticos* between 1185 and 1195, i.e. after the Council of Verona[g] to be brought in chains to the Bishop for punishment[g]
1194	U.S. constitutional laws against "unlawful search and seizure," for "freedom of speech," "freedom to peaceably gather," "freedom of conscience"		Raymond VI succeeded his father as Count of Toulouse; he sought to keep peace between the two rival religions in Languedoc[O]	**Alphonsus II, King of Aragon**, decreed (applying the 3rd Lateran Council to the evangelism of the "heretics"): "If from this day on, any one shall receive said **Waldenses** and **Insabbathi**, or other heretics of whatever confession, into his house, or hear their pernicious preaching in any place, or give them food, or dare to show them any favor, be it known to the same, that he has incurred the disfavor of God and us, that he is punishable for the crime of leze-majesty, and that his goods shall be	
1194				confiscated without appeal."[b] He then commanded that this decree be read every Sunday, perpetually, throughout his dominion. If the heretics did not leave his lands they were to be plundered, robbed, and beat with sticks [!][b]	
1194				[History apparently records no results of the 1192/94 decree of **Alphonsus II of Aragon**, which was repeated by his successor **Peter II** in 1197/98]	
1195			Disputation between Bernard, archbishop of Narbonne and Waldenses[S2] (see above 1190)	The regional councils of Lerida (1194) and Gerona (1198) repeated the anathema of the 1194 decree, Peter II adding burning at the stake for receiving, aiding, or abedding them.	
1198 Papal Inquisition established	The College of Cardinals seems to have violated Vatican I (1123), Canon 6, by electing **Innocent III** as Pope, as he may have not beforehand even been a priest		Cistercians **Reynier** [Reinerius] and **Gui** [Guido] sent to act against the Heretics[O]	Though not a priest, the 38 year old Lothario Conti was elected Pope on the day of **Celestius III's** death; he took the name **Innocent III**; he established the Roman Church's "absolute supremacy" over kings and emperors, including the capture of Constantinople by his French crusaders[O]	
1198				Innocent III's "**Vergentes in Senium**" established episcopal or Legate's inquisition; it was one of three letters sent that year that established Reinerius and Guido as inquisitors of the heretics, on his behalf[b]	
1199	Denzinger's titled on this section: "On the necessity of the Magisterium of the Church for the interpretation of Scripture" (DS 770)	Innocent III's "**Cum ex Iniuncto**" To the inhabitants of Metz [12 July 1199] "Our venerable brother, the Bishop of Metz [Lorraine, France], We have come to know from his letter that in his diocese as well as in the town of Metz a rather important number of lay people and of women, drawn in some way by a desire for the Scriptures, made for themselves			Innocent III's "**Cum ex Iniuncto**" condemned the translation of the Psalms, the Gospels, and the epistles of Paul into Roman (proto-French), and

1199	translations into the French language of the Gospels, the epistles of Paul, the Psalter, the Moralia of Job, and many other books; … (with the result being) that in the secret gatherings lay people and woman dare to belch forth to each other and to mutually preach, and they equally despise the company of those who are not mixed up in such things … Some of them also despise the simplicity of their priests, and when a word of salvation is proposed to these latter, they whisper in secret that they have better in their writings and that they are capable of express them more judiciously.			prohibited the meetings taking place in the diocese of Metz, Lorraine, France, being guilty of studying the Scriptures; Cistercian monks were sent to burn all vulgar translations they founds
1199	"Even if a desire to understand the divine Scriptures and the care to exhort in conformity with them is not to blame but quite the opposite commendable, these people deserve nevertheless to be reprimanded that they hold secret conventicles, and that they usurp the office of preaching, that they scoff at the simplicity of the priests and that they distain the company of those that do not attach themselves to such practices. God in fact … hates to this point the works of darkness that he commanded and said (to the apostles): "What I tell you in the dark, say it in the daylight; that which you hear in the deep of your ear proclaim it from the rooftops" (Matt 10:27); by this it is clearly manifest that the preaching of the Gospel ought to be proposed not in secret conventicles, as is done by the heretics, but publicly in the Church, in conformity with Catholic custom. …			
1199	"Such is the depth of the holy Scriptures that not only simple and uncultivated people, but even those who are wise and learned are not able to scrutinize the meaning. This is why the Scripture says: "For many of those who sought failed in their search" (Psa 64:7). Also was it correct that it was established in the divine Law that if an animal touches the Mountain (of Sinai)			
1199	he should be stoned (cf. Heb 12:20; Ex 19:12ff), in order that in fact no simple or uncultivated man should have the presumption to touch upon the sublimities of the holy Scripture or to preach it to others. It is written in fact: "Do not seek that which is too high for you" (Sir 3:22). This is why the apostle said: "Do not seek more than what is necessary to seek, but seek with sobriety" (Rom 12:3).			
1199	"Similarly just as the body numbers many members, but not all the members have the same activity, likewise, the Church counts many levels, but not all have the same duty, for according to the Apostle "The Lord has given some as apostles, others as prophets, but others as doctors, etc." (Eph 4:11). Therefore the doctor is in some ways the principal in the church and this is why no one ought to usurp without deference the office of preacher" (DS 770-771)			
1200		**Five men and three women** burned in Troyes (Champagne) on the charge of heresyob		Certain **Waldenses** were expelled from Metz (in Lorraine), and their Bibles burned
1201		An **Albanian** leader visited southern France, leading to further revivalb2	A **knight** burned at the stake in Nevers0	**Joachim of Flores**, head of Cistercian monastery in Corazzo, founded the "**Joachimite sect**" (parallel to strict Franciscans), died in 1202; he was a neo-Montanist reformer from within Catholicism, preaching against its "secularization" as especially noted in its taking up of arms in the crusades; he was condemned in 1215 (for his doctrine of the Trinity) and by **Alexander IV** in 1255 (for the apocalyptic elements);j
1201		"**Perfects**" began to travel, preaching the Gospel door-to-door, converting many	Persecution of Catharist colony at **Charité-sur-Loire**0	the **Fourth Lateran Council** (1215), Article 2, was in part directed against **Joachim**
1203		Peter de Castelnau became Papal Legate0		
1204	Crusaders who were part of the Fourth Crusade invaded Constantinople, instituting the **Latin Empire** (1204-1261),	**Raymond de Perella** rebuilt Montségur, at the request of Cathars in the area0	**Peter II of Aragon** instigated debate between Catholics and Cathars in Carcassonne0	As part of Rome's rule, when they took Constantinople, three eighths of the **Byzantium Empire** was given to the Republic

COLOR GUIDE: YELLOW=Roman Catholic areas; TAN=Bad years for Anabaptists; GOLD=Important events for Catholicism; RED=Evangelicals martyred; ORANGE=Catholics "martyred"; GRAY=Other martyred; Disclaimer: some dates may vary
PINK=Marriage issues; PURPLE= Crusades or massacres; TURQUOISE=Martyrology info; BLUE=Part Protestant areas; AQUA=U.S. Const and Rel.; LT GREEN=Disputed areas; LIME=Bible issues; GREEN=Major dates. (Page 25)

Geographic History

Date	Germany-Austria-Scandinavia	Switzerland	France-Alsace			British Isles	Italy, Spain, Low Lands
1204	the Pope crowning **Baldwin IX, count of Flanders** (Belgium), as first Latin Emperor in Constantinople					Durand d'Osca debated Bishop of Osma, Diego, in Palmiers, presumably the "last debate"	of Venice, as part of the *Partitio terrarum imperii Romanie* signed on 1 Oct 1204
1206	→		Esclarmon-de, sister of the Count of Foix, received Cathar *consolamentum*	Bishop Diego and Dominic stoppe-d in Toulouse and led an Albigensian innkeeper to the Catholic faith	Domi-nic estab-lished a founda-tion [home] for "conver-ted" Cathar wo-men0		"**An Extract of certain Rules of Caution, whereby the Inquisitours formerly regulated their Prosecution of the Waldenses.**" "1. It is not expedient to dispute concerning Matters of Faith before Laymen.
1206	→						"2. None ought to be reputed as true Repentants, but such as discover all those whom they knew to be of the same principles and profession with themselves. "3. He that accuses and discovers not those of the same profession with himself, ought to be cut off from the Church as a rotten and putrified member, lest he should corrupt and infect the rest.
1206	→						"4. After any is admitted to the secular power, he must not be at all permitted to excuse himself, or to declare his innocence before the people, for, if such a one be put to death, it scandalizes the Lay-men; and if he escape, it becomes prejudice to our religion.
1206	→						"5. There must be great caution had of promising life to any man who is condemned, before the people; because there's no Heretick who would ever be burnt, if he could escape by virtue of a promise. And in the case he should promise Repentance before the people, and then be put to death, that would necessarily scandalize the people, and make them believe that such were wrongfully put to death.
1206	→						"6. The Inquisitour ought always to presuppose the Fact, and (waving that) onely to inquire the Circumstances of the Fact, after this manner. How many times hast thou confessed thyself to the Hereticks? In what Chamber in thy House did they lie? And such like Questions.
1206	→						"7. The Inquisitour must hold some Book before the accused Party, during the Examination, as if he had there written the whole Life of him who he examines.
1206	→						"8. He must threaten him with Death, in case he will not confess, and tell him that he is a dead man, that he ought to think upon his Soul, and wholly renounce his Heresie, since that I must die, he ought to take patiently whatever befalls him. And if he answer, 'I had rather die in this my faith, than in that of the *Roman* church.' Then be sure there's no hope at all for such a one, and therefore he must be delivered forthwith to justice.
1206	→						"9 There is no hope at all of convincing Hereticks by the knowledge of the Scriptures, and Learning, for as oft times it falls out, that very learned men are confounded by them, and by that means, the Hereticks fortifie themselves, when they thus learn that even learned men themselves are deceived by them. "10. Hereticks must never be suffered to answer directly to anything. And when they are pressed by frequent Interrogatives, they have a Custome to make an answer, that they are poor ignorant men, and are not able to answer. And if they perceive that the Standers by are any whit moved with compassion toward them, as being poor harmless men, and wrongfully accused, then they take courage, and seem to cry and take on, like poor miserable Wretches, and so flattering and smoothing the Judge, endeavor to escape the Inquisition; saying, 'Sir, if I have offended in any thing, I shall willingly do penance, but I beseech you assist and deliver me from this Infamy, which has been cast upon me by pure malice and envy, and altogether undeservedly.' But then must the couragious Inquisitour not at all bend, or be moved by these Flatteries, nor give the least ear or credence to any such Fables.
1206	→						"11. Lastly, the Inquisitour must prevent them, by assuring them, that they shall gain nothing by Swearing falsely, for as much as they have sufficient proofs to convict them otherwise; and therefore that they should not at all think to escape the Sentence of Death thereby. But withall, he must promise them, that if they confess freely their errour, they shall find Mercy. For, in such a perplexity as this, there are many that will confess their Errour, in hopes to escape."m2

1206							→	**Durand d'Osca**, Waldensian who was to return to the Church of Rome, wrote *Liber antiheresis* sometime after the writings of **Bernard de Foucault** and **Jean de Lille**, and prior to 1207, when he returned to Rome[g]	**Pope Innocent III** wrote letters to the leader and counselors of Faenza against the preaching of the Waldenses[g]
1206							→	In his *Liber antiheresis*, **Durand d'Osca** argued against the "false teachings" of the Cathars, while highlighting the teachings and methods of the Waldenses:[b]	The **Pope** began to exercise great cruelty against the followers of **Peter the Bruys** and **Henry of Toulouse**[b]
1206							→	For example, when speaking of the right of the preacher to partake of the altar: "If the Lord had desired that the Apostles would consecrate themselves to earthy work and to the accumulation of wealth, he would not have preached the parable of the birds of the sky or the lily of	
1206							→	the field. But because he knew that whoever was involved in earthly negotiations cannot preach freely, he sequestered them from earthly work so that their spirit may not be under the weight of worldly preoccupations	
1206							→	and so that they could give themselves with greater care to preaching, to exhortation, and to the salvation of the other"[g]	
1206							→	When speaking of the heavenly call, **Durand** wrote: "In order that our spirits may not be hindered by the love of riches, we propose, according to the grace that has been conferred to us by God, to attend to preaching and prayer, accepting, according to the order of the Lord, that	
1206							→	workers be sent out into the harvest field, meaning that preachers go out to preach into the midst of the people. By consequence, imitating the primitive Church, we dare to engage ourselves in the work that the Lord confided to	
1206							→	the Seventy-two"[g]	
1207						**U.S. constitution** guarantees: "no establishment of religion," "right to bear arms," "self-rule" (for the people,		**Pope** confirmed **Peter of Castelnau's** excommunication (=death sentence, see Aquinas below [1265-1271]) against the **Raymond VI**, Count of Toulouse (29 May)[O]	At Arles, **Pope Innocent III** sought to persuade **Raymond VI of Toulouse** to expulse all Heretics from his lands[b]
1207						by the people), "freedom of speech," and "freedom of conscience"			Finally the **Pope** excommunicated **Raymond VI**, deeding his land to any who could take it[b]

COLOR GUIDE: YELLOW=Roman Catholic areas; TAN=Bad years for Anabaptists; GOLD=Important events for Catholicism; ORANGE=Catholics "martyred"; RED=Evangelicals martyred; GRAY=Other martyred; Disclaimer: some dates may vary
PINK=Marriage issues; PURPLE=Crusades or massacres; TURQUOISE=Martyrology info; BLUE=Part Protestant areas; AQUA=U.S. Const and Rel.; LT GREEN=Disputed areas; LIME=Bible issues; GREEN=Major dates. (Page 27)

Thomas P. Johnston
Geographic History
Page 28

Date	Germany-Austria-Scandinavia	Switzerland	France-Alsace	British Isles	Italy, Spain, Low Lands
1208	→				Durand d'Osca appears to have left the **Waldenses**, as we shall see from his "Profession of Faith" upon returning into the Catholic Church, whereupon he was said to have founded the "Lower Order" of the **Poor Catholics**g →	Durand d'Osca's founding of the "Poor Catholics" predated: • 1208-1209, Franciscans of [St] Francis (OFM); • 1210, Poor Reconciled of the "first" Bernard; • 1215, "Brothers Preachers" (Dominicans, OFP or OP) of [St] Dominic
1208	The Pope released **Roman Catholics** from the rights of citizenship (fealty) to a heretical governor, see also on this same issue: (1) Gregory VII (1073-1085); (2) **Fourth Lateran Council** (1215); (3) Innocent IV (1243). By 1487, all the rulers were Catholic, and needed only to be compelled to use the sword on their heretical citizens.		The **Waldensian, Durand d'Osca** (from Aragon, Spain), returned to the Roman Catholic church in 1207, his profession of the faith was preserved in **Innocent III's** letter to the **Archbishop of Tarragone** *Eius Exemplo* (18 Dec 1208). Gonnet and Molnar wrote that this letter also mentioned some companions of **Durand d'Osca: Jean de Narbonne**, and **Ermengaud** and **Bernard de Beziers**g The entire text of **Denzinger** is here reproduced in its entirety as it is quite fascinating from an Evangelical point-of-view.		
1208			"May all believers know that I, Durand of Osca… and all our brothers, we believe from our mouth and we affirm by these simple words: "The Father and the Son and the Holy Spirit are three persons, one God, and the entire Trinity is coessential, consubstantial, coeternal, and all powerful, and each of the persons of the Trinity are fully God, as is found in the 'I believe in God' [Apostles Creed], in the 'I believe in one God' [Creed of Constantinople], and 'Whosoever will' [Pseudo-Athanasian Creed].		
1208			"We equally believe from our heart and confess from our mouth that the Father and the Son and the Holy Spirit, one God of whom we speak, created, made, governs, and ordains all things corporal and spiritual, visible and invisible. "We believe that the author of the New and of the Old Testament is one and only: God who, as it is said, remains in Trinity, created all things from nothing; and that John the Baptist was sent by him, holy and righteous, and full of the Holy Spirit from the womb of his mother.		
1208	→		"We believe with our heart and we confess with our mouth that the Incarnation was not accomplished in the Father nor in the Holy Spirit, but only in the Son; resulting that he who was divinely Son of God the Father, was, in humanity, the Son of man, true man of the mother, having a true flesh from the womb of his mother and a reasonable soul; simultaneously of both natures, meaning God and man, one person, one Son, one Christ, one God with the Father and the Holy Spirit, author of everything, and director of everything, born of the Virgin Mary of a natural fleshly birth; he ate and drank, he slept and, fatigued on his route, he rested; he suffered a true Passion in his flesh, and died a true death in his body, and he was resurrected by true Resurrection of his body and of a true return of the soul to the body; in this flesh, after having eaten and drunk, he rose to heaven, sits at the right hand of the Father, and he will return from there to judge the living and the dead.		
1208	→		"We believe from our heart and confess with our mouth one Church, not that of the heretics, but the holy Roman Church, catholic, apostolic, and outside of which we believe that none are saved.		
1208	→		"Similarly we reject in no manner the sacraments that are celebrated in it [the Church], and through which the Holy Spirit cooperates by his inestimable and invisible virtue, even if they be administered by a sinful priest, from the moment that the Church recognizes him; and we do not despise any more the ecclesial actions and the blessings conferred by him, but we accept them as from a heart of goodwill just as if they came from the most righteous of men, for the malice of a bishop or of a priest does not negate either the baptism of an infant, nor the consecration of the Eucharist, nor the other ecclesiastical offices celebrated for their subjects.		
1208	→		"We approve therefore of the baptism of infants, and if they are dead after baptism, before having committed sins, we confess and believe that they are saved; and we believe that in baptism all sins areremitted, including both original sin that has been contracted as well as those that have been committed voluntarily. "We esteem that the confirmation bestowed by a bishop, that is the laying on of hands, is holy and must be received with veneration.		
1208	→		"We firmly and immovably believe from a sincere heart, and we simply affirm by our words full of faith, that the sacrifice, that is the bread and the wine, is, after consecration, the true body and the true blood of our Lord Jesus Christ, and that nothing more is accomplished by a good priest and nothing less is effectuated by the merits of the person who consecrates, but by the word of the Creator and the virtue of the Holy Spirit. This is why we believe and firmly confess that no one, neither so honest, neither so holy and neither so prudent as he may be, can nor may consecrate the mass nor offer the sacrifice of the altar, unless he is a priest and is regularly ordained to this office by a visible		

1208	→	and tangible bishop. For this office three things are necessary, we believe: a determinant person, that is a priest established particularly for this office by a bishop, as we have said; the solemn words are expressed by the holy Fathers in the canon; and the intention of the faith of he who consecrates them; this is why we believe and firmly confess that whosoever, without the ordination of a bishop as we have said, thinks and pretends to be able to effectuate the sacrifice of the Eucharist, is a heretic; he participates and takes part in the perdition of Korah and his accomplices [see Num 16], and he must be separated from the holy Roman church.
1208	→	"We believe that for sinners who truly repent pardon is accorded to them by God, and it is with great joy that we are in communion with them. "We venerate the anointing of the sick with oil. "We do not deny that carnal marriages ought to be solemnized, according to the Apostle [see 1 Cor 7], and we absolutely prohibit the breaking of those which were regularly done. We believe and confess that a man can be saved with his wife, and we no longer condemn the second and other wedding.
1208	→	"We do not reprove in any way the consumption of meat. We do not condemn taking a vow, but even more, we believe from a sincere heart that it is permitted to swear according to truth, judgment, and righteousness [added in 1210: On the subject of the secular authorities, we affirm that he can, without mortal sin, exercise judgment by the shedding of blood, given that, when exercising the penalty, he does not proceed with hatred but in judgment, nor with rashness but with moderation.] "We believe that preaching is very necessary and commendable, nevertheless we believe that it should be accomplished in virtue of the authority or with the permission of the sovereign
1208	→	**Herein, Durand d'Osca** affirmed that he will seek unto death to confound the heretical preachers pontiff or his prelates. But in all the places where reside the manifest heretics who renounce and blaspheme God and the faith of the Roman church, we believe that we must, according to the will of God, confound them through disputation and exhortation, and to oppose them with the Word of the Lord, with head high and until death, as unto adversaries of Christ and the Church. "Ecclesiastical ordinations and all that is read or sung according to what has been established, we approve with humility and we venerate it in the
1208	→	and oppose them at all cost! Yes, re-converted heretics became Rome's most formidable inquisitors in the history of the inquisition, e.g. **Reinerius Saccho** (see 1250) faith. "We believe that the devil did not become evil by his condition, but by his free will. "We believe with all of our hearts and we verbally confess the resurrection of this body which is ours and not another. "We believe and firmly affirm that there will be a judgment by Jesus Christ and that everyone, according to what he has done in this flesh, will receive
1208	→	"We believe that almsgiving, sacrifice, and other good deeds can benefit the deceased. "Those that remain in this world and possess goods, we profess and believe that they will be saved if they give alms and other goods that they possess, and if they observe the commandments of God. We believe that according to the precepts of the Lord, tithes, firstfruits, and offerings must penalties or rewards.
1208	→	be paid to clerics" (DS 790-797).
1208	→	**Inquisitor Peter of Castelnau** murdered (15 Jan)ᴼ **Peter of Castelnau** canonized (10 Mar)ᴼ **Francis of Assisi** devoted his life to "apostolic work"ᴼ
1208	→	**Synodal Constitution of Odon of Paris** condemned the **Waldenses**g
1209	→	Crusade led by [St] **Simon de Monfort** and [St] **Dominic** **Raymond VI** submitted to Roman church, **Jacques de Vitry** preached for a crusade against the **Simon de Montfort** accepted Pope's challenge to conquer the Languedoc region [of France] for the Church of Rome

COLOR GUIDE: YELLOW=Roman Catholic areas; TAN=Bad years for Anabaptists; GOLD=Important events for Catholicism; ORANGE=Catholics "martyred"; RED=Evangelicals martyred; GRAY=Other martyred; Disclaimer: some dates may vary
PINK=Marriage issues; PURPLE=Crusades or massacres; TURQUOISE=Martyrology info; BLUE=Part Protestant areas; AQUA=U.S. Const and Rel.; LT GREEN=Disputed areas; LIME=Bible issues; GREEN=Major dates. (Page 29)

Thomas P. Johnston — Geographic History — Page 30

Date	Germany-Austria-Scandinavia	Switzerland	France-Alsace		British Isles	Italy, Spain, Low Lands
1209	→			marched on Languedoc (Albigenses area) in	Cathars, in which he likely coined the term "Albigenses" was publicly scourged at St. Gilles (June 18)o	
1209	→			Southern France; took: Béziers (22 July),	Because the town would not turn over the 222 known Albigenses or Cathars in their midst, on 22 July 1209, the entire population of the city of Béziers	
1209	→			Carcassonne (15 Aug), Castres, Caussade,	(chief city of 4 departments) was massacred as part of the extirpation required by the Pope; the crusade was led by Simon de Monfort; when asked	
1209	→			Fanjeaux, Gontaud, Mirepoix, Puy-la-Roque,	about Catholics in the Cathedral prior to setting it on fire, Papal Legate Arnaud-Amaury, Abbot of Citeaux, famously replied, "Kill them all,	
1209	→			Saverdun, Tonneins, etc.o	God will know His own" [Neca eos omnes omnes. Deus suos agnoscet] (which statement is disavowed by some)	
1209	→			General Simon de Montfort was named Viscount of the captured	Council held at Avignon proscribed 21 canonical decrees against Heretics and Jewso	
1209	→			Carcassonne and Béziers (Aug)o	Death of Raymond-Roger Trencavel, [former] Viscount of Carcassonne and Béziers (10 Nov)o	
1210	→	Innocent III's Conjectured Three Way Approach to the Waldensian "Problem" (1) Crusade against compromising political leaders, who sheltered the same;		At the capture of Minerve (22 July), 140	Raymond VI was excommunicated a second time in St. Gilleso	24 Waldensian hereticsb burned in Paris; 40	Francis of Assisi's Franciscan Order [OFM—Ordo Fratrum Minorum) officially recognized by
1210	→	(2) Unleashing wandering Franciscan monks to imitate and bring back the Waldenses into the Church of Rome; and (3) Provide the incentive and teaching of a Waldensian leader who returned to the Church of Rome, Durand d'Osca.		Catharso [or 180]b Cathars walk into fire rather than	heretics burned in Narbonne [130 put to death who reproved the	Waldensian man burned in Londonb	Innocent III to assist in combating heresy in Southern Franceo
1210	→			recant in La Minerve [3 women apostacized to	abuses and idolatry of the Pope]b: Philip II burned disciples of Waldo", who later converted back to Catholicism,		By 1210 the word "Roman" is added to the symbol of belief: Durand d'Osca "a remarkable disciple of Waldo", who later converted back to Catholicism,

1210	Mandate of **Emperor Otto IV** of Germany, to the **Bishop of Turin**, against the **Waldenses**g		avoid the flames]b	**Amaury de Bène** in Paris for heresyo	writing *Liber antiheresis*, wrote that the Symbol of faith in his day included belief in the "Holy, **Roman**, Catholic, and Apostolic" churchg	
1210		Crusaders capture Alayrac (**massacre** garrison), Bram (**mutilate** garrison), Pennautier, etc.o			Also by 14 June 1210, the **Waldensian** leader, **Bernard Prim**, had suscribed to the formula of **Durand d'Osca** (found above in 1208)	
1211		First seige of Toulouse (May); siege of Castelnaudary (Sept); took Cahuzac, Coustaussa, Gaillac, La Garde, La Grave (**garrison**	Fall of Castelnaudary: 50 **Cathars**b burned; all of Lavaur: **400**		By order of **Pope Innocent III**, **Bishop of Metz** [Lorraine, France], **Bertram**, organized crusade against readers of the	
1211		**massacred**), La Guépie, Montaigu, Moncuq, Monteferrand, Montgey (**complete destruction**), Puy-Celsi, Rabastens, etc.o	**Cathars**ob burned (3 May); fall of Cassès: **94** [~**100**]b **Cathars**o burned		Bible in the vulgar tongue and all Bibles found were to be burneds	
1211						18 **Heretics** burned in Metzb
1212	**39 Heretics** (from Metz) burned alive at Bingenb	**Pierre de Vaux de Cernay** sent to **Albigensian** districto	Nearly 80 **Heretics** put on trial in Strasbourg, the			
1212		**Simon de Montfort** summoned assembly at Pamiers to settle legal status of the conquered (1 Dec)o	majority sent to the stakeo: van Bracht stated ~**100 persons**b			
1212		Crusaders took: Ananclet (**massacre**), Auterive (**burnt**), Biron, Castelsarrasin, Cauzac, Hautpoul (siege and massacre), L'Isle, Moissac (siege and **massacre of mercenaries**), Montaut, Muret,				
1212		Penne d'Agenais (siege), Penne d'Albigeois (siege), Saint-Antonin (sack of outer borough), Saint-Gaudens, Saint-Marcel, Saint-Michel, Samatan, Verdun-sur-Garonneo				
1213		Battle of Muret (12 Sept)o				
1213		**Prince Louis**, son of **Philip II**, joined crusade (end of year)o				

[St] **Simon de Monfort** led crusade (with help from [St] **Dominic**)

COLOR GUIDE: **YELLOW**=Roman Catholic areas; **TAN**=Bad years for Anabaptists; **GOLD**=Important events for Catholicism; **ORANGE**=Catholics "martyred"; **RED**=Evangelicals martyred; **GRAY**=Other martyred; Disclaimer: some dates may vary
PINK=Marriage issues; **PURPLE**=Crusades or massacres; **TURQUOISE**=Martyrology info; **BLUE**=Part Protestant areas; **AQUA**=U.S. Const; **LT GREEN**=Disputed areas; **LIME**=Bible issues; **GREEN**=Major dates.

Thomas P. Johnston   Geographic History   Page 32

Date	Germany-Austria-Scandinavia	Switzerland		France-Alsace	British Isles	Italy, Spain, Low Lands
1213	→			Siege of Casseneuil (capture, massacre, demolition of walls)°		
1214	→		→	Battle of Bouvines (27 July)°		
1214	These same tests of **Conrad of Marburg** were used to ferret out witches and Heretics in the infamous *Malleus Maleficarum* of 1484; note the use of the hot iron test on "Heretics" in Strasbourg in 1215		→	Captured of the fortresses of Dome, in Perigord	"**Bishop Diego**, borrowing from **the enemy**, recommended to the legates a new type of apostolate. They should give up their other business and devote themselves zealously to preaching. They should send away their followers, travel on foot without money and beg their bread from door to door, imitating the way of life and preaching of the apostles" (Hinnebusch)	[Founding of Dominican Order] ←
1214			→	(kept demolished), and of Montfort°		Grand Inquisitor **Conrad of Marburg [Marpurg]**, so appointed by **Pope** (which office he dispensed for 19 years); **Conrad** used a red hot iron placed in the hand to test for heresy, complete with Mass and a special prayer; the burning iron was placed in the hand and carried 9 paces, then the hand was wrapped; after three days, if they were not burned, they were acquitted, otherwise they were burned alive; **Conrad** also used boiling water, wherein the hand was dipped up to the elbow; also the cold water test, in which the presumed guilty was cast: if he sank, he was considered innocent, if he floated, he was guilty[b]
1214	→		→	Toulouse; they were to [1] *extirpate heresy*,		
1214	→		→	[2] combat vice, [3] teach the faith, and [4] train men in		
1214	→		→	good morals" (Mandonnet)		
1215 Fourth Lateran Council 1215	**Innocent III** called **Fourth Lateran Council**, a.k.a. the 12th Ecumenical Council (opened 11 Nov 1215). The following is the complete text of Section 3, "On Heretics" (From: http://www.dailycatholic.org/history/12ecume1.htm; accessed: 28 June 2003): "We excommunicate and anathematize every heresy raising itself up against this holy, orthodox and catholic faith which we have expounded above. We condemn all heretics, whatever names they may go under. They have different faces indeed but their tails are tied together inasmuch as they are alike in their pride. Let those condemned be handed over to the secular authorities present, or to their bailiffs, for due punishment. Clerics are first to be degraded from their orders. The goods of the condemned are to be confiscated, if they are lay persons, and if clerics they are to be applied to the churches from which they received their stipends. Those who are only found suspect of heresy are to be struck with the sword of anathema, unless they prove their innocence by an appropriate purgation, having regard to the reasons for suspicion and the character of the person. Let such persons be avoided by all until they have made					
1215	adequate satisfaction. If they persist in the excommunication for a year, they are to be condemned as heretics. Let secular authorities, whatever offices they may be discharging, be advised and urged and if necessary be compelled by ecclesiastical censure, if they wish to be reputed and held to be faithful, to take publicly an oath for the defence of the faith to the effect that they will seek, in so far as they can, to expel from the lands subject to their jurisdiction all heretics designated by the church in good faith. Thus whenever anyone is promoted to spiritual or temporal authority, he shall be obliged to confirm this article with an oath. If however a temporal lord, required and instructed by the church, neglects to cleanse his territory of this heretical					

1215	filth, he shall be bound with the bond of excommunication by the metropolitan and other bishops of the province. If he refuses to give satisfaction within a year, this shall be reported to the supreme pontiff so that he may then declare his vassals absolved from their fealty to him and make the land available for occupation by Catholics so that these may, after they have expelled the heretics, possess it unopposed and preserve it in the purity of the faith—saving the right of the suzerain provided that he makes no difficulty in the matter and puts no impediment in the way. The same law is to be observed no less as regards those who do not have a suzerain.
1215	"Catholics who take the cross and gird themselves up for the expulsion of heretics shall enjoy the same indulgence, and be strengthened by the same holy privilege, as is granted to those who go to the aid of the holy Land. Moreover, we determine to subject to excommunication believers who receive, defend or support heretics. We strictly ordain that if any such person, after he has been designated as excommunicated, refuses to render satisfaction within a year, then by the law itself he shall be branded as infamous and not be admitted to public offices or councils or to elect others to the same or to give testimony. He shall be intestable, that is he shall not have the freedom to make a will nor shall succeed to an inheritance. Moreover nobody shall be compelled to answer to him on any business whatever, but he may be compelled to answer to them. If he is a judge sentences pronounced by him shall have no force and cases may not be brought before him; if an advocate, he may not be allowed to defend anyone; if a notary, documents drawn up by him shall be worthless and condemned along with their condemned author; and in similar matters we order the same to be observed. If however he is a cleric, let him be deposed from every office and benefice, so that the greater the fault the greater be the punishment. If any refuse to avoid such persons after they have been pointed out by the church, let them be punished with the sentence of excommunication until they make suitable
1215	Herein unauthorized satisfaction. Clerics should not, of course, give the sacraments of the church to such pestilent people nor give them a christian burial nor accept alms or offerings from public or private them; if they do, let them be deprived of their office and not restored to it without a special indult of the apostolic see. Similarly with regulars, let them be punished with preaching is losing their privileges in the diocese in which they presume to commit such excesses. "There are some who holding to the form of religion but denying its power (as the absolutely forbidden Apostle says), claim for themselves the authority to preach, whereas the same Apostle says, How shall they preach unless they are sent? Let therefore all those who
1215	have been forbidden or not sent to preach, and yet dare publicly or privately to usurp the office of preaching without having received the authority of the apostolic see or the catholic bishop of the place", be bound with the bond of excommunication and, unless they repent very quickly, be punished by another suitable penalty. We add further that each archbishop or bishop, either in person or through his archdeacon or through suitable honest persons, should visit twice or at least once in the year any parish of his in which heretics are said to live. There he should compel three or more men of good repute, or even if it seems expedient the whole neighbourhood, to swear that if anyone knows of heretics there or of any persons who hold secret conventicles or
1215	who differ in their life and habits from the normal way of living of the faithful, then he will take care to point them out to the bishop. The bishop himself should summon the accused to his presence, and they should be punished canonically if they are unable to clear themselves of the charge or if after compurgation they relapse into their former errors of faith. If however any of them with damnable obstinacy refuse to honour an oath and so will not take it, let them by this very fact be regarded as heretics. We therefore will and command and, in virtue of obedience, strictly command that bishops see carefully to the effective execution of these things throughout their dioceses, if they wish to avoid canonical penalties. If any bishop is negligent or remiss in cleansing his diocese of the ferment of heresy, then when this shows itself by unmistakeable signs he shall be deposed from his office as bishop and there shall be put in his place a suitable person who both wishes and is able to overthrow the evil of heresy."
1215	Note the U.S. constitutional ammendments act which protect U.S. citizen's from the canons of the **Fourth Lateran Council**: unlawful seizure of property without just compensation, probable cause prior to arrest, innocent until proven guilty, no self-incrimination, trial by jury of impartial peers, no double-jeopardy, speedy and public trial, no cruel and unusual punishment. Note the **Fourth Lateran's** overthrow of constituted government (expanded	In **Prince Louis'** first crusade; he and **Simon de Montfort** entered Toulouse (Apr-Oct)o	~80 person called **Waldenses**, arrested by **Conrad of Marburg**, tested using the red-hot iron method, found guilty, and burned alive in Strasbourgb
		Wealthy Toulouse burgher **Pierre Seila** (Cella) "presented" several homes to [St] **Dominic**,	Persecution of **Heretics** in Colmaro	**Innocent III** called **Fourth Lateran Council** (opened 11 Nov) to deal in a firm a final way with the "heresy" of the Albigenses and Waldenses; his purpose was to once and for all extirpate the "heretics" in
1215	from 1207): "If however a temporal lord, required and instructed by the church, neglects to cleanse his territory of this heretical filth, he shall be bound with the bond of excommunication by the metropolitan and other bishops of the province. If he refuses to give satisfaction within a year, this	**Prince Louis** (of France) joined the crusade	Several **Waldenses**	Southern France, the number one "problem" of his papacy, as they had the audacity to "claim for themselves the authority to

(Page 33)

COLOR GUIDE **YELLOW**=Roman Catholic areas; **TAN**=Bad years for Anabaptists; **GOLD**=Important events for Catholicism; **ORANGE**=Catholics "martyred"; **RED**=Evangelicals martyred; **GRAY**=Other martyred; Disclaimer: some dates may vary **PINK**=Marriage issues; **PURPLE**= Crusades or massacres; **TURQUOISE**=Martyrology info; **BLUE**=Part Protestant areas; **AQUA**=U.S. Const; **LIME**=Bible issues; **LT GREEN**=Disputed areas; **GREEN**=Major dates.

Thomas P. Johnston — Geographic History — Page 34

Date	Germany-Austria-Scandinavia	Switzerland	France-Alsace	British Isles	Italy, Spain, Low Lands
1215	→	shall be reported to the supreme pontiff so that he may then declare his vassals absolved from their fealty to him and make the land available for occupation by Catholics so that these may, after they have expelled the heretics, possess it unopposed and preserve it in the purity of the faith --	which became the headquarters and prisons for the **Dominican** inquisition	burned alive in Toulouse, sent to the secular judge by **Dominic**,	preach" without being sent [by the Pope or his Bishops]s
1215	→	saving the right of the suzerain provided that he makes no difficulty in the matter and puts no impediment in the way. The same law is to be observed no less as regards those who do not have a suzerain" (op. cit.)	→	founder of the **Dominicans**b	**Dominicans** published **"On the Manner of Conducting Trials"** explaining the manner of
1215			→		questioning Heretics in the Netherlandsb
1216	→		**Simon de Montfort** received investiture as **Lord of Languedoc** (10 Apr)o	Siege of Beaucaire brought	Death of Innocent III (6 July)
1216	→		**Simon de Montfort** entered Toulouse, crushing the revolt and dismantling defenseso	crusaders their first defeat (May-Aug) o	**Papal Bull of Honorius III** confirmed the Order founded by **Dominic** [OFP—Ordo Fratrum Praedicatorum or O.P. Ordo Praedicatorum], or simply **Dominicans**o
1217	**Peter Waldo** died in Bohemia		**Simon de Montfort** captured fortresses of Crest in Dauphiné, La Bastide, Monteil, Montgrenier, and Pierre-pertuseo	Persecution of **Heretics** of Cambraio	
1217	→		→ Opening of siege of Toulouseo		
1218	→		→	Gérard de la Motte, "A Summary of the Doctrine of the Papists" [1218] A. D. 1218—In a certain ancient history of the martyrs of this time, I have found the following account, in which one of the orthodox believers presents a summary of the doctrine of the papists, as opposite to the true doctrine of the true church of God in those times; it reads as follows:	
1218	→		→	1. "They found their church upon the succession and derivation of the bishops (though erroneously) from the time of the apostles. 2. "They call those bishops, who consecrate churches, chapels, and altars; who make mass priests and sanctuaries of altars.	
1218	→		→	3. "They regard the pope as the supreme bishop, the head of their churches; who may be reproved by none but God. 4. "They are divided into many contending sects; some a ecclesiastics, some seculars. The ecclesiastics have separated themselves from the common people—whom they call the laity—and are themselves	

Date				Event
1218	→			variously divided. Some are called monks and nuns; who vow, not to marry; to submit to voluntary poverty; to observe human institutions, such as, to have nothing to do with money; to a wear gray, white, or black cap; to eat no flesh; to be dumb at times; and similar other false and invented forms of holiness. Others are called secular priests; who also may not marry, but like the others, have to do a great amount of muttering and reading.
1218	→			5. "They have priests, who are consecrated by bishops, to offer up sacrifice for the living and the dead.
1218	→			6. "All these ecclesiastics hold themselves exempt from punishment by civil authority, and bear no burdens with the citizens, since they are exempt.
1218	→			7. "They seek their salvation out of Christ, in their own works and merits, which they also sell to each other for money; such as masses, indulgences, pilgrimages, and the merits of departed saints, which they also sell to the dead, who, they say, are in purgatory.
1218	→			8. "They have an idol or patron for every city, village or hamlet.
1218	→		**Simon de Montfort** led crusade with help from **Prince Louis**	9. "They divide the power and honor of God among the departed saints; thus seamen invoke St. Nicholas, St. Christopher, and St. Anna; women in travail, St. Mary; for gum-boils, St. Appolonia; against pestilence, St. Rochus and St. Anthony.
1218	→			10. "They set up images in their churches; they light tapers, torches, and lamps before them; they clothe them in cloth, silk, velvet, silver, and gold; they carry them with great reverence on their shoulders; they visit them in different places, and offer gifts to them (to which practice the popes and bishops append indulgence for sins); they kneel before them; they kiss, and worship them.
1218	→			11. "In their oaths they swear by God and all His saints, etc.
1218	→			12. "They pray to, and call upon God, without considering their need, and without thinking why they call upon Him; they give Him their prayers by the number, as apples are bought; they read, in the hours, rosaries, etc.
1218	→			13. "They create many sabbaths, which they call holidays, in honor of the departed saints; on which days manual labor is forbidden on pain of punishment; while drinking to excess, bartering, and gambling remain unpunished. On these days they generally commit shameful idolatry; the services are read in an unknown tongue; water is conjured; the organ is played; and the dead are called upon for help or assistance.
1218	→		→	14. "To the two sacraments, or signs of grace, instituted by Christ in His church, namely, holy baptism and the holy Supper, which they have shamefully corrupted, they have added five others, namely, confirmation, matrimony, ordination of mass priests, auricular confession, and extreme unction.
1218	→		→	15. "In baptism they leave out the most important part, namely the preaching of the Gospel; and add their own, conjure salt, grease, spittle, and tapers, and exorcise the devil from children which he never possessed.
1218	→			16. "They also baptize bells, giving them names.
1218	→		→	17. "They have changed the Lord's Supper into an offering for the living and the dead; they conjure bread with five words ["Hoc est enim corpus meum", i.e. for this is my body]; and persuade the people, that the bread is changed into flesh, and the wine into blood.
1218	→			18. "They withhold wine from the laity, contrary to the command of Christ, who said: *'Drink ye all of it.'*
1218	→		→	19. "They worship the bread, and say that it is their God; they enclose it in coffers and ciboria; they carry it

COLOR GUIDE: YELLOW=Roman Catholic areas; TAN=Bad years for Anabaptists; GOLD=Important events for Catholicism; ORANGE=Catholics "martyred"; RED=Evangelicals martyred; GRAY=Other martyred; Disclaimer: some dates may vary. PINK=Marriage issues; PURPLE=Crusades or massacres; TURQUOISE=Martyrology info; BLUE=Part Protestant areas; AQUA=U.S. Const; LT GREEN=Disputed areas; LIME=Bible issues; GREEN=Major dates. (Page 35)

Thomas P. Johnston — Geographic History — Page 36

Date	Germany-Austria-Scandinavia	Switzerland		France-Alsace	British Isles	Italy, Spain, Low Lands
1218			→	through the streets; they burn torches and tapers before it, also at noonday; they address and salute it; but it answers not. 20. "In their churches they have altars draped with linen, upon which burning tapers are placed at daytime, when the mass is read.		
1218			→	21. "Mass is read by a mass priest, who is hired to do it for money, or a yearly salary; he comes clothed in strange attire, after Jewish fashion, with a drinking cup of silver or gold in his hand, and accompanied by an attendant. He then says his confession before the altar, in Latin (though the attendant does not understand it), and invokes the assistance of the dead saints. Then, having kept up his mummery for a		
1218			→	considerable time, having spoken loud and low, turning himself hither and thither, kissing and licking, he finally takes bread and wine, and forthwith offers the same to God, for the redemption of souls, for the hope of salvation, and the health of those present. Thus they reject Thy sacrifice, O Christ Jesus, which Thou once didst make for our salvation. O God, says the writer, how canst Thou suffer this? He then		
1218			→	calls the dead saints to the feasts, desiring to be aided by their merits. Over the bread he breathes these five words: *Hoc it enim corpus meum*, that is: For this is my body; supposing that thereby the bread will be changed into flesh. He then holds it over his head, for the people to worship it. So he does also with the cup. Then he prays for all those who sleep in Christ, that they may obtain a place of		
1218			→	refreshing. Thereupon he prays to the Father, to accept the Son, whom they believe to have there, as graciously as He accepted the offerings of Melchisedek and of Abel. Finally, he worships the bread, calling it the Lamb of God. Having worshiped the Lamb, he breaks it in pieces, and eats it up, also quaffing the wine, which he imagines to be the Lamb's blood. This is the glorious mass of the papists,		
1218			→	which, says the author, is a shameful corruption of the Supper of Christ, and has been reprehended by many godly men, who on account of this had shed their blood. 22. "Such masses are read in honor of the dead saints, of the sacrament, of the cross, the spear, and the nails.		
1218			→	23. "They sell the same remedy against all sickness, against storm, thunder, lighting, hail, tempests at sea, and every calamity. Every man is served according to his money; they who give little, have a dry mass, or a wet mass without singing; those who give much, get a half-sung mass, or one partly sung, according to how much they give.		
1218			→	24. "They teach that their invented sacrament of confirmation is of more importance than the sacrament of baptism, instituted by Christ; and that baptism is incomplete without confirmation. 25. "They dissolve marriage, in order that the husband or the wife may become spiritual, that is a priest, monk, or nun, contrary to the command of Christ: What God hath joined together, let no man put asunder."		
1218			→	"Time would fail me," writes this zealous man, "if I were to recount all the falsities of the papists, in life, doctrine, and the sacraments; and still they can endure no admonition to reform, but persecute with fire and sword, those who admonish and reprove them."b [Gerard was burned alive in 1227]		
1218	**Beghart burned in Erfurt**		→	Death of **Simon de Montfort** (25 June)o		

1218	→				Death of **Pierre de Vaux de Cernay** (late Dec)o					
1219	→				**Prince Louis**' second crusade; capture of Marmande, unsuccessful siege of Toulouse (May-June)o					
1220	→	**Frederick II** of Hohenstaufen succumbed to demands of clerics and published laws to give them further rights in **"Privilegium"**			**Heretics** persecuted at Troyeso	Theologian **Almaricus**, who reproved the invocation of the saints as idolatry, burned alive in Parisb				
1221	→				Death of [St] **Dominic** (6 Aug)o					
1222	→				Death of **Raymond VI** (Aug)o		**Deacon** burned at Oxford			
1223	→				Death of **Raymond-Roger**, Count of Foix (Apr)o	Death of **Philip II** (4 July)o				
1223	→					**Louis VIII** crowned at Rheims (6 Aug)o				
1224	→				**Amaury de Montfort** left Languedoc (15 Jan)o					
1225	→				Cathar churches assemble at Pieusseo	Death of **Arnald-Amalric**, Archb. of Narbonne (29 Sept)o			**T. Aquinas** born in kingdom of Naples	
1226	→				**Raymond VII** excommunicated by Council of Bourges (28 Jan)o				Death of [St] **Francis of Assisi**	

King **Louis VIII** led crusade (from 1223)

COLOR GUIDE: YELLOW=Roman Catholic areas; TAN=Bad years for Anabaptists; GOLD=Important events for Catholicism; ORANGE=Catholics "martyred"; RED=Evangelicals martyred; GRAY=Other martyred; Disclaimer: some dates may vary
PINK=Marriage issues; PURPLE= Crusades or massacres; TURQUOISE=Martyrology info; BLUE=Part Protestant areas; AQUA=U.S. Const; LT GREEN=Disputed areas; LIME=Bible issues; GREEN=Major dates. (Page 37)

Thomas P. Johnston — Geographic History — Page 38

Date	Germany-Austria-Scandinavia	Switzerland	France-Alsace	British Isles	Italy, Spain, Low Lands
1226	→		Louis VIII's crusade (June-Nov)o		
1226	→		Louis VIII died at Montpensier (8 Nov)o		
1227	→		The King of France left Humbert of Beaujeu to conquer the area for himself and Rome;		Gregory IX became Pope (1227-1241); early in his rule he gave extraordinary powers to judge matters of faith, turning those convicted over to the secular arm in *Inquisitio haereticae pravitatis*h3
1227	→		Humbert besieged a suspicious town named Borriens; upon entering the town he burned alive the Borriens Deacon and others burned alive in Borriens		
1227	→		all who would not become Catholic, including their pastor, G. de la Motteb G. de la Motte, Albigensian-Waldensian		
1228	→		Archbishops of Aix, Arles, and Narbonne assembled in Navignon [?] to ask inquisitors to forbear, "that they		
1228	→		had apprehended so many *Waldenses*, that it was not possible to get a sufficient quantity of Lime and Stone to build prisons for them, and therefore		
1228	→		desired them to forbear the imprisoning of them, till they had heard further from the Pope"m2		
1229	Contra U.S. law: no freedom of conscience, guilty until proven innocent, and the "lawful" seizure of		Treaty of Meaux signed, Raymond VII scourged before the altar of Notre Dame de Paris (12 Apr)o		Council of Toulouse, chapter 5, "We ordain, that the house in which a heretic is discovered shall be razed to the ground; and the farm or land upon which a heretic is found, shall be confiscated"b
1229	and destruction of any property on which a heretic is found; these laws continued after the Reformation, as lands and homes were taken from		Council of Toulouse (Nov)o →		Council of Toulouse, canon 14, "We prohibit lay persons to have books of the Old and New Testament, with the exception of the Psalter, and the

Year	Left content	Center	Right content
1229	Anabaptists in the Netherlands and divided with the Emperor or Duke		portion of the Psalms contained in the Brevary, or in the Hours of the Very Blessed Virgin. But we prohibit them very vigorously from being in the vulgar tongue even in the books listed"S
1229	→		From the **Council of the Prelates of France**: "*Of the abjuration of heresy*.—'In order that, through the help of God, the heretics may be more easily exterminated, and the Roman Catholic faith may be the sooner planted in the land, we decree, that you shall perfectly observe all the statutes, ecclesiastical ordinances, laws, and commandments that have been enacted regarding this matter, by the apostolic see (the pope and his legates), and by princes. Moreover, that you make all males as well as females, the male sex
1229	Again the destruction of property and the confiscation of all the goods of the presumed heretics		from fourteen years and upwards, and the female sex from twelve year and upwards, abjure all heresy, and besides, promise with an oath, that they will observe the Roman Catholic faith, defend the Catholic church, and persecute the heretics. All those who, after
1229	→		such abjuration, shall be found to have apostacized, and not to observe or fulfill the penance imposed upon them, shall be punished with the proper punishment, such as apostates deserve."b
1229	→	**Council of Beziers**b →	**Council of Beziers**, chapter 35, "Also the houses in which any heretic shall be found, living or dead, accused or condemned, being with the knowledge and consent of the proprietors of said houses, provided said proprietors have achieved their legal age, you shall cause to be demolished, and shall confiscate all the goods of those who live in them, unless they can legally prove or show their innocence or ignorance"b
1230	Severe persecution of **Waldenses** in Germany (French Rhine area), many burned for their faith; confessions on the rack led to the knowledge of many adherents and accomplishes throughout Germany, France, Italy, and especially Lombardyb	**Cathar New Testament**, titled "**Waldensian Bible**" dated by Jean Duvernoy from 1230-1330, written in Occitan or Languedoc	Excerpt of the three letters/decrees of **Holy Roman Emperor Frederic II**: 1st: "Men, as well as women, whatever name they may bear, we sentence to perpetual infamy, that neither oath nor faith shall be kept towards them [foreshadowing of John Hus' death]; but we banish them, and order that their goods be confiscated, never
1230		language; known as Manuscript #AP36 at the municipal library in	more returned to them. We likewise ordain … that all officers … swear an oath that they will … expell from their jurisdictions all heretics, indicated by the church.…" 2nd: "We therefore decree and ordain that heretics, of whatever name, shall receive condign punishment, throughout the empire, wherever the church shall condemn them
1230	→ Three decrees of **Holy Roman Emperor Frederick II** (at the request of **Pope Gregory IX**)	Lyons, France; included in this manuscript is a New Testament,	as heretics, and deliver or indicate them to the secular judge. … "We ordain like punishment for those whom the crafty enemy stirs to be their advocates, or who are their improper protectors.…" 3rd: "The sects of the heretics, are not called by the name of any ancient heretics, lest
1230	→ issued against the **Albigenses** and **Patarini**, leading to severe persecutions in 1231b →	and a "**Cathar Ritual**," which included two Gospel	they should be known; … but after the example of the ancient martyrs, who suffered martyrdom for the Catholic faith, they likewise, from their suffering, call themselves Patarini, that is, *delivered unto passion or suffering*. "But these miserable Patarini, who are estranged from the holy faith of the eternal
1230	Again the confiscation of goods, "never to be returned to them" "Squanderers of their own lives" and		Godhead, destroy with one sweep of their heretical wickedness, God, their neighbor, and themselves.… they destroy their neighbor because, under the cover of spiritual food, they administer heretical wickedness; but far more cruelly they rage against themselves, because, after destroying their souls they, as extravagant squanderers of

COLOR GUIDE: YELLOW=Roman Catholic areas; TAN=Bad years for Anabaptists; GOLD=Important events for Catholicism; ORANGE=Catholics "martyred"; RED=Evangelicals martyred; GRAY=Other martyred; Disclaimer: some dates may vary PINK=Marriage issues; PURPLE=Crusades or massacres; TURQUOISE=Martyrology info; BLUE=Part Protestant areas; AQUA=U.S. Const; LT GREEN=Disputed areas; LIME=Bible issues; GREEN=Major dates. (Page 39)

Geographic History

Date	Germany-Austria-Scandinavia	Switzerland	France-Alsace	British Isles	Italy, Spain, Low Lands
1230			presentations and advice for those evangelizing two-by-two ["double"]	"seekers of their own death" repeated in the questioning of Huguenot martyrs after the Reformation. their life, and improvident seekers of their death, also ultimately expose their bodies to a cruel death, which they might have escaped by a true confession of, and constancy in, the orthodox faith.	
1230			in dangerous areas: Gospel presentations emphasized	The Evangelical Faith of the Waldenses was called "superstition" (later being associated with "And what is hardest of all to say, those who survive are not only not deterred by the example of others whom they see die before their eyes, but they even strive to be burnt alive in the sight of men.	
1230			baptism in the Holy Spirit by the laying on of hands and separation from the world	witchcraft (*Malleus Maleficarum*, 1484) "Therefore we cannot refrain from drawing the sword of just vengeance against them the more vigorously to persecute them, as it is judged that they practice the more extensively the knavery of their superstition, to the exclusion of the Christian faith, on account of the Roman church, which is held to be the head of all other churches, as it is known that they came from the borders of Italy, and especially from Lombardy, as we have ascertained, their wickedness overflows far and wide...."b	
1231	Repercussions of the decrees of the Emperor, let to greater persecution of **Anabaptistic Waldenses** in the				
1231	Rhine valley of Germany and France: who were informed against, and made manifest by torture on the rack, and who were burned alive		Montségur became Cathar strongholdº	Death of Foulques de Marseilles, Bishop of Toulouseº	
1231	under the vigilant eyes of the Dominican monk, **Conrad of Marburg**b				
1232	→		Guilhabert de Castres convened the Synod of Montségurº	19 Waldenses burned alive in Toulouseb	
1233 Monastic [itinerating] Inquisition Codified	Gregory IX appointed Conrad of Marburg to impliment "*Excommunicatus*" in Germany; Conrad asked for assistance →		Pope Gregory IX appointed Robert le Petit (a.k.a. Robert le Bougre) to impliment "*Excommunicatus*" in France, with the assistance of the Dominican prior of Besançonº	Pope Gregory IX's "*Excommunicatus*" established a special **permanent tribunal** to combat the heresies of the Cathari (Albigenses) and Waldenses ←	Raymond Lull (1232-1315) born in Mallorca (now Spain), became prominent Franciscan missionary to the Muslims
1233	from Dominican priors of Regensberg, Friesach, and Strasbourg (using Bull "Ille Humani Generis") →			Pope Gregory IX declared "We excommunicate and anathematize all heretics, Cathars, Patarenes, Poor Men of Lyons, Passagini, Josepini, Arnaldistae, and others by whatever names they may be known, having indeed different faces but being united by their tails and meeting in the same point through their vanity"	
1233	→		Pope Gregory IX granted Dominicans general authority for monastic [itinerating] inquisition (13 Apr)º		

1233	Inquisitor **Conrad of Marburg** died at the hand of Heretics⁰			**Three Dominicans** thrown into a well at Cordes⁰					**Council of Tarracon** prohibited the owning Old or New Testaments	
1234				**Inquisitor Arnald Cathala** exhumed certain dead Heretics; he was roughly treated by a mob⁰						
1234				**Raymond VII** published his "statutes against heretics"⁰						
1234				**Inquisitors William Arnald** and **Pierre Celan** [Seila?] condemned **210 persons** to be burned alive at Moissac⁰						
1234										
1235				**Count of Toulouse** and council expelled Dominicans from Toulouse (Nov)⁰						
1237				**Franciscans** join the Inquisition in Languedoc by order of **Gregory IX** to temper the cruelty of the **Dominicans**⁰³						
1238									**Pope Gregory IX** sent **Robert Boulgre O.P.** as an inquisitor to France and Flanders on account of the increase of the **Waldenses** in those regions	
1238										
1239				**183 Cathars** burned alive in the presence of the **Count of Champagne** in Montwimer (Marne)⁰						

COLOR GUIDE
YELLOW=Roman Catholic areas; TAN=Bad years for Anabaptists; GOLD=Important events for Catholicism; ORANGE=Catholics "martyred"; RED=Evangelicals martyred; GRAY=Other martyred; Disclaimer: some dates may vary
PINK=Marriage issues; PURPLE= Crusades or massacres; TURQUOISE=Martyrology info; BLUE=Part Protestant areas; AQUA=U.S. Const; LIME=Bible issues; GREEN=Major dates.
LT GREEN=Disputed areas; (Page 41)

Thomas P. Johnston — Geographic History — Page 42

Date	Germany-Austria-Scandinavia	Switzerland	France-Alsace		British Isles	Italy, Spain, Low Lands
1240	→		Raymond Trencavel besieged Carcassonne (Sept)o			
1241	→		Raymond VII promised Louis IX to destroy fortress of Montségur o	Pierre Celan d con-		Council of Lomberts b2
1241	→		11 inquisitors, including William Arnaud and Stephen of Narbonne, murdered in Avignonet	tinued his inquisi-tion		
1242	→		Raymond VII's rebellion (Apr-Oct) o	→		
1242	→		Massacre of Avignonet (28 May) o	→		
1243	Pope reminded "local authorities" to work with inquisitor; or a threat of the "absolution of fealty" as found in the Fourth Lateran Council (1215)!		Treaty of Lorris (Jan) o	Inquisi-tion of Bernard de	Inquisi-tion of Ferrier and Gary d	224 Waldenses apprehended by the Bishop of Narbonne and Albi, and the Seneschal of Carcassonne,	"Processus Inquisitionis" was published to provide assistance and further guidance to inquisitors
1243	→			Caux d in Lauran-gais and	→	burned alive near Toulouse b	Pope Innocent IV reminded local authorities to work with inquisitors under penalty
1243	→			Tou-louse [apparen-tly the	→		of severe censure if they did not
1243	→			only inquisi-tion record	→	Council of Beziers decided to destroy Montségur o	
1243	→		Began siege of Montségur (13 May) o	available to Penn. State Profes-	→		

1243	→	Ramon Damors brought letter from **Cathar Bishop of Cremona** to Bertrand Marty at Montségur○	→ sor Henry Charles Lea (1887)]l2	→ Pierre Celan conducted inquisitions in Southern France (continued into the 1250s)d	**Council of Beziers** prohibited owning heretical books (see below)
1243	→		→	→ Bernard de Caux conducted his inquisition in Lauragais region and city of Toulouse (May 609)d	**Pope Innocent IV** grants absolution to **Raymond VII** (2 Dec)
1243	→	**Durand, Bishop of Albi**, brought reinforcements for siege of Montségur (Nov)○	→	→ Pons de Parnac and **Ferrer** conducted inquisitions in Montségur following the murder of 11 inquisitors in Avignonet	**Council of Narbonne** attended by army commanders besieging Montségur
1244	→	Night attack attempted (5 Jan?)○	→	→	
1244	→	Night sortie of garrison failure (1 Mar)○	→	→	
1244	→	Truce concluded between besiegers and besieged (2 Mar)○			
1244	→	Capitulation of Montségur (14 Mar)○			
1244	→	**Massacre of Montségur** (16 Mar)○; approx **250 burned alive**			
1245	→				**First Council of Lyons** to clarify laws on excommunication and to provide plenary absolution for participation in crusades
1245	→				At the University of Paris **Thomas Aquinas** joined the Dominicans and argued for their

Disclaimer: some dates may vary (Page 43)

COLOR GUIDE: YELLOW=Roman Catholic areas; TAN=Bad years for Anabaptists; GOLD=Important events for Catholicism; ORANGE=Catholics "martyred"; RED=Evangelicals martyred; GRAY=Other martyred; PINK=Marriage issues; PURPLE=Crusades or massacres; TURQUOISE=Martyrology info; BLUE=Part Protestant areas; AQUA=U.S. Const; LT GREEN=Disputed areas; LIME=Bible issues; GREEN=Major dates.

Thomas P. Johnston — Geographic History — Page 44

Date	Germany-Austria-Scandinavia	Switzerland	France-Alsace			British Isles	Italy, Spain, Low Lands
1245	→		→	→	→		cause [as an apologist for the inquisition in Southern France? Was this not his ultimate purpose in writing his *Summa*?]
1246	→		→	→	→	Louis IX (aka St. Louis) ordered the construction of a special prisons to house Heretics in Carcassonne and Béziers[o]	**Council of Beziers** [1243 or 1246], Canon 36 stated, "You will fully watch, according to all that is right and legal, that theological
1246	→		→	→	→		books not be possessed, even in Latin, by lay people, nor in the vulgar language by clerics."
1247	→		→	→	→	→ Waldenses inquisited in Southern France[b] →	
1248	→			Count of Toulouse had 80 *credentes* [Heretics] burned at Barleigh (Agen)[o]			**Aragonese Inquisition** established boundaries
1249	→			Death of Raymond VII (27 Sept)[o]			
1249	→						
1250	→			Pierre Celan inquisited in Quercy[d]			Inquisitor Reinerius Saccho wrote his "Of the Cathars and the Poor Men of Lyons" (first date, 1250, also 1254)
1251	→	Dominicans **Conrad Dorfo** and his disciple **John** were sent to					Pope Innocent IV appointed and sent Dominican and Franciscan inquisitors to Toulouse; Dominicans **Conrad Dorfo** and his disciple **John** were sent to Worms[b]
1251	→	Worms by the **Pope Innocent IV**; condemned many Heretics to the fire[b]					

1252	→									Inquisitor of Lombardy, **Peter Verona**, assassinated near Milan; he was raised to sainthood 24 days later by the **Pope Innocent Iv**[b]
1252	→								Death of Spanish **King Ferdinand III** who was made a saint in 1671 for his efforts in burning heretics	
1253	→					**Jean de St. Pierre** (brother of **B de Caux**) continued inquisition of his brother			**Pope Innocent IV** deposed **Robert, Bishop of Lincoln**, who "reproved the avarice, ambition, arrogance, and tyranny of the Pope… in order to enrich his illegitimate children, nieces and nephews"[b]	11 years of severe inquisitions in Lombardy (1251-1262)[b]
1253	→									→
1254	→									Former Waldensian, **Reinerius Saccho**, who became their inquisitor, wrote "*Summâ de hæreticis*", describing them, and inadvertently affirming their orthodox beliefs
1254	→					**Fragments of the inquisitions of Jean de Saint-Pierre and Réginald de Chartres**[d]				→
1255	→						End of **Albigensian Crusade** in Southern France, begun in 1181 and/or 1209			11 years of severe inquisitions in Lombardy (cont.)[b]
1255	→						Capture of Quéribus, one of the last Cathar strongholds in Languedoc[o]			
1258	→									In Cambray [Belgium], **Jacobines and Dominicans** caused many to be burned alive[b]
1258	→								**Aquinas** began writing *Summa contra Gentiles* partly directed to assist in detecting and converting "heretics"	

COLOR GUIDE: YELLOW=Roman Catholic areas; TAN=Bad years for Anabaptists; GOLD=Important events for Catholicism; ORANGE=Catholics "martyred"; RED=Evangelicals martyred; GRAY=Other martyred; Disclaimer: some dates may vary
PINK=Marriage issues; PURPLE=Crusades or massacres; TURQUOISE=Martyrology info; BLUE=Part Protestant areas; AQUA=U.S. Const; LT GREEN=Disputed areas; LIME=Bible issues; GREEN=Major dates.

(Page 45)

Thomas P. Johnston — Geographic History — Page 46

Date	Germany-Austria-Scandinavia	Switzerland	France-Alsace	British Isles	Italy, Spain, Low Lands
1259	→		Italian physician in Paris, **Gerard Sagarellas**, wrote a book against the Franciscans; **Bonaventura**, general of the order, replied that **Sagarellas** believed like the Waldenses[b]		11 years of severe inquisitions in Lombardy (cont)[b]
1259	→			Death of **Reinerius Saccho**, former Waldensian, become their inquisitor, and author of *Summā de hæreticis*	
1260	→			Letter of **Pope Alexander IV** to the Dominican inquisitors of Lombardy to persecute the Christians there, and excommunicate any secular authorities that did not execute suspects of heresy	
1261	**Latin Empire fell to Emperor Michael VIII Palaiologos** of the Empire of Nicaea, Latin Emperor **Baldwin II** went into exile				
1262			Records of inquisitions of **Pierre de Fenouillet** and **Hugue de Saissac**[d]	Decree of Pope Urban IV against **Waldenses** and **Albigenses** of Lombardy and Margravate of Genoa; there is no writing extant which explains the suffering and deaths that ensued	
1265	Aquinas on "**Whether a prince forfeits his dominion over his subjects, on account of apostasy from the faith, so that they no longer owe him allegiance?**" (*Summa*, SS, Q[12], A[2]): "On the contrary, Gregory VII [1073–1085] says (Council, Roman V): 'Holding to the institutions of our holy predecessors, we, by our apostolic authority, absolve from their oath those who through loyalty or through the sacred bond of an oath owe allegiance to excommunicated persons: and we absolutely forbid them to continue their allegiance to such persons, until these shall have made amends.' Now no apostates from the faith, like heretics, are excommunicated, according to the Decretal [*Extra, De Haereticis, cap. Ad abolendam]. Therefore princes should not be obeyed when they have apostatized from the faith"			**Thomas Aquinas'** *Summa Theologica* — **Thomas Aquinas**, O.F.P., that "Great Angelic Doctor," wrote his *Summa Theologica* as an apologetic for Roman Catholic theology and its inquisition, as well as for the practices of his Order, the Dominicans, and their primary role in the inquisition of and extirpation of the Evangelical Albigenses (from: http://www.ccel.org/ccel/aquinas/summa.html) SS, Q[10], "**Unbelief in General**", A[6], "**Whether the unbelief of pagans or heathens is graver than other kinds?**": "In this way the unbelief of heretics, who confess their belief in the Gospel, and resist that faith by corrupting it, is a more grievous sin than that of the Jews, who have never accepted the Gospel faith. Since, however, they accepted the figure of that faith in the Old Law, which they corrupt by their false interpretations, their unbelief is a more grievous sin than that of the heathens, because the latter have not accepted the Gospel faith in any way at all" … "Now the heathens deny the faith in more numerous and more important points than Jews and heretics; since they do not accept the faith at all. Therefore their unbelief is the gravest." … "Hence, speaking absolutely, the unbelief of heretics is the worst"	
1265					
1266			→ inquisition in Carcassonne	SS, Q[10], A[7], "**Whether one ought to dispute with unbelievers in public?**": "On the other hand, in the second case it is dangerous to dispute in public about the faith, in the presence of	
1266			→	SS, Q[10], A[8], "**Whether unbelievers ought to be compelled to the faith?**": "On the other simple people, whose faith for this very reason is more firm, that they have never heard anything differing from what they believe. Hence it is not expedient for them to hear what unbelievers have to say against the faith."	

Year	Content	Event 1	Event 2	Commentary
1266	hand, there are unbelievers who at some time have accepted the faith, and professed it, such as heretics and all apostates: such should be submitted even to bodily compulsion, that they may fulfil what they have promised, and hold what they, at one time, received. … For, Augustine says (Contra Ep. Parmen. iii, 2) 'these words show that when this is not to be feared, that is to say, when a man's crime is so publicly known, and so hateful to all, that he has no defenders, or none such as might cause a schism, the severity of discipline should not slacken.'" SS, Q[10], A[11], **"Whether the rites of unbelievers ought to be tolerated?"**: "On the other hand, the rites of other unbelievers, which are neither truthful nor profitable are by no means to be tolerated, except perchance in order to avoid an evil, e.g. the scandal or disturbance that might ensue, or some hindrance to the salvation of those who if they were unmolested might gradually be converted to the faith. For this reason the Church, at times, has tolerated the rites even of heretics and pagans, when unbelievers were very numerous."	Records of inquisitions of **Pierre de Fenouillet** and **Hugue de Saissac**d →	inquisition in Carcassonne (Registre Doat XXV)d →	
1266	SS, Q[11], **"Heresy"**, A[1]: **"Whether heresy is a species of unbelief?"**: "Therefore heresy is a species of unbelief, belonging to those who profess the Christian faith, but corrupt its dogmas."	→	→	
1266	SS, Q[11], A[2]: **"Whether heresy is properly about matters of faith?"** Quoted Jerome: "If anything therein has been incorrectly or carelessly expressed, we beg that it may be set aright by you who hold [Aquinas' Summa cont.] the faith and see of Peter. If however this, our profession, be approved by the judgment of your apostleship, whoever may blame me, will prove that he himself is ignorant, or malicious, or even not a catholic but a heretic."	→	→	Notice that **Aquinas** distinctly taught in SS, Q[10], A[11] that Roman Catholics ought to "by no means" tolerate the rites of heretics (e.g. Baptists or Protestants), unless they themselves are in a minority, in which case they may tolerate those rites.
1266	SS, Q[11], A[3]: **"Whether heretics ought to be tolerated?"** "I answer that, With regard to heretics two points must be observed: one, on their own side; the other, on the side of the Church. On their own side there is the sin, whereby they deserve not only to be separated from the Church by excommunication, but also to be severed from the world by death. … much more reason is there for heretics, as soon as they are convicted of	→	→	
1271	heresy, to be not only excommunicated but even put to death. On the part of the Church, however, there is mercy which looks to the conversion of the wanderer, wherefore she condemns not at once, but 'after the first and second admonition,' as the Apostle directs: after that, if he is yet stubborn, the Church no longer hoping for	Death of **Alphonse of Poitiers** and **Jeanne of Toulouse**;	→	
1271	his conversion, looks to the salvation of others, by excommunicating him and separating him from the Church, and furthermore delivers him to the secular tribunal to be exterminated thereby from the world by death."	Languedoc region annexed to **French crown**o	→	
1272	"Reply to Objection 3: According to Decret. (xxiv, qu. iii, can. Notandum), 'to be excommunicated is not to be uprooted.' A man is excommunicated, as the Apostle says (1 Cor. 5:5) that his "spirit may be saved in the day of Our Lord." Yet if heretics be altogether uprooted by death, this is the Church no longer hoping for his conversion, looks to the salvation of others, by excommunicating him and separating		→	Notice how **Aquinas** again provided an apologetic for Rome's (and his Dominican Order's) execution of the Albigensian so-called "Heretics", calling on Inquisitors to put heretics to death, by them being: (1) severed from the world by death; (2) put to death and (3) exterminated thereby from the world by death (SS, Q[11], A[3]).

COLOR GUIDE: **YELLOW**=Roman Catholic areas; **TAN**=Bad years for Anabaptists; **GOLD**=Important events for Catholicism; **ORANGE**=Catholics "martyred"; **RED**=Evangelicals martyred; **GRAY**=Other martyred; Disclaimer: some dates may vary **PINK**=Marriage issues; **PURPLE**= Crusades or massacres; **TURQUOISE**=Martyrology info; **BLUE**=Part Protestant areas; **AQUA**=U.S. Const; **LT GREEN**=Disputed areas; **LIME**=Bible issues; **GREEN**=Major dates.

(Page 47)

Date	Germany-Austria-Scandinavia	Switzerland	France-Alsace	British Isles	Italy, Spain, Low Lands
1273			Inquisitions in Toulouse by R. de Plassac, Pons de Parnac, P. Arsieu, H. Amiel, H. Bouniols		him from the Church, and furthermore not contrary to Our Lord's command, which is to be understood as referring to the case when the cockle cannot be plucked up without plucking up the wheat, as we explained above (Q[10], A[8], ad 1), when treating of unbelievers in general."
1273			→		SS, Q[33], A[6], "A[6] **Whether one ought to forbear from correcting someone, through fear lest he become worse?**" **Answer to Objection 3**: Whatever is directed to end, becomes good through being directed to the end.
1273			→		SS, Q[33], A[7]. "**Whether the precept of fraternal correction demands that a private admonition should precede denunciation?**" "I answer that … For certain secret sins are hurtful to our neighbor either in his body or in his soul, as, for instance, when a man plots secretly to betray his country to its enemies, or when a heretic secretly turns other men away from the faith. And since he that sins thus in secret, sins not only against you in particular, but also against others, it is necessary to take steps to denounce him at once, in order to prevent him doing such harm, unless by chance you were firmly persuaded that this evil result would be prevented by admonishing him secretly."
1273			→		
1273			→		
1273			→		SS, Q[69], A[4]: "**Whether a man who is condemned to death may lawfully defend himself if he can?**" "I answer that, A man may be condemned to death in two ways. First justly, and then it is not lawful for the condemned to defend himself, because it is lawful for the judge to combat his resistance by force, so that on his part the fight is unjust, and consequently without any doubt he sins. "Secondly a man is condemned unjustly: and such a sentence is like the violence of robbers, according to Ezech. 22:21, "Her princes in the midst of her are like wolves ravening the prey to shed blood." Wherefore even as it is lawful to resist robbers, so is it lawful, in a like case, to resist wicked princes; except perhaps in order to avoid scandal, whence some grave disturbance might be feared to arise."
1273			→		
1273			→		
1274					**Second Council of Lyons** reaffirmed celibacy of priests, detailed issues of ordination, excommunication, etc.
1274					**Aquinas** died
1274					

1280	Consultation of **four Bishops** (Narbonne, Arles, Aix, and Alban) against the **Waldenses**: "Who is so great a stranger in France, as to be ignorant of the damnatory sentence which has now, for a long time, been most justly used against these						
1280	heretical Waldenses; and should we doubt a matter of so notorious and common, which has cost the Catholics so much money, sweat, and labor, and has sealed so many condemnations and executions of unbelievers"b						
1283	Increased search and persecution of **Waldenses** that were again increasing in Franceb						
1283		Increased persecution of **Waldenses** that were again increasing in Franceb					
1284		Continued executions to utterly exterminate the Waldenses	→				
1284		astonished certain Avignon bishops and advocatesb	→				
1285			J. Galand and G. de Sainte-Seine conducted inquisitionsd				
1285						**Gerard Sagarellus** in Parma and **Dulcinus of Novaria** declared heretics by Roman adherents, as having borrowed the beliefs of the Waldenses; **Sagarellus**b burned alive in Parma (of **Dulcinus** and his wife, see 1308)	
1286							
1287							

COLOR GUIDE: YELLOW=Roman Catholic areas; TAN=Bad years for Anabaptists; GOLD=Important events for Catholicism; ORANGE=Catholics "martyred"; RED=Evangelicals martyred; GRAY=Other martyred; Disclaimer: some dates may vary
PINK=Marriage issues; PURPLE= Crusades or massacres; TURQUOISE=Martyrology info; BLUE=Part Protestant areas; AQUA=U.S. Const; LT GREEN=Disputed areas; LIME=Bible issues; GREEN=Major dates. (Page 49)

Thomas P. Johnston — Geographic History — Page 50

Date	Germany-Austria-Scandinavia	Switzerland	France-Alsace		British Isles	Italy, Spain, Low Lands
1288			10 Jews and their books burned at the stake in Troyes	→		
1289				→		
1294			Pope Celestin V gave permission for a group of Strict Franciscans to form their own congregation, "Poor Hermits";	Records of inquisitions of P. de Fenouillet and H. de Saissac →		
1294				→		
1294			later called *Fraticelli* (DS910)	→		
1295			Pope Boniface VIII rescinded the rights of the "Poor Hermits" to be independent of the strict Franciscans in an	→		Boniface VIII's sixth book of Decretals "confirmed the order of friars, and privileged the with great freedoms; as appeareth by his constitution, 'Super Cathedram'"f
1295				→		
1295			8 April 1295 decree (DS910)	→		
1299			25 leading citizens d2 from Albi arrested, inquisited, and	Council of Toulouse prohibited persons from owning Old and New Testaments		Pope Boniface VIII declared the *Fraticelli* heretics; they were hunted down and burned, the living and the dead were exhumed for burning; hence the bodies of **Herman, Andrew,** and
1299			imprprsoned indefinitely on charges of heresy	→		

1299						Guillemete were exhumed and their bones burned[b]
1302 *Unum Sanctum* 1302	→					Boniface VIII's *"Unum Sanctum"* (18 Nov 1302) established the Pope as head over all religious and secular realms, by virtue of the "two Swords"; he died the next year
		Records of inquisitions of **Pierre de Fenouillet** and **Hugue de Saissac**[d]	Master **William of Nogaret** provided a discourse to the French King, in which he stated, "Boniface is a manifest heretic, and utterly cut off from the body of the holy church"[f]			
1303						"About this time **Peter Joannis** taught that the pope was the antichrist, and the Roman synagogue the great Babylon. About his martyrdom we have not been able to learn anything"[b]
1303						
1305			The **Avignon Papacy** established near the disputed region of Southern France (see 1167)			Pope **Clement V** left Rome for Avignon, France
1305	→		**Inquisitor Geoffroy d'Albis** arrested the entire population of the city of Verdun, and brought them to Carcassonne for interrogation[o3]			→
1305	→			**Bernard Gui**, inquisitor of Toulouse →		→
1307	[Sample] **Rules for Inquisitors**[b] (1) It is not permitted or advisable to dispute concerning the faith in the presence of the laity;	→				Letter of **Cassiodorus** to the church in England concerning the abuses of the Romish Church[f]	Pope **Clement V** condemned **Dulcinus** and his **wife** as archheretics, and →
1307	(2) No one is to be regarded as converted, if he will not accuse all those whom he knows to be such as he is;	→		Gui also wrote a manual on inquisition;			commanded them, as well as their adherents to be exterminated →

COLOR GUIDE: YELLOW=Roman Catholic areas; GOLD=Important events for Catholicism; ORANGE=Catholics "martyred"; RED=Evangelicals martyred; GRAY=Other martyred; Disclaimer: some dates may vary TAN=Bad years for Anabaptists; PINK=Marriage issues; PURPLE=Crusades or massacres; TURQUOISE=Martyrology info; BLUE=Part Protestant areas; AQUA=U.S. Const; LIME=Bible issues; LT GREEN=Disputed areas; GREEN=Major dates. (Page 51)

Thomas P. Johnston
Geographic History
Page 52

Date	Germany-Austria-Scandinavia	Switzerland	France-Alsace		British Isles	Avignon Papacy	Italy, Spain, Low Lands
1308	(3) He who does not accuse such as he is, must be severed from the church as a diseased member; that the sound members may not become		→	**Geoffroy d'Albis** inquisition in Carcassonne		(temporary move closer to the disputed territory with the Orthodox Bishops, as noted in the "Charter of Niquinta")	Leader of an Evangelical-type of sect, **Dulcinus**[b], and his wife **Margaret**[b],
1308	corrupted by it; (4) After one is delivered to the secular judge, great care must be exercized, that he be not allowed to		→	area (Ms 4269)d	Gui's manual was entitled, "*Pracuca officci Inquisitionis heretice pravitatis.*"			torn limb from limb, and with them **140 others**[b] burned alive in Novaria, Lombardy [northern
1308	prove his innocence, or show his harmlessness before the people; for it he is put to death, the people will take offense; and if he is discharged, the		→		For example, Gui wrote: "The goal of Inquisition is			Italy]; **400 more**[b] **people** surrounded and died in the crusade of the **Pope Clement V**
1308	(Catholic) faith will be endangered; (6) Observe: The inquisitor must always take the deed for granted, without any consideration, and ask questions only		→		the destruction of heresy; wherefore			
1309	in regard to the circumstances of the matter, Not saying: Have you made confession to the heretics? but, how often have you made your confession		→		heresy cannot be destroyed if heretics			
1310	to the heretics? Again, do not ask: Have they slept in your house? but, In what room of your house did they sleep? and the like. (continued below)				are not destroyed; and heretics cannot be	**Worker** burned in a barrel in London		
1311	(7) The inquisitor may look into a book, as though he had noted in it, the life and conduct of the accused together with everything in regard to which he is interrogating him;				destroyed if at the same time are not destroyed			
1312	(8) The accused must be threatened with death, if he will not confess, and be told that his doom is sealed; that		**Clement V** issued a decree against the "Poor Hermits" *Exivi de Paradiso* (6 May 1312) because of their refusal to rejoin the strict Franciscans (DS910)		those who receive them, favor them, or		→	**Council of Vienna** dealt with the Order of the Knights Templar
1312	he must regard his soul, and, first of all, forsake his heresy.[b]				defend them[h3]		→	→
1315	In Crema [Austria], **very many Waldenses**,[b] condemned by Dominican inquisitors,	In Zuidenitz, Poland, a **great number of**	→				→	

1315	were burned alive as heretics; one of their martyred leaders, named **Lolhard**[b], stated that there were 80,000 believers in Austria and Bohemia					→				
1315		**Waldenses**[b] were burned alive				→				
1315	In Steyer [Austria], three large books of [additional martyrs'] confessions and examinations[b] were found					→				
1315						→				
1317					**Pope John XXII** issued a papal decree, *Gloriosam Ecclesiam* (23 Jan 1318) against the "Poor Hermits" (or *Fraticelli*) prohibiting them from meeting publicly or in secret, from electing pastors or teachers over them, and from practicing worship; apparently, the Poor Hermits were antagonistic to **John XXII**, stating that he was an enemy of the Gospel and had lost all power of jurisdiction and order (DS 910); likewise, it was said that they did not follow the sacramental system of the Church of Rome	→ [See **papal decree** given in Avignon France] ←				
1317						→				
1317						→				
1317						→				
1317					In Marseille, **four former Franciscans**[b] burned alive as heretics (they were against "apostolic poverty") [named "Beguins" and burned in 1318]d3	→				
1317						→				

COLOR GUIDE: YELLOW=Roman Catholic areas; TAN=Bad years for Anabaptists; GOLD=Important events for Catholicism; ORANGE=Catholics "martyred"; RED=Evangelicals martyred; GRAY=Other martyred; Disclaimer: some dates may vary
PINK=Marriage issues; PURPLE=Crusades or massacres; TURQUOISE=Martyrology info; BLUE=Part Protestant areas; AQUA=U.S. Const; LT GREEN=Disputed areas; LIME=Bible issues; GREEN=Major dates. (Page 53)

Thomas P. Johnston — Geographic History — Page 54

Date	Germany-Austria-Scandinavia	Switzerland	France-Alsace		British Isles	Italy, Spain, Low Lands
1318			→	→		"Guido the Carmelite." **Guy de Perpignan**, "Doctor Parisiensis,"
1318			→	→		became General of the Carmelite Order until 1320
1319			**Jacques Fournier**[d] (later Pope Benedict XII of Avignon) conducted inquisitions in Pamiers; in 1320 he was accompanied by Jean de Beaune	**Jean de Beaune** conducted inquisitions in Carcassonne		**Bernard Gui**, Inquisitor of Toulouse · **Pope John XXII** unleashed further persecution of the
1319			→	→		Waldenses in France through his Jacobite (Dominican) inquisitors[b]
1323			Inquisitions in Lodève[d]	**Four heretics burned in Carcassonne 24 Apr 1323**l2		**Avignon Papacy** (temporary move closer to the disputed territory with the Orthodox Bishops, as noted in the "Charter of Niquinta")
1323			→	→		
1324			Inquisitions in Pamiers[d]	→		
1325			→	→		
1326				Inquisition of **Carcasonne**, Pamiers, (Man DDD);[d]		
1326						A so-called heretical sect in Portugal called "Gendarmes de

1327					→	Jesus"c [Police of Jesus] appeared in Portugal
1328		**Carcasonne** (GGG, Doat XXVII)d			→	
1329		→		Birth of **John Wycliffe** in Hipswell, Yorkshire	→	
1330	Intense persecution of **Waldenses** in Bohemia and Poland; "very many" b were executed by the inquisition	→		**John Aston**b apprehended by the Archbishop of Canterbury, died in prison	→	
1330	Former Dominican monk from Heidelberg, **Eckhart**b [aka **Richard**], condemned as a heretic and publicly burned				→	
1334	There seems to be nothing new under the sun in the history of the churches. Compare with the writing of **Gérard de la Motte** from 1218	John XXII, in *Gloriosam Ecclesiam* (DS 910-916)			→	
1334	Notice how the "**Poor Hermits**" felt about the Sacraments of the Church of Rome, along with their vocalized antagonism to the primacy of Rome	This Pontifical Constitution condemned the *Fraticelli*, the 1294 "spirituals" offshoot of the **Franciscans** (also known as **Poor Hermits**), who identified their rule as the proper interpretation of the Gospel itself. **John XXII** condemned their teachings, which he likened to the poisonous teaching of the **Donatists** and **Waldenses**:			→	
1334	These men made a distinction between the spiritual and temporal church, one that is regularly made in Protestant writings; however they	910: "§12.... The aforesaid sons of boldness and wickedness have fallen, as is noted by the indications worthy of faith, to the point where in poverty of spirit they are thinking with wickedness against the most imminent and salvific truths of the Christian faith, [to the point] that they despise the venerable Sacraments of the Church and that, driven by a desire to see her [the church] quickly ruined, they seek, filled with blind fury, to shake the glorious primacy of the Roman Church before all the nations.			→	
1334	went one step farther by likening the carnal church to the luxury and power of the Church of Rome. An interesting mention of inward	911: "(1) §14. The first error therefore that is emitted from their laboratory filled with darkness is the invention of two Churches, one carnal, crushed by riches, overflowing with riches and soiled by wickedness, and over whom reigns, say they, the Roman Pontiff and all the inferior prelates; the other [Church] spiritual, pure from its frugality, adorned with virtue, upheld by poverty, in which they find themselves unique along with those who are alike, and over whom they preside equally by the merit of their spiritual life, if one can give credit to their lies.			→	
1334	spiritual life, almost akin to the "new birth"! Note that Rome paralleled the teachings of the 5th Century **Donatists**	912: "(2) §16. The second error clamoring from the soiled consciences of these boastful people [is that] the venerable priests and the other servants of the Church are destitute at this point of the power of jurisdiction and order, that they cannot carry [out] any decrees, nor confer the Sacraments, nor teach and instruct the people who are subject to them, and they portend that all who are strangers to their disloyalty are deprived of ecclesiastical power, because it is in them only (according to their meanderings) that resides spiritual life and due to this fact the authority; and in this they follow the error of the Donatists. …			→	

COLOR GUIDE YELLOW=Roman Catholic areas; TAN=Bad years for Anabaptists; GOLD=Important events for Catholicism; ORANGE=Catholics "martyred"; RED=Evangelicals martyred; GRAY=Other martyred; Disclaimer: some dates may vary
PINK=Marriage issues; PURPLE= Crusades or massacres; TURQUOISE=Martyrology info; BLUE=Part Protestant areas; AQUA=U.S. Const; LT GREEN=Disputed areas; LIME=Bible issues; GREEN=Major dates.   (Page 55)

Thomas P. Johnston
Geographic History
Page 56

Date	Germany-Austria-Scandinavia	Switzerland	France-Alsace	British Isles	Italy, Spain, Low Lands
1334	and the 13th Century **Waldenses**, against their normal guarded approach to historiography. Was the taking of an oath a concept	913: "(3) §18. Their third error conspires with the error of the Waldenses, as the one and the other affirms that one must not swear [by an oath] in any case, and teach that they are soiled by the stain of a mortal sin and are devoted to eternal punishment who find themselves bound by the obligations of an oath. 914: "(4) §20. The fourth blasphemy of these wicked [ones], bubbling forth from the poisonous source of the			→
1334	which proved one's belief in literal interpretation of Scripture (much like premillennialism)? This fourth issue was also the	aforementioned Waldenses, invents that priests that have been rightly and legitimately ordained according to the right of the Church, but who are charged with a crime, cannot accomplish or confer the Sacraments of the Church. 915: "(5) §22. The fifth blind error at this point of these men, [is] that they affirm that the Gospel is accomplished only through them in the present time, and that up until now (according to their meanderings) it has been veiled,			→
1334	centerpiece of Augustine's *Contra Donatisten*! Note that the "**Poor Hermits**," as they are called, considered that they were	seeing totally extinguished. 916: "§24. There are many other things, it is said, that these presumptuous men argue against the venerable Sacrament of Marriage, many other things that they distort on the subject of the end of the world, many things that in their deplorable lies they spread among the people on the subject of the coming of the Antichrist which they affirm			→
1334	unique in propagating the true Gospel! They also believed in the imminent return of Christ and the Antichrist! Notice also Rome's guarded approach	is imminent. All this, that we consider in part heretical, in part as invented, We think that it should be condemned along with those who are their authors, rather than to refer to it in writing. …"			→
1334 Inquisitor as	to putting further things in writing!				Chief Inquisitor of Pamiers, France, **Jacques Fournier** →
Pope 1334					became Avignon Pope **Benedict XII** (20 Dec 1334-25 April 1342) →
1342			1340 A.D. Death of **Jehan de Vignay**, translator of an enormous number of works from Latin into French (fr.wikipedia.org)		Death of **Guy de Perpignan**; his chief work was the "Summa de Haeresibus." →
1347 Bubonic Plague 1347					**Bubonic Plague** began sweeping across Europe via shipping lanes beginning in Turkey →
1348			**Bubonic Plague** came to France via shipping lanes, and quickly spread to England	**Bubonic Plague** spread to England, killing as much as 30-40% of the urban	**Bubonic Plague** reached Italy →

Date			Papacy	
1349	**Bubonic Plague** spread to Germany and Scandinavia	population; the plague recurred several other times, decimating the population (1360, 1369, 1364)	→	
1356		**Wycliffe** became teacher at Merton College, then appointed master of Balliol College w2	→	
1361		**Wycliffe** resigned his post at Balliol, remaining a lecturer at Oxford and serving churches in Fillingham,	→	
1361		Lincolnshire and then Lutterworth, 15 miles from Oxford w2	→	
1361		From his teaching, **Wycliffe's** followers began to preach on the streets throughout England, they were called	→	
1361		**"Lollards"** probably pejorative for "Lowlanders" w2	→	
1365	**Milic of Kromeriz** (of Prague) released from the Inquisition prison, proposed to **Pope Urban V** that a missionary campaign should be		Avignon Papacy	
1365	launched to reach the whole known Christian world; he founded a school for preachers in Prague which was			
1365	destroyed by violence; **Milic** died in Avignon, France (date unknown) m6			
1366			→	Roman Papacy reinstated	"Police of Jesus" C spread to

COLOR GUIDE: YELLOW=Roman Catholic areas; TAN=Bad years for Anabaptists; GOLD=Important events for Catholicism; ORANGE=Catholics "martyred"; RED=Evangelicals martyred; GRAY=Other martyred; Disclaimer: some dates may vary PINK=Marriage issues; PURPLE= Crusades or massacres; TURQUOISE=Martyrology info; BLUE=Part Protestant areas; AQUA=U.S. Const; LT GREEN=Disputed areas; LIME=Bible issues; GREEN=Major dates. (Page 57)

Thomas P. Johnston — Page 58

Geographic History

Date	Germany-Austria-Scandinavia	Switzerland	France-Alsace	British Isles	Italy, Spain, Low Lands		
1366					Tuscany and Senes		
1372			Waldensian "heretics" called **Turilupins** by John Tylius in his *Chronicle of the Kings of France* (1372)[b]		→	→	
1373			Books of the **Turilupins** burned in Paris, along with a woman, **Peronne of Aubeton**,[b] who was publicly burned		→	→	
1373					→	→	
1373					→	→	
1376	At Vienna, **Henry de Haffra**, wrote on Genesis, against the merits of the saints, and reproving the clergy and Pope for its many errors[b]				→	→	
1378		Antipope **Robert of Geneva** (aka **Clement VII**) began his	Faithful to **Avignon Papacy** were: France, Scotland, Castile, Aragon, Navarre, Portugal, Savoy, some German states, Denmark, Norway		**Pope Urban VI** elected as Second Pope in Rome	→	
1378		papacy (20 Sept 1378)			→	→	
1380	The Bohemian, **M. Matthaeus Parisiensis**, wrote a large book against the Pope, saying that he was the	→	Catholic scholar, **Nicholas Clemangis**, opposed certain superstitions of the Church of Rome: feast days, excessive eating and drinking, and evil speaking[b]		Minorite friar, **M. Cesenas**, wrote against the Pope; he was deposed[b]	→	
1380	antichrist, as did Lupoldus de Bedenborgh[b]	→				→	
1380		→			**Avignon Pope Clement VII** sent a	→	

Date	Roman Catholic		Important events		Avignon Papacy / Roman Papacy reinstated	Martyrology
1381 Wycliffe NT	If the Pope tells the people to revolt against their constituted government (cf. Fourth Lateran Council [1225]), then it is justified; but if the people stop attending the Catholic Church or push back on the government for "**Freedom of Conscience**", then it is called a "**Peasant's Revolt**", may this contradiction not signal a double-standard?	→	**Wycliffe** completed his first edition of his New Testamentw2	"**Peasant's Revolt**" blamed on growth of Lollard movement	Avignon Papacy →	monk as an inquisitor to deal with heretics in certain partsb2, in the next 13 years, 230 heretics were burned aliveb2
1381		→				
1382 Wycliffe Bible		→	**Wycliffe** completed his first edition of the Bible	**Pope Gregory XI** published Bull against Wycliffe	[Had the Avignon location achieved its original purpose of suppressing the Cathar "heresy" in Southern France?]	
1384		→		Wycliffe responded to Pope Gregory XI's bull against him Wycliffe died		
1388 Wycliffe Bible		→	**John Purvey** completed 2nd edition Wycliffe Bible, among other things removing 33 of Wycliffe's 36 uses of the verb "evangelize"			
1389		→		**W. Swinderby**, a priest of Lincoln, arrested for preaching contrary to the Church of Rome; was compelled by fire to read a recantation; rearrested and burned in 1401		
1389		→		→		
1390	36 **Waldenses** burned alive in Bingen, Germanyb	→			→ Roman Papacy reinstated →	
1391	443 **Waldenses** inquisited (many tortured on the rack), refusing to recant they were put to death in Pomeria on the Baltic Seab	→			→ →	
1391	In Prague, the "**Bethlehem Chapel**" continued the work of **Milic**m6	→			→ →	

COLOR GUIDE: **YELLOW**=Roman Catholic areas; **TAN**=Bad years for Anabaptists; **GOLD**=Important events for Catholicism; **ORANGE**=Catholics "martyred"; **RED**=Evangelicals martyred; **GRAY**=Other martyred; Disclaimer: some dates may vary
PINK=Marriage issues; **PURPLE**= Crusades or massacres; **TURQUOISE**=Martyrology info; **BLUE**=Part Protestant areas; **AQUA**=U.S. Const; **LT GREEN**=Disputed areas; **LIME**=Bible issues; **GREEN**=Major dates. (Page 59)

Geographic History

Date	Germany-Austria-Scandinavia	Switzerland	France-Alsace	British Isles	Italy, Spain, Low Lands	
1392		→		W. Brute appeared before John, Bishop of Hereford, holding to articles against the Church of Rome b	→	→
1394		Antipope Robert of Geneva ended his papacy (16 Sept 1394)			→	→
1395			"Twelve Conclusions of the Lollards" (from http://sites.fas.harvard.edu) "We poor men, treasurers of Christ and his Apostles, denounce to the Lords and the Commons of the Parliament certain conclusions and truth for the reformation of the Holy Church of England, the which has been blind and leprous many years by the maintenance of the proud prelacy, borne up with flattering of private religion, the which is multiplied to a great charge and onerous [to] people here in England. **The First Conclusion: State of The Church** "When the Church of England began to dote in temporality after her stepmother, the great Church of Rome, and		→	→
1395			churches were slain by appropriation to diverse places. Faith, Hope, and Charity began for to flee out of our Church. For Pride with his sorry genealogy of deadly sins challengeth it by title of heritage. This conclusion is general and proved by experience, custom, and manner, as you shall after hear. **The Second Conclusion: The Priesthood** "The Second Conclusion is this: Our usual priesthood, the which began in Rome feigned of a power higher than angels, is not the priesthood the which	"Twelve Conclusions of the Lollards" presented to English Parliament and nailed to the doors of Westminster Abbey and St. Paul's Cathedral ←	→	→
1395			Christ ordained to his Apostles. This conclusion is proved: for the priesthood of Rome is made with signs, rites, and bishops' blessings, and that is of little virtue. nowhere ensampled in the Holy Scripture, for the bishops ordinals in the New Testament be little of record. And we can not see that the Holy Ghost, for any such signs, gives any gifts, for he and his noble gifts may not stand with deadly sin in no matter person. The corollary of this conclusion is that it is full uncouth to many that be wise to see bishops play with the holy ghost in making of their orders, for they give crowns in characters in stead of white harts, and that is the livery of Antichrist, brought into Holy Church to color idleness. **The Third Conclusion: Clerical Celibacy**		→	→
1395			"The Third Conclusion, sorrowful to hear, is: That the law of continence annexed to priesthood, that in prejudice of women was first ordained, induces sodomy in Holy Church; but we excuse us by the Bible, for the suspect decree that says we should not name it. Reason and experience prove this conclusion. For delicious meats and drinks of men of Holy Church will have needful purgation or worse. Experience for the privy assay of such men is that they like not women. The corollary of this conclusion is that the private religions. beginners of this sin, were most worthy to be annulled but God, for his might, of privy sin send open vengeance. **The Fourth Conclusion: Transubstantiation**		→	→
1395			"The Fourth Conclusion that most harms the innocent people is this: That the sacrament of bread induces all men but a few to idolatry, for they ween that Christ's body, that never shall out of heaven, by virtue of the priest's word should be essentially enclosed in a little bread, that they show to the people. But would God that they would believe that the Doctor Evangelicus says in his Trialogue, *quod panis materialis est habitudinaliter corpus Christi*. For we suppose that on this wise may every true man and woman in God's law make the sacrament of the bread without any such miracle. The corollary of this conclusion is that if Christ's body be endued with everlasting joy, the service of Corpus Christi made by Friar Thomas is untrue and painted full of false miracles, and that is no wonder, for Friar Thomas that same time, holding with the Pope, would have made a miracle of a hen's egg, and we know well that every lie openly preached turns itself to villainy that ever was true and without lack. **The Fifth Conclusion: Exorcisms and Hallowings**		→	→

1395	"The fifth conclusion is this: that exorcisms and hallowings, made in the church, of wine, bread, and wax, water, salt, oil and incense, the stone of the altar, upon vestment, miter, cross, and pilgrim staffs be the very practice of necromancy rather than of the holy theology. This conclusion is proved thus: For by such exorcisms creatures be charged to be of higher virtue than their own kind, and we see no thing of change in no such creature that is so charmed but by false belief, the which is the principal of the Devil's craft. The corollary is that holy water used in holy church should be the best medicine to all manner of sickness. *Cuius contrarium experimur.*	→	→
1395	**The Sixth Conclusion: Clerics in Secular Offices** "The sixth conclusion that maintaineth much pride is: that a king and a bishop all in one person, a prelate and a justice in temporal cause, a curate and an officer in worldly service, make every realm out of good rule. This conclusion is openly showed, for temporality and spirituality be two parts of Holy Church and therefore he that hath taken him to the one should not meddle him with the other, *quia nemo potest duobus dominis servire*. Us thinketh that hermaphrodite or ambidexter were a good name to such men of double estate. The corollary is that for we, procurators of God, for this cause pursue to this Parliament that all manner of curates, both high and low, be fully excused of temporal office and occupy them with their cure and naught else.	→	→
1395	**The Seventh Conclusion: Prayers for the Dead** "The Seventh conclusion that we mightily affirm is: that special prayers for dead men's souls made in our church, preferring one by name more than another, this is the false ground of alms deeds, on the which all alms houses in England be wickedly grounded. This conclusion is proven by two skills. One is for prayer meritorious and of value should be a work proceeding from high charity, and perfect charity accepts no persons, *quia diliges proximum tuum, etc.* Wherefore us thinks that the gifts of temporal goods to priests and to alms houses is the principal cause of special prayers, the which is not far from simony. Another skill for special prayer made for men damned to everlasting pain is to God greatly displeasing, and though it be doubt, it is lightly to true Christian people that the founders of the alms houses for their venomous dotacion be for the most part passed the broad way. The corollary is the prayer of value stringing out of perfect charity should embrace in general all those that God would have saved and leave their merchandise now used for special prayers made to mendicants and possessioners and other souls' priests, the which be a people of great charge to all the realm maintained in idleness, for it was proved in a book that the king heard that an hundred of alms houses sufficed to the realm and thereof should fall the greatest increase possible to temporal part.	→	→
1395	**The Eighth Conclusion: Pilgrimages** "The eighth conclusion needful to tell the people beguiled is the pilgrimage, prayers, and offerings made to blind roods and deaf images of tree and stone be near kin to idolatry and far from alms deeds. And though this forbidden imagery be a book of errors to the lewd people, yet the image used of Trinity is most abominable. This conclusion God openly showeth, commanding to do almsdeeds to men that be needy. for they be the image of God in a more likeness than the stock of the stone, for God sayeth not *Faciamus lignum ad ymaginem et similitudinem nostram aut lapidem*, but *faciamus hominem etc.* For the high worship that clerks call *latria* longeth to the godhead alone and the lower worship that is called *dulia* longeth to man and to angel and to lower creatures. The corollary is that the service of the Rood, done twice every year in our church, is fulfilled of idolatry, for if the Rood tree, nails, and the spear, and the crown of God should be so holy worshipped, then were Judas' lips, whoso might them get, a wonder great relic. But we pray thee, pilgrim, us to tell when thou first offerest to saints' bones enshrined in any place, whether relieves thou the saint that is in bliss or the alms house that is so well endowed. For men be canonized, God knows how, and for to speak more in plain, true Christian men suppose that the points of that noble man that men call Saint Thomas, were no cause of martyrdom.	→	→
1395	**The Ninth Conclusion: Confession** "The ninth conclusion that holdeth the people low is, that the articles of confession that is said necessary to the salvation of man, with a feigned power of absolution enhanceth priests' pride, and giveth them opportunity of calling other than we will not say. For lords and ladies be arrested that for fear of their confessors, that they dare not say a truth, and in time of confession is the best time of wooing and of privy continuance of deadly sin. They say that they be commissaries of God to deem of every sin, to foul and cleanse whomso they like. They say that they have the keys of heaven and of hell, they may curse and bless, bind and unbind at their own will, in so much that for a bushel of wheat or twelve pence by year they will sell the bliss of heaven by charter of clause of warranty, ensealed with the common seal. This conclusion is seen in use that it needeth none other proof. *Correlarium*: The Pope of Rome that	→	→

COLOR GUIDE: YELLOW=Roman Catholic areas; TAN=Bad years for Anabaptists; GOLD=Important events for Catholicism; ORANGE=Catholics "martyred"; RED=Evangelicals martyred; GRAY=Other martyred; Disclaimer: some dates may vary
PINK=Marriage issues; PURPLE= Crusades or massacres; TURQOUISE=Martyrology info; BLUE=Part Protestant areas; AQUA=U.S. Const; LT GREEN=Disputed areas; LIME=Bible issues; GREEN=Major dates. (Page 61)

Thomas P. Johnston — Geographic History — Page 62

Date	Germany-Austria-Scandinavia	Switzerland	France-Alsace	British Isles	Italy, Spain, Low Lands	
1395				feigneth him high treasurer of holy church, having the worthy jewel of Christ's passion in his keeping, with the deserts of all hallows of heaven, by which he giveth the pardon *a pena et a culpa*. He is a treasurer most banished out of charity, since he may deliver the prisoners that be in pain at his own will, and make himself so that he shall never come there, Here may every true Christian well see that there is much privy falseness hid in our church. **The Tenth Conclusion: War, Battle, and Crusades**	→	→
1395				"The tenth conclusion is that manslaughter by battle or law of righteousness for temporal cause or spiritual with out special revelation is express contrary to the New Testament, the which is a law of grace and full of mercy. This conclusion is openly proved by example of Christ's preaching here on earth. the which most taught to love and to have mercy on his enemies. and not for to slay them. The reason is of this, that for the more party, there men fight, after the first stroke charity is broken; and who so dyeth out of charity goth the high way to hell. And over this, we know well that no clerk can find by scripture or	→	→
1395				by reason lawful punishment of death for one sin and not for another. But the law of mercy, that is the New Testament, forbade all manslaughter: *in euangelio dictum est antiquis. Non occides.* The corollary is: it is an holy robbing of poor people when lords purchase indulgences *a pena et a culpa* to them that helpeth with his host. and gathereth to slay the Christian men in far lands for good temporal, as we have seen. And knights, that run to heathenness to get them a name in slaying of men, get much maugré of the King of Peace; for the meekness and sufferance our belief was multiplied, and fighters and manslayers Jesu Christ hateth and menaceth. *Qui gladio percutit, gladio peribit.* **The Eleventh Conclusion: Female Vows of Continence and Abortion.**	→	→
1395				"The eleventh conclusion is shameful for to speak: that a vow of continence made in our church of women, the which be fickle and imperfect in kind, is cause of bringing in of most horrible sin possible to man kind. For though slaying of children ere they be christened, abortion, and destroying of kind by	→	→
1395				medicine be full sinful, yet knowing with themselves [i.e., *having intercourse with*] or [*either*] unreasonable beast or creature that beareth no life passeth in worthiness to be punished in pains of hell. The corollary is that widows and which as have taken the mantle and the ring, deliciously fed, we would they were wedded for we can not excuse them from privy sins. **The Twelfth Conclusion: Arts and Crafts**	→	→
1395				"The twelfth conclusion is that the multitude of crafts not needful used in our church nourisheth much sin in waste, curiosity, and disguising. This showeth experience, and reason proveth, for nature with a few crafts sufficeth to need of man. The corollary is, since Saint Paul sayeth, we having our bodily food and clothing, we should hold ourselves satisfied, us thinketh that goldsmiths and armourers and all manner crafts not needful to men, after [*according to*] the Apostle, should be destroyed for the increase of virtue. For though to these crafts named were much more needful in the Old Law, the New testament hath voided these and many others.	→	→
1395				"This is our embassy, that Christ has commanded us to pursue, at this time most acceptable for many causes. And though these matters be here shortly knit they be in another book longly declared, and may another more, all in our language, the which we would were communed to all true Christian men. We pray God of his endless goodness reform our church. all out of joint, to the perfections of the first beginning. Amen."	→	→
1400	John Tauler called the Roman Church to reform in his many writings[b]		[Here began the *Martyrology* of Jean Crespin, Book I]	**W. Sautre**[cf] burned in London; Meanwhile, **J. Purvey** (and many others) recanted[f]	**Persecution expanded**[b2]	→
1401				**Henry IV** published *Statutum ex Officio* against 15 articles of the **Wycliffites**; the 7th read: "That any layman, though he have not studied at college, has the		→
1401				right to preach the Gospel everywhere, and that he may teach upon his own authority, without permission from his ordinary bishop"[b]		→

1401					Henry IV passed *De Heretico Comburendo* against translating or owning a Bible, and authorizing burning heretics at the stake	→		→			
1401					W. Swinderby[b], former priest, burned alive in Smithfield, London; J. Baldy[f] burned in a barrel, Smithfield, London	→		→			
1402	John Hus began his association with the "Bethlehem School" (started by disciples of Milic) in Prague[m6]					→		→			
1407		The Five Articles by which W. Thorpe, former priest, apprehended, was charged: 1. That the sacrament of the altar, also after the consecration, that is, after the priest has read the canon, it still remains bread;			W. Thorpe[bcf] severely mistreated and burned at the Caslte of Saltwoden (taken from a writing of William Tindal)[f] ←	→		→			
1407		2. The images are not to be worshiped, nor any honor shown to them; 3. That no pilgrimages ought to be made; 4. That the priests have no right to appropriate tithes for themselves| 5. That men ought not to swear[b]									
1408					Council of Oxford forbade the public or private reading of the Wycliffe Bible, with the penalty of death	→	← Roman Papacy	← Pisan Papacy	Pope Alexander V, elected as third Pope in Pisa, Italy		
1408					(excommunication) as a heretic, also forbading the translation of Scriptures into English.						
1409					Constitution of T. Arundel, Archbishop of Canterbury, against the Gospelers[f]	→	←	→			
1410					Following Council of Oxford, J. Wycliffe's bones exhumed, burned, and scattered over the Thames; his books confiscated and burned	→	←	→			
1410					A certain tradesman[b] burned over a slow fire in London	→	←	→			

COLOR GUIDE: YELLOW=Roman Catholic areas; TAN=Bad years for Anabaptists; GOLD=Important events for Catholicism; ORANGE=Catholics "martyred"; RED=Evangelicals martyred; GRAY=Other martyred; Disclaimer: some dates may vary
PINK=Marriage issues; PURPLE=Crusades or massacres; TURQUOISE=Martyrology info; BLUE=Part Protestant areas; AQUA=U.S. Const; LT GREEN=Disputed areas; LIME=Bible issues; GREEN=Major dates. (Page 63)

Thomas P. Johnston
Geographic History
Page 64

Date	Germany-Austria-Scandinavia	Switzerland	France-Alsace	British Isles	Italy, Spain, Low Lands			
					Avignon Papacy (cont.) →	Roman Papacy (cont.) →	Pisan Papacy (cont.) →	
1413				**R. Acton**[C], **J. Brown**[C], and **J. Beverlau**[C] burned in London; **J. Claydon**[C], **R. Turming**[C], totalling **36**[C] burned in London	→	→	→	
1414					→	→	→	**Council of Constance** (Constance, Austria); Condemned 260 teachings of **Wycliffe**, and all his Writings; damned as heretic any who cited them
1415 Council of Constance	**Council of Constance, Session 8** (5 May 1415), "After these things had again been brought to the notice of the apostolic see and a general council, the Roman pontiff condemned the said books, treatises and pamphlets [of Wycliffe] at the lately held council of Rome [24], ordering them to be publicly burnt and strictly forbidding anyone called a Christian to dare to read, expound, hold or make any use of any one or more of the said books, volumes, treatises and pamphlets, or even to cite them publicly or privately, except in order to refute them. In order that this dangerous and most foul doctrine might be eliminated from the church's midst, he ordered, by his apostolic authority and under pain of ecclesiastical censure, that all such books, treatises, volumes and pamphlets should be diligently sought out by the local ordinaries and should then be publicly burnt; and he added that if necessary those who do not obey should be proceeded against as if they were promoters of heresy." **Sentence against John Hus**: "Since a bad tree is wont to bear bad fruit, as truth itself testifies, so it is that John Wyclif, of cursed memory, by his deadly							Condemned **J. Hus** as Wycliffite heretic;
1415	teaching, like a poisonous root, has brought forth many noxious sons, not in Christ Jesus through the gospel, as once the holy fathers brought forth faithful sons, but rather contrary to the saving faith of Christ, and he has left these sons as successors to his perverse teaching. This holy synod of Constance is compelled to act against these men as against spurious and illegitimate sons, and to cut away their errors from the Lord's field as if they were harmful briars, by means of vigilant care and the knife of ecclesiastical authority, lest they spread as a cancer to destroy others. Although, therefore, it was decreed				→	→	→	ordered the burning of all
1415	at the sacred general council recently held at Rome [1412] that the teaching of John Wyclif, of cursed memory, should be condemned and the books of his containing this teaching should be burnt as heretical; although his teaching was in factcondemned and his books burnt as containing false and dangerous doctrine; and although a decree of this kind was approved by the authority of this present sacred council [36]; nevertheless a certain **John Hus**, here present in person at this sacred council, who is a disciple not of Christ but rather of the heresiarch John Wyclif, boldly and rashly contravening the				→	→	→	his books;
1415	condemnation and the decree after their enactment, has taught, asserted and preached many errors and heresies of John Wyclif which have been condemned both by God's church and by other reverend fathers in Christ, lord archbishops and bishops of various kingdoms, and masters in theology at many places of study. **[order the public burning of J. Hus' books]** …On account of the above, moreover, all his teaching is and shall be deservedly suspect regarding the faith and is to be avoided by all of Christ's faithful. In order that this pernicious teaching may be eliminated from the midst of the				→	→	→	degraded him from his religious
1415	church, this holy synod also orders that local ordinaries make careful inquiry about treatises and pamphlets of this kind, using the church's censures and even if necessary the punishment due for supporting heresy, and that they be publicly burnt when they have been found. This same holy synod decrees that local ordinaries and inquisitors of heresy are to proceed against any who violate or defy this sentence and decree as if they were persons suspected of heresy" **[Sentence of degradation then condemnation of J. Hus]**: "This holy synod of Constance, seeing that God's church has nothing more that it can				→	→	→	orders; and sentenced him to be turned over
1415	do, relinquishes John Hus to the judgment of the secular authority and decrees that he is to be relinquished to the secular court."		A vow of safe passage was almost meaningless for a heretic, as the Catholic leader and ruler was absolved from fealty to the heretic (see 1073, 1207, 1215, 1243), as well as absolved from all contracts with a heretic (see also 1487)		→	→	→	to the secular arm for burning ↓
1415	**John Hus**[C] burned at the stake at Council of Constance				→	→	→	
1415	**Council of Constance, Session 13** (15 June 1415), the Lord's Supper "was received under both kinds only by those confecting it, and by the laity only under the form of bread. … Those who stubbornly assert the opposite of the aforesaid are to be confined as heretics and severely punished by the local bishops or their officials or the inquisitors of heresy…"				→	→	→	Condemned taking the Lord's Supper in both kinds

1415	**Council of Constance**, Session 19 (23 Sept 1415), "Jerome of Prague finally abjures his faith publicly and solemnly. … It is also decreed that, *notwithstanding safe conducts of emperors and kings and others, a competent judge can inquire into heresy*" **Council of Constance**, Session 21 (30 May 1416), "It notes the public talk and loud outcry against the said master **Jerome of Prague**, master of arts, layman. From the acts and proceedings of the case it is evident that the said Jerome has held, asserted and taught various heretical and erroneous	→	→	→	→	**Jerome of Prague** abjured his faith
1416	articles, which were long ago condemned by holy fathers, some of which are blasphemous, others scandalous and others offensive to the ears of the devout as well as rash and seditious. They were long ago asserted, preached and taught by John Wyclif and John Hus, of cursed memory, and were included in various of their books and pamphlets. These articles, doctrines and books of the aforesaid **John Wyclif** and **John Hus**, as well as the memory of Wyclif, and finally the person of Hus, were condemned and damned by this same holy synod and its sentence of heresy. … This holy synod has	→	→	→	→	**J. of Prague** condemned of being a Wycliffite
1416	therefore decreed and now declares that the said Jerome is to be cast away as a branch that is rotten, withered and separated from the vine; and it pronounces, declares and condemns him as a heretic who has relapsed into heresy and as an excommunicated and anathematised person." **Jerome of Prague**c burned at the stake in Constance		→	→	→	**J. of Prague** condemned and burned ←
1417	**Council of Constance**, Session 29 (8 March 1417), **Peter de Luna**, Avignon Pope Benedict XIII is cited for contumacy [stubborn resistance to the will of the Council] **Council of Constance**, Session 30 (10 March 1417), Process against **Peter de Luna** continued	→	→	→	→	Process to depose Avignon
1417	**Council of Constance**, Session 32 (1 April 1417), **Peter de Luna** is again accused of contumacy and an inquiry about him is established **Council of Constance**, Session 33 (12 May 1417), The process against **Peter de Luna**, who is deemed contumacious, continues **Council of Constance**, Session 34 (5 June 1417), Everything is made ready for the condemnation of **Peter de Luna** **Council of Constance**, Session 36 (22 July 1417), It is decreed that **Peter de Luna** is to be cited to hear the council's sentence	→	→	→	→	Pope, **Peter de Luna**, aka. **Benedict XIII**
1417	**Council of Constance**, Session 37 (26 July 1417), Definitive sentence whereby **Peter de Luna**, pope **Benedict XIII**, is divested of the papacy and deprived of the faith.	→	→	→	→	Final process deposing Avignon Pope
1417	**Council of Constance**, Session 40 (30 Oct 1417), enacted as the Seventh Reform, the office of the chancery and penitentiary; the former led to the selling of indulgences, as noted in 1471, when **Pope Sixtus IV** published "Taxation of the Casuistic Parties of the Papal Shop…" [after the invention of movabletype in 1455]	→	→	Papacy restored to Rome; laws enacted to avoid future schism	The "Reform" of the Papal chancery led to the development of the system of indulgences	
1417		**Catherine Saube**bc burned at the stake in Montpelier for Waldensian heresy ↑	Jean Crespin described the propositions by which Catherine Saube of Lorraine was determined guilty and burned at the stake in 1417 at Montpellier, France (which he took from the writings of Le Talamus): "That the Catholic Church consists only of men and women, holding to			
1417			and following the lives of the Apostles: and that it would be better to die than to offend God. "Item, that she did not worship the consecrated host of the priest, insofar as she did not believe that it was the body of Christ.			
1417			"Item, that it is not necessary to confess to a priest: for it is sufficient to confess to God and it is of the same value to confess to a lay good man, than to a cappelan or a priest.			
1417			"That after this life there will be no purgatory: but only in the present			

COLOR GUIDE: YELLOW=Roman Catholic areas; TAN=Bad years for Anabaptists; GOLD=Important events for Catholicism; ORANGE=Catholics "martyred"; GRAY=Other martyred; Disclaimer: some dates may vary
PINK=Marriage issues; PURPLE= Crusades or massacres; TURQUOISE=Martyrology info; BLUE=Part Protestant areas; AQUA=U.S. Const; LT GREEN=Disputed areas; GREEN=Major dates. (Page 65)
RED=Evangelicals martyred; LIME=Bible issues;

Date	Germany-Austria-Scandinavia	Switzerland	France-Alsace	British Isles	Italy, Spain, Low Lands
1417				life… Crespin added these four propositions, which he considers show Catherine's lack of learning, as well as the ambiguity of those who recorded her inquisition:	
1417				"That there was not a true Pope, Cardinal, Bishop, nor Priest, since the election of the Pope was not done by virtue of a miracle of faith or faithfulness. "That the evil priests or cappelans cannot consecrate the body of Christ, though they say the sacramental words	
1417				"That the baptism administered by wicked priests does not profit unto salvation.	
1417				"That children who die after baptism, before they have faith are not saved (for they do not believe) if it is not by the faith of their godfather, godmother, and parents."c	
1418			**Questionnaire destined for the Wycliffites and Hussites** [Martin V, "**Inter Cunctas**" 22 Feb 1418 (DS 1247-1279)] (P.S. Certain numbers are missing in my edition of Denzinger) "(5) Likewise, if he believes, holds and affirms that all general councils, and also that of Constance, represents the universal Church. "(6) Likewise, if he believes that the **holy council of Constance**, representing the universal Church, approved or approves in favor of the faith and for salvation of souls, this must be approved and held by all the faithful of Christ: and that which it has condemned and condemns as contrary to the faith and good works, this must be held, believed and affirmed as such by every catholic.		
1418			"(7) Likewise if he believes that the condemnations of **John Wyclif** of England, of **John Hus** of Bohemia and of **Jerome of Prague** pronounced by the holy general council of Constance concerning their persons, their writings and their doctrines, where done legitimately and rightly, and that they must be held and firmly affirmed as such by every catholic. "(8) Likewise if he believes, holds and affirms that **John Wyclif** of England, **John Hus** of Bohemia and **Jerome of Prague** were heretics and ought to be designated and recognized as such, and that there writings and their doctrines were and are false, and it is because of them and their obstinacy that they were condemned as heretics by the **holy council of Constance**."		
1418	Hence one's view of **John Wycliffe** or **John Hus** became a touchstone for adherence or antagonism to Rome's doctrines		"(37) Likewise if he thinks that it is permitted lay people of one or the other sex, that being to men and women, to freely preach the Word of God." "(38) Likewise if he thinks that it is permitted to all priests to freely preach the Word of God, where, when and to whom he desires, even if he has not received a mission."		
1418	Herein is addressed and forbidden New Testament evangelism!				
1419	"Hussite Revolution" (1419-1436) founded on the "**Four Articles of Prague**" (written up as manifestos or			J. **Oldcastle**c, Lord of Cobham, burned at the stake in London	
1419	tracts): (1) to give freedom for the preaching of the word in the mother-tongue; (2) to administer Communion in both				

1419	kinds; (3) to dispossess the Church of its earthly wealth; and (4) to organize political life according								
1419	to God's law, a public sin to receive public punishmentm6								
1419	One **Taborite** (during Rome's attempt to regain Bohemia), **Nicolas of Pelhrimov**, wrote that "faith can in no								
1419	way be awakened by violent measures," affirming that since Papism was anti-Christianity, war was necessarym6								
1420	H. Grunfelder[C] burned at Ratisbonne (Reinsbourg)								
1420 First Anti-Hussite Crusade	**Sigismund** sought Rome's assistance to affirm his crown over Bohemia;						**Pope Martin V** issued a Bull proclaiming a crusade against the Hussites [17 Mar 1420] to gain back the territory of Moravia under the control of the Church of Rome		
	Pope Martin V responded by issuing a Bull against the Hussite "revolutionaries"								
1420	The **Taborite**, **Pierre Chelcicky**, in *Net of the True Faith*, wrote that the Church of Christ ceased to exist with								
1420	the liaison between Church and State under Constantine, encouraging a minority church, not fearing martyrdom; he wrote with admiration								
1420	of the missionary dynamism of the first Christiansm6								

COLOR GUIDE: YELLOW=Roman Catholic areas; TAN=Bad years for Anabaptists; GOLD=Important events for Catholicism; ORANGE=Catholics "martyred"; RED=Evangelicals martyred; GRAY=Other martyred; Disclaimer: some dates may vary PINK=Marriage issues; PURPLE=Crusades or massacres; TURQUOISE=Martyrology info; BLUE=Part Protestant areas; AQUA=U.S. Const; LT GREEN=Disputed areas; LIME=Bible issues; GREEN=Major dates. (Page 67)

Thomas P. Johnston Geographic History Page 68

Date	Germany-Austria-Scandinavia	Switzerland	France-Alsace	British Isles	Italy, Spain, Low Lands
1421	Second Anti-Hussite Crusade led to the defeat of the Roman Crusaders			J. Purvey[c] died in prison after 25 years of cruelty	In Flanders, many Waldenses burned alive[b]
1422	Bohemia briefly ruled by Lithuanian prince Sigismund Korybut			W. Taylor[c] burned for heresy in London	
1423	H. Radtgeber[b] burned in Ratisbonne (Reinsbourg)				
1424	J. Draendorf executed in Worms				
1424	Third Anti-Hussite Crusade was called by the Pope, who wanted to regain control over the land; it again failed				
1426	P. Toraw [Torea][b] martyred in Spire				
1426	Foreign troops again sought to attack the Hussites, but the Hussite troops led by Prokop the Great soundly defeated them				
1427					J. Savonarola[b] burned alive in Florence
1428				Young King Henry VI wrote a letter to John Extor on the 6th of July that he should apprehend the priest W. White, chaplain Thomas of Settling, the priest W. Northhampton, "and all others that are suspected of heresy, whoever they may be, and wherever they may be	
1428					

1428									found, whether in free cities or without…"[b]
1428								W. Whyte[c] [White][b], Abraham[b], J. Waddon[b] burned in Norwich	
1429							Jacobel of Stribro, a collaborator with Hus, died (circumstances unknown)		
1430								R. Hovenden[c] burned at the stake in London	
1430									Margaret Backster[b] imprisoned until death or secretly put to death in England
1431								P. Craw[bc], a Bohemian, burned at the stake in Scotland	T. Bugle[c] burned at the stake in London
1432							Waldensian inquisitor Pierre Fabri renewed the prior work of Francois Borel, in extirpating heresy from the Alpine valleys		
1433				An Ecumenical Conference was held in Basel; Rome accepted the presence of the Hussites, but did not agree to allow members of the Greek church				The "English Hussite" Peter Payne arrived in Basel for the negotiations with Rome	Rome attended negotiations with the Hussites, calling for an
1433			Hussites were involved in the Basel Ecumenical Conference (3 Mar 1433); their request for participants from the Greek church were rejected by Rome						Ecumenical Conference in Basel, Switzerland; locally elected John of Rokycany,
1433		Upon pressure from Rome, Frederick, Margrave of Brandenburg sent as large army to fight the Hussites (1 Aug 1433); on							Archbishop of Prague, was [later] not recognized by Rome,

Disclaimer: some dates may vary (Page 69)

COLOR GUIDE: YELLOW=Roman Catholic areas; TAN=Bad years for Anabaptists; GOLD=Important events for Catholicism; ORANGE=Catholics "martyred"; RED=Evangelicals martyred; GRAY=Other martyred; PINK=Marriage issues; PURPLE= Crusades or massacres; TURQUOISE=Martyrology info; BLUE=Part Protestant areas; AQUA=U.S. Const; LT GREEN=Disputed areas; LIME=Bible issues; GREEN=Major dates.

Geographic History

Date	Germany-Austria-Scandinavia	Switzerland	France-Alsace	British Isles	Italy, Spain, Low Lands
1433	14 Aug the crusaders sent by Rome crossed the border; they took flight when the Hussites came out to fight				who also refused the participation of the Greek church in these negotiations
1434	A war broke out between the Taborites and the Ultraquists (referring to taking communion in both kinds) allowing the Polish Hussites to gain the upper hand in Bohemia; Wladyslaw III of Varna definitively defeated the Hussites in the Battle of Grotniki, ending the Hussite wars				
1434					
1434	Inquisitor Johannes Nider began writing *Formicarius* (1434-1436), which content was used in the publication of *Malleus* in 1484m3				
1436	Peace Agreement King Sigismund of Moravia, the Hussite delegates, and the Church of Rome agreed to modify the 1419 "Four Articles" as follows:				T. Rhedonbc, a Frenchman, went to Rome to preach reform, was imprisoned and burned at the stake
1436	(1) Holy Sacrament is to be given freely in both kinds to all Christians in Bohemia...				In its "Peace Agreement" with Bohemia, Rome refused to recognize John of Rokycany as archbishop of Prague, who had been elected to that dignity by the estates of Bohemia*
1436	(2) All mortal sins shall be punished and extirpated by those whose office it is to do so				
1436	(3) The word of God is to be freely and truthfully preached by the priests of the Lord, and by worthy deacons				*Herein Rome followed the precedent of Gregory VII's *Dictatus Papae* (1075)
1436	(4) The priests in the time of the law of grace shall claim no ownership of worldly possessions				
1438			King of France, Charles VII signed the "Pragmatic Sanction of Bourges" which affirmed a conciliar approach to local control over absolute Papal		

1438									primacy; the document was never approved by Rome, who followed Boniface VIII, *Unam Sanctum* (1302) which affirmed that "outside the	
1438									Church there is no salvation"; the French King, **Francis I**, in 1516, later accepted the Bull of the **5th Lateran Council** by **Leo X**, *Pastor aeternus*	
1438									*gregem*, which gave Rome unopposed absolute primacy (DS 1445)	
1439					**Council of Basel** among other things affirmed the doctrine of the Immaculate Conception of Mary in their 36th Session (DS 1400)			**Antipope Amadeus of Savoy** (aka. **Felix V**) became pope (basdd on the Council of Bale); the following regions were faithful to his papacy: Savoy,		
1439					**Eugene IV** wrote that a council is inferior to the word of the Pope (DS 1309), contra **Basel's** 33rd session		In Basel, **A. de Roma**[b] condemned as a heretic	Switzerland, Austria, Tyrol, Bayen-Munchen, Simmen, Teutonic orders, and other German orders		
1441					**Father**[c] of the Duchesse of Crete burned by a Papal legate	**R. Dule**[c] hung and strangled in England		→		
1442					From "**Cantate Domino**" from the Council of Florence, a decree for the Jacobites (DS 1336): "This is why she [the Church] anathematizes the folly of the **Manicheans** who are founded on two first principles, one of visible	Jean Voyle inquisited Waldenses in the Provence region of France		Could not this anathema against the **Manicheans** be applied to: (1) those who disbelieve that the Host is the		
1442					things, the other of invisible and have said that there is one God of the New Testament and another of the Old" (DS 1351) "She [the Church] firmly believes, professes and preaches that 'none of those who find themselves outside of the Catholic Church' [note: Fulgence de Ruspe, *De fide seu de regula fidei ad Petrum* 38, n.81], not			very Body of Christ; (2) those who disbelieve in holy "things" such as holy garments, holy water, holy oil, etc.; (3) those who do believe in being born		
1442					only pagans, but also Jews or heretics and schismatics can become participants to eternal life, but will go "into the eternal fire which is prepared for the Devil and his angels" (Matt 25:41)"			again of the Spirit; and (4) those who believe in a level of discontinuity between the sacrifices of the Old Covenant and the need for		
1442								Sacraments under the New Covenant?		

COLOR GUIDE: YELLOW=Roman Catholic areas; TAN=Bad years for Anabaptists; GOLD=Important events for Catholicism; ORANGE=Catholics "martyred"; RED=Evangelicals martyred; GRAY=Other martyred; Disclaimer: some dates may vary
PINK=Marriage issues; PURPLE=Crusades or massacres; TURQUOISE=Martyrology info; BLUE=Part Protestant areas; AQUA=U.S. Const; LT GREEN=Disputed areas; LIME=Bible issues; GREEN=Major dates. (Page 71)

Thomas P. Johnston   Geographic History   Page 72

Date	Germany-Austria-Scandinavia	Switzerland	France-Alsace	British Isles	Italy, Spain, Low Lands
1449	End of **Antipope Amadeus of Savoy**'s papacy				
1450		**A. Chartetius**b wrote a book against the unmarried life of the priests	**J. Lefevre** d'Etaples born in Picardy, France		
1450		[former Avignon Pope] **P. de Luna**b wrote against the papacy and chuch			
1452	Hussite town of Tabor was captured by **George of Podebrady**, establishing Ultraquist worship there				
1455	**Guttenberg Press** invention of moveable type			**Pope Nicholas V**'s Bull, *Romanus Pontifex* (8 Jan 1455) gave Portugal claim to the "New World"	
1457	Many **Waldenses**b put to death in Eichstaedt, Germany				
1458	**M. Hager**c executed in Berlin				
1459					**Pius II** anathematized **Zaninus de Solcia** as a heretic [he combined elements the licenciousness and Socinianism] (DS 1361-1369)
1459					
1460	"**Unity of the Czech Brethren**" church of the Reformed type was foundedm6				

1460	Birth of **Luke of Prague**s3							
1465					A **Waldensian** burned in Lille			**L. Valla**b arrested for repudiating papacy and its vows, banished and died in Naples
1466								**Erasmus** born
1470	**J. de Wesalia**b began preaching in Worms against the supremacy of	**G. Mortgenstern**b began preaching against the lack of virtue of the monks; nothing else is known of his fate						**Pope Sixtus IV** published *Cum praexcelsa* (27 Feb 1477) reaffirming the Immaculate
1470	the Pope; he was later arrested in 1479 and burned →							Conception of Mary confirmed by the 36th session of the **Council of Basel** (1439) DS 1400
1471, Sale of Indulgences became big business 1471	Rome's **"Taxation of the Casuistic Parties of the Papal Shop..."** published in Cologne (1515, 1522)p	**Stephen** b an elder of the Waldenses burned alive in Vienna; persecution spread to many other Waldenses in Bohemia and Austria		Rome's "Taxation of the Casuistic Parties of the Papal Shop..." published in Paris (16 editions up to 1545)p			**Pope Sixtus IV** published "Taxation of the Casuistic Parties of the Papal Shop..." to provide monetary uniformity for sellers of indulgences (Rome: [2 early eds no date], 1486, 1492, 1503, 1508, 1509, 1512, 1514; Venice eds: 1532, 1584)p	
							Pope Sixtus IV further authorized the inquisition in Spainc	
1471	**Sample Indulgences** "Absolution for the one who reveals the confession of any penitent is taxed at seven *carlins*. "Absolution for the one who abuses a young girl is taxed at six *carlins*. "Absolution for a priest who lives with a concubine is taxed at seven *carlins*. "Absolution for a lay person guilty of the same is taxed at eight *carlins*. "Absolution for the one who has killed his father, his mother, his brother, his sister, his wife, or any other relative or associate, being a lay person, is taxed at five *carlins*.							
1471	"Absolution for a current lay person who has killed an Abbot or another ecclesiastic inferior to a Bishop, is taxed at seven, eight, or nine *carlins*.							

COLOR GUIDE: YELLOW=Roman Catholic areas; TAN=Bad years for Anabaptists; GOLD=Important events for Catholicism; RED=Evangelicals martyred; GRAY=Other martyred; Disclaimer: some dates may vary PINK=Marriage issues; PURPLE=Crusades or massacres; TURQUOISE=Martyrology info; BLUE=Part Protestant areas; AQUA=U.S. Const; LT GREEN=Disputed areas; LIME=Bible issues; GREEN=Major dates.

(Page 73)

Thomas P. Johnston — Geographic History — Page 74

Date	Germany-Austria-Scandinavia	Switzerland	France-Alsace	British Isles	Italy, Spain, Low Lands
1471					"Absolution for a husband who strikes his wife in such a way that she has an abortion or a pre-term delivery, is taxed at eight *carlins*. "Absolution for a woman who takes any remedy to cause her to have an abortion, or who does anything else with the design of causing the fetus to perish, is taxed at five *carlins*. "The father, the mother, or whatever other relative who suffocates a child, will pay for each murder four *tournois*, one *ducat*, eight *carlins*. "The one who has committed anyone of these crimes (blasphemies [lit. *sacrilèges*], thefts, arsons, perjury, or other similar) is fully absolved, and his honor reestablished in every form and without forfeiture, comes to thirty-six *tournois* and nine *ducats*.
1471					"The absolution for all acts of impurity, of whatever nature they may be, committed by a [religious] clerk, be it with a nun, in the cloister or elsewhere, or with his/her parents or relatives, or with a spiritual daughter, or with another woman, whomever that may be; being that the absolution be requested not simply by the clerk, or by he himself or his concubines, with the exemption of being able to keep his orders [religious position] and of holding its benefits, and with no claim of forfeiture, costs only thirty-six *tournois* and nine *ducats*.
1471					"Absolution for a lay person for the crime of adultery given for the inner heart of his conscience, costs four *tournois*. "A religious woman who has fallen several times in the sin of luxury [i.e. coveting things] will be absolved and will be reestablished in her order, even if she is the *abesse* [superior of a female abbey], comes to thirty-six *tournois*, nine *ducats*. "Absolution for a priest who keeps a concubine, with the exemption to keep his orders and to hold its benefits, costs twenty-one *tournois*, five *ducats*, six *carlins*.
1471					"If there is adultery and incest one the part of lay people, they will need to pay for each head six *tournois*. "Permission to eat milk products when it is forbidden [prohibited] costs, for only one person, six *tournois*."p
1473					J. Veyllet O.F.M. (Franciscan) was named inquisitor of Waldenses in the Piedmont valleys of Farissimere, Argenteria, and Loysiam2
1476					Pope Sixtus IV decreed on 28 February that all who should assist at the Divine Office of the Solemnity of the Feast of Our Lady's Conception would be granted an indulgence (*Malleus*)
1478				T. More born	
1479	J de Wesaliab burned alive in Mentz				Another **Papal Bull** of **Sixtus IV** authorized the inquisition in Spain4
1479			The heretical propositions of **Peter Martinez d'Osma**, master at Salamanque, condemned by **Sixtus IV** in the bull "Licet ea quae de nostro mandato" (DS 1411-1419) "(1) The detailed confession of sins, which proceeds in reality from a statute of the Universal Church, is not known in the divine law; "(2) As regards the culpability and the punishment, mortal sins are erased in the other world without confession only by contrition of soul. "(3) And depraved thoughts [are erased] only by mere displeasure. "(4) That confession must be in secret is not required as a necessity		
1479			"(5) That those that confess ought not be absolved before they have fulfilled their penitence [or, in reality: ought not be absolved if they are not repentant?] "(6) The Roman Pontif cannot remit the punishment of purgatory "(7) Nor [has he the authority] to bestow what has been determined by the Universal Church		

1479				"(8) As concerns the conferring of grace, the Sacrament of Penitence is a natural [carnal] sacrament, but not the institution of the New or of the Old Testaments
1479				[Censure:] To take a larger measure of prudence, We declare… that the preceding propositions are false, all and each, contrary to the holy catholic faith, erroneous and scandalous and completely foreign to the truth of the Gospel, and contrary to the decrees of the Holy Fathers and of the other apostolic constitutions, and that they contain manifest heresy"
1480		Luke of Prague joined Moravian Brethrens3		Spanish Inquisition established under **Ferdinand and Isabella**, primarily against **Jews** and **heretics**l4
1480				"In 330 years (1478-1808), the merciless **Spanish Inquisition** had **323,362 persons** burned alive, and **17,659 persons** burned in effigy" (Joseph F. Conley, *Drumbeats that Changed the World*, 32).
1483			M. Luther born in Eisleben	**Pope Sixtus IV** published *Grave nimus* (4 Sept 1483) affirming the Immaculate Conception of Mary against those who preached a contrary doctrine; some where preaching that the doctrine of the immaculate conception was a mortal sin and heresy (DS 1425-1426)
1483				
1484 *Malleus*	*Malleus* [→] first published in German by two Dominican Inquisitors, H. Kramer and J. Sprenger as *Hexenhammer*m3			**Pope Innocent VIII** pre-affirmed the publication of *"Malleus Maleficarum"* [hammer of wickedness] (9 Dec 1484), which described witchcraft (including refusal to baptize infants), with appropriate methods of torture, and how to deal with heretics; *"Malleus"* was first written in German as *Hexenhammer* by Dominican Inquisitors Heinrich Kramer and Jacob Sprenger in 1486; Its Third Section described with how to deal with heretics; *Malleus* was presumably prohibited by **Pope Innocent VIII** in 1490, and yet it allowed its publication 13 times (1487-1520), and 16 times (1574-1669) with the 1484 endorsement of **Pope Innocent VIII**; one must remember the Papal control of most Western European printing presses
Maleficarum 1484		B. Hubmaier born in Friedberg	U. Zwingli born in Wildhaus	**A Portion of Pope Innocent VIII's Endorsement of *Malleus*:**m3
1484	By *Malleus*, refusal to baptize infants remained a capital crime, and was now associated with unbelief, atheism, and witchcraft.			"Innocent, Bishop, Servant of the servants of God, for an eternal remembrance. "Desiring with the most heartfelt anxiety, even as Our Apostleship requires, that the Catholic faith should especially in this Our day increase and flourish everywhere, and that all heretical depravity should be driven far from the frontiers and bournes of the Faithful, We very gladly proclaim and even
1484	Grand Inquisitor **Conrad of Marburg** (Marpurg), sent by **Pope Innocent III**, used tests similar to those described in *Malleus* against Heretics in 1214.			restate those particular means and methods whereby Our pious desire may obtain its wished effect, since when all errors are uprooted by Our diligent avocation as by the hoe of a provident husbandman, a zeal for, and the regular observance of, Our holy Faith will be all the more strongly impressed upon the hearts of the Faithful. "It has indeed lately come to Our ears, not without afflicting Us with bitter sorrow, that in some parts of Northern Germany, as well as in the provinces,

(Page 75)

COLOR GUIDE: YELLOW=Roman Catholic areas; TAN=Bad years for Anabaptists; GOLD=Important events for Catholicism; ORANGE=Catholics "martyred"; RED=Evangelicals martyred; GRAY=Other martyred;   Disclaimer: some dates may vary
PINK=Marriage issues; PURPLE= Crusades or massacres; TURQUOISE=Martyrology info; BLUE=Part Protestant areas; AQUA=U.S. Const; LT GREEN=Disputed areas; LIME=Bible issues; GREEN=Major dates.

Thomas P. Johnston
Geographic History
Page 76

Date	Germany-Austria-Scandinavia	Switzerland	France-Alsace	British Isles	Italy, Spain, Low Lands
1484	By his choice of the surname "Innocent", **Pope Innocent VIII** seems to show a common spirit with **Pope Innocent III**, the Fourth Lateran Council, and the crusade against the Albigenses and Waldenses.		townships, territories, districts, and dioceses of Mainz, Cologne, Tréves, Salzburg, and Bremen, many persons of both sexes, unmindful of their own salvation and straying from the Catholic Faith, have abandoned themselves to devils, incubi and succubi, and by their incantations, spells, conjurations, and other accursed charms and crafts, …; over and above this, they blasphemously renounce that Faith which is theirs by the Sacrament of Baptism, and at the instigation of the Enemy of Mankind they do not shrink from committing and perpetrating the foulest abominations and filthiest excesses to the deadly peril of their own souls, whereby they outrage the Divine Majesty and are a cause of scandal and danger to very many. And although Our dear sons Henry Kramer and James Sprenger, Professors of Theology, of the Order of Friars Preachers, have been by Letters Apostolic delegated as Inquisitors of these heretical pravities, and still are Inquisitors, the first in the aforesaid parts of Northern Germany, …, and further since the two delegates themselves and the abominations they are to encounter are not designated in detailed and particular fashion, these persons are not ashamed to contend with the most unblushing effrontery that these enormities are not practised in these provinces, and consequently the aforesaid Inquisitors have no legal right to exercise their powers of inquisition in the provinces, townships, dioceses, districts, and territories, which have been rehearsed, and that the Inquisitors may not proceed to punish, imprison, and penalize criminals convicted of the heinous offences and many wickednesses which have been set forth. Accordingly in the aforesaid provinces, townships, dioceses, and districts, the abominations and enormities in question remain unpunished not without open danger to the souls of many and peril of eternal damnation."		
1484			**Excerpts of the Text of *Malleus Maleficarum***		
1484			[a very long text benefiting from the invention of the printing press in 1455] Part 1, Ques 2, "Let us especially note too that in the practice of this abominable evil, four points in particular are required. First, most profanely to renounce the Catholic Faith, or at any rate to deny certain dogmas of the faith; secondly, to devote themselves body and soul to all evil; thirdly, to offer up unbaptized children to Satan; fourthly, to indulge in every kind of carnal lust with Incubi and Succubi and all manner of filthy delights" … Part 2, Ques 1, Chap 2, "But these [powerful witches] are only the children who have not been re-born by baptism at the font." [quoting a witch] "This is the manner of it. We set our snares chiefly for unbaptized children, and even for those that have been baptized, especially when they have not been protected by the sign of the Cross and prayers' (Reader, notice that, at the devil's command, they take the unbaptized chiefly, in order that they may not be baptized)." … "And although the devil for the most part performs this by means of this unguent, to the end that children should be deprived of the grace of baptism and of salvation, yet he often seems to affect the same transvection without its use." … Part 2, Ques 2, Chap 6, "Therefore, since the first act of reconciliation by which a man is consecrated to God is in baptism, it is necessary that man should be exorcised before he is baptized; indeed in this it is more imperative than in any other circumstance." … Part 3, Intro, "This being so, whatever crime a man commits, if he acts without an error in his understanding he is not a heretic. … Similarly, since an error in the understanding is a necessary condition of heresy, no action which is done entirely without any such error can make a man a heretic. … Therefore they are rather sorcerers than heretics, and are to be classed with those whom the above Canon *accusatus* declares are not properly subject to the Inquisitorial Court, since they do not manifestly savour of heresy; their heresy being hidden, if indeed it exists at all." … "So when there is no doubt about the effect, still it is necessary to inquire farther into the cause; and if it be found that a man has acted out of a perverse and erroneous opinion concerning the faith, then he is to be judged a heretic and will be subject to trial by the Inquisitors together with the Ordinary. … For the spirit of faith is known by the act of faith; as the spirit of chastity is shown by a chaste life; similarly the Church must judge a man a heretic if his actions show that he disputes any article of the faith." … "For they cannot proceed against schismatic Bishops and other high Dignitaries, as is shown by the chapter of the Inquisition *Concerning Heretics*, Book VI, where it says: The Inquisitors of the sin of heresy deputed by the Apostolic See or by any other authority have no power to try such offenders on this sort of charge, or to proceed against them under pretext of their office, unless it is expressly stated in the letters of commission from the		

Date		Content
1484		Apostolic See that they are empowered to do so." … "But an error against Holy Scripture, against the articles of the faith, or against the decision of the Church, as has been said above, is heresy (art. 24, q. 1, *haec est fides*)." … "For just as he who obstinately argues against the articles of the faith is a heretic, so also is he who stubbornly maintains his opinion against the determination of the
1484		Church in matters concerning the faith and that which is necessary for salvation. For the Church herself has never been proved to be in error over matter of faith (as it is said in art. 24, q. 1, *a recta*, and in other chapters). And it is expressly said, that he who maintains anything against the determination of the Church, not in an open and honest manner, but in matters which concern faith and salvation, is a heretic." "The third condition required is that he who holds the error should be one who has professed the Catholic faith. For is a man has never professed the
1484		Christian faith, he is not a heretic but simply an infidel, like the Jews or the Gentiles who are outside the faith. Therefore S. Augustine says in the *City of God*: The devil, seeing the human race to be delivered from the worship of idols and devils, stirred up heretics who, under the guise of Christians, should oppose Christian doctrine. So for a man to be a heretic it is necessary that he should have received the Christian faith in baptism." "Fourthly, it is necessary that the man who so errs should retain some of the true belief concerning Christ, pertaining either to His divinity or to His
1484		humanity. For if he retains no part of the faith, he is more rightly to be considered an apostate than a heretic." "Applying this to our discussion of the heresy of witches and to the modern laws, we say that in law there are three degrees of suspicion in the matter of heresy: the first slight, the second great, and the third very great." … "As an example of simple heresy, if people are found to be meeting together secretly for the purpose of worship, or differing in their manner of life and
1484		behaviour from the usual habits of the faithful." … "The second or grave suspicion is in law called grave or vehement…" "As, to take an example of simple heresy, when people are found to shelter known heretics, and show favour to them, or visit and associate with them and give gifts to them, receive them into their houses and protect them, and such like: such people are vehemently suspected of heresy" …
1484		"For example, in simple heresy, if persons are found to show a reverent love for heretics, to receive consolation or communion from them, or perpetrate any other such matter in accordance with their rites and ceremonies: such persons would fall under and be convicted of a violent suspicion of heresy and heretical beliefs." … "But if he does not confess his crime after he has been convicted, and does not consent to abjure his heresy, he is to be condemned as an impenitent
1484	Contra the U.S. Constitution's Fifth Amendment, *Malleus* allowed for a death sentence for heresy under suspicion only (without due process); similarly, allowing for double jeopardy	heretic. For a violent suspicion is sufficient to warrant a conviction, and admits no proof to the contrary"
1484	With the prominence given to the "Salem Witch Trials" in Salem, Massachusetts between February	**[The following are sample convictions provided in *Malleus* for witches/heretics; *Malleus*, Part 3, Ques. 20-29]** "Of the **First Method** of Pronouncing Sentence: SINCE, therefore, the accused is either found innocent and is to be altogether absolved, or is found only to be generally defamed as a heretic, or is found a proper subject for the questions and the torture on account of her reputation, or is found to be lightly suspected of heresy, or is found to be strongly or gravely suspected of heresy" (following questioning by torture, discharged)
1484	1692 and May 1693, it is helpful to know that these trials did not take place in a historical vacuum.	"The **Second method** of delivering judgement is to be employed when he or she who is accused, after a diligent discussion of the merits of the case in consultation with learned lawyers, is found to be no more than defamed as a heretic in some village, town, or province … a canonical purgation shall be imposed upon him. That is, he must produce some seven, ten, twenty, or thirty men, according to the extent to which he has been defamed and the size and important of the place concerned, and these must be men of his own station and condition. … And if he accepts the purgation and fails
1484		in it; that is, if he cannot find sponsors of the number and quality desired; he shall be considered as convicted, and is to be condemned as a heretic." "The **Third method** of bringing a process on behalf of the faith to a conclusive termination is when the person accused of heresy, after a careful consideration of the merits of the process in consultation with learned lawyers, is found to be inconsistent in his statements, or is found that there are sufficient grounds to warrant his exposure to the question and torture: so that if, after he has been thus questioned, he confesses nothing, he may be

COLOR GUIDE YELLOW=Roman Catholic areas; TAN=Bad years for Anabaptists; GOLD=Important events for Catholicism; ORANGE=Catholics "martyred"; RED=Evangelicals martyred; GRAY=Other martyred; Disclaimer: some dates may vary
PINK=Marriage issues; PURPLE= Crusades or massacres; TURQUOISE=Martyrology info; BLUE=Part Protestant areas; AQUA=U.S. Const; LT GREEN=Disputed areas; LIME=Bible issues; GREEN=Major dates. (Page 77)

Thomas P. Johnston   Geographic History   Page 78

Date	Germany-Austria-Scandinavia	Switzerland	France-Alsace	British Isles	Italy, Spain, Low Lands
1484					considered innocent.... But if, after having been fittingly questioned and tortured, he will not discover the truth, let him not be further molested, but be freely allowed to depart.... If, on the other hand, he confesses the truth, but is not penitent but obstinately persists in his heresy, but is not a relapsed heretic, then according to the Canon, after a decent interval and due warning, he is to be condemned as a heretic and handed over to the secular Court to suffer the extreme penalty, as we show later in the tenth method"
1484					"The **Fourth method** of concluding the process on behalf of the faith is used when, after the merits of the process have been diligently examined in consultation with expert lawyers, the accused is found to rest under only a light suspicion of heresy. .... For such an accused, if the matter be a public one, will publicly make the following abjuration in the Church: I, N., of such a Diocese, a citizen of such a city or place, being on my trial, do swear before you the Lord Bishop of such a city, and upon the Holy Gospels placed before me and upon which I set my hand, that I believe in my heart and
1484					profess with my lips that Holy Catholic and Apostolic Faith which the Holy Roman Church believes, confesses, preaches, and observes. Also I swear that I believe in my heart and profess with my lips that the Lord JESUS Christ, in company with all the Saints, abominates the wicked heresy of witches; and that all who follow or adhere to it will with the devil and his Angels be punished in eternal fire unless they turn their hearts and are reconciled by the penitence of the Holy Church. And there I abjure, renounce, and revoke that heresy of which you, my Lord Bishop, and your
1484					Officers hold me suspected: namely, that I have been familiar with witches, have ignorantly defended their errors, have held in detestation their Inquisitors and prosecutors, or that I have failed to bring their crimes to light. Also I swear that I have never believed the aforesaid heresy, nor do I believe, nor have I adhered, nor do I adhered to it, nor shall I ever believe, adhere to, or teach it, nor do I intend to teach it"
1484					"The **Fifth method** of concluding a process on behalf of the faith is used when she who is accused of heresy, after a careful examination of the merits of the process in consultation with learned lawyers, is found to be strongly suspected of heresy. .... she must abjure that specific heresy. .... But it must be noted that those who are suspected, but not taken in heresy, whether they be strongly or lightly suspected, must not be imprisoned or confined for life. For this is the punishment of those who have been heretics and afterwards repented. But they may, because of their deeds for which they have come under suspicion, be sent to prison for a time, and afterwards, as will be seen, released. Neither are they to be branded with
1484					the sign of the Cross, for such is the sign of a penitent heretic; and they are not convicted heretics, but only suspected, therefore they are not to be marked in this way. But they can be ordered either to stand on certain solemn days within the doors of a church, or near the altar, while Holy Mass is being celebrated, bearing in their hands a lighted candle of a certain weight; or else to go on some pilgrimage, or something of the kind, according to the nature and requirements of the case"
1484	Against the First and Fifth Amendments of the U.S. Constitution, there was no possibility				"The **Sixth method** of bringing to a conclusion a process on behalf of the faith is used when the person accused of heresy, after a careful examination of the merits of the process in consultation with learned lawyers, is found to be gravely suspected of heresy. .... And if he remained obstinate in that excommunication for a year, then he would be gravely suspected of heresy; for then the strong suspicion would become a grave one, against which no defence is admitted. .... For in the case of one gravely suspected of simple heresy, the following is the procedure. Although he may not in actual
1484	of a defense against the charge of being "gravely suspect" of heresy				truth be a heretic, since there may not be any error in his understanding, or if there is, he may not cling obstinately to it in his will: nevertheless he is to be condemned as a heretic because of the said grave suspicion, against which no proof is admitted. .... [after full abjuration] First, you shall put on over all the garments which you wear a grey-blue garment after the manner of a monk's scapulary, made without a hood either before or behind, and having upon it crosses of yellow cloth three palms long and two palms wide, and you shall wear this garment over all others for such a length of time
1484					(setting a period of one or two years, more or less as the guilt of the person demands), And in the said garment and crosses you shall stand in the door of such a church at such a time for so long, or on the four major Feasts of the Glorious Virgin, or in such and such cities in the doors of such and such churches; and we sentence and condemn you for life, or for such a period, to such a prison. (Let this be set down as seems most to the honour of the faith, and according to the greater or less guilt and obstinacy of the accused.) And we expressly, and in the sure knowledge that it is so
1484					ordained by canonical institution, reserve to ourselves the right to mitigate the said penance, to increase it, change it, or remove it, in whole or in part, as often as seems good to us."
1484					"The **Seventh method** of bringing to a conclusion a process on behalf of the faith is employed when the person accused of the sin of heresy, after a careful examination of the merits of the process in consultation with men learned in the law, is found to be both suspected and defamed of heresy.

Date		Content
1484		And this is when the accused is not legally convicted by his own confession or by the evidence of the facts or by the legitimate production of witnesses; but is found to be publicly defamed, and there are also other indications which render him lightly or strongly suspected of heresy: as that he has held much familiarity with heretics. … And let them pronounce sentence as shall seem most to the honour of the faith and the extermination of the sin of heresy: as that on certain Sundays and Festivals he must stand at the door of such a church, holding a candle of such a weight, during
1484		the solemnization of Holy Mass, with head uncovered and bare feet, and offer the said candle at the altar; and that he must fast on Fridays, and that for a certain period he must not dare to depart from that place, but present himself before the Bishop or Judge on certain days of the week; and any similar penance which seemed to be demanded by the particular nature of his guilt; for it is impossible to give a hard-and-fast rule. This sentence was given, etc. And let it be put into execution after it has been pronounced; and it can be cancelled, mitigated or changed as may be required by the
1484		condition of the penitent and for his correction and humiliation; for the Bishop has this power by law." "The **Eighth method** of terminating a process on behalf of the faith is used when the person accused of heresy, after a careful examination of the merits of the process in consultation with learned lawyers, is found to have confessed his heresy, but to be penitent, and not truly to have relapsed into heresy. And this is when the accused has himself confessed in a Court of law under oath before the Bishop and Inquisitor that he has for so long
1484		lived and persisted in that heresy of which he is accused, or in any other, and has believed in and adhered to it; but that afterwards, being persuaded by the Bishop and others, he wishes to be converted and to return to the bosom of the Church, and to abjure that and every heresy, and to make such satisfaction as they require of him; and it is found that he has made no previous abjuration of any other heresy, but is now willing and prepared to abjure." …. My son, your sentence or penance consists in this, that you bear this cross during the whole period of your life, that you stand so
1484	The ninth method explained the method of degrading of clerics experienced by the many Catholic	bearing it on the altar steps or in the door of such churches, and that you be imprisoned for life on bread and water" "The **Ninth method** of arriving at a conclusive sentence in a process on behalf of the faith is used when the person accused of heresy, after a careful investigation of the circumstances of the process in consultation with men of good judgement, is found to have confessed her heresy and to be penitent, but that she has truly relapsed. …. The following procedure must be observed in this case. When, after mature and careful and, if
1484	clerics who later became Protestant before they were burned alive, as explained in Crespin's *Martyrology*	necessary, repeated investigation by learned men, it has been concluded that the said prisoner has actually and prepense relapsed into heresy, the Bishop or Judge shall send to the said prisoner in the place of detention two or three honest men, especially religious or clerics, who are zealous for the faith, of whom the prisoner has no suspicion, but rather places confidence in them; and they shall go in to her at a suitable time and speak to her sweetly of the contempt of this world and the miseries of this life, and of the joys and glory of Paradise. And leading up from this, they shall indicate
1484		to her on the part of the Bishop or Judge that she cannot escape temporal death, and that she should therefore take care for the safety of her soul, and prepare herself to confess her sins and receive the Sacrament of the Eucharist. And they shall visit her often, persuading her to penitence and patience, strengthening her as much as they can in the Catholic truth, and they shall diligently cause her to confess, so that she may receive the Sacrament of the Eucharist at her humble petition. For these Sacraments are not to be denied to such offenders. And when she has received these
1484		Sacraments, and been well disposed by these men to salvation; after two or three days during which they have strengthened her in the Catholic faith and induced her to repentance, the Bishop or Judge of that place shall notify the bailiff of the place or the authorities of the secular Court, that on such a day at such an hour (not a Feast Day) he should be with his attendants in such a square or place (but it must be outside a church) to receive from their Court a certain backslider whom the Bishop and Judge will hand over to him. … It must also be remarked that such a sentence which
1484		delivers up a person to the secular Court ought not to be pronounced on a Festival or Solemn Day, nor in a church, but outside in some open space. For it is a sentence which leads to death; and it is more decent that it should be delivered on an ordinary day and outside the church; for a Feast Day and the church are dedicated to God. "The **Tenth method** of completing a process on behalf of the Faith by a final sentence is used when the person accused of heresy, after a careful
1484		examination of the circumstances of the process in consultation with skilled lawyers, is found to have confessed his heresy and to be impenitent, though he has not relapsed into the heresy. …they shall give notice to the herald or bailiff or secular authorities that on such a day, not a Feast, and at such an hour they should be in such a place with their attendants outside a church, and that they will deliver to them a certain impenitent heretic. None the less they shall themselves make public proclamation in the customary places that on such a day at such a time in the aforesaid place a

COLOR GUIDE YELLOW=Roman Catholic areas; TAN=Bad years for Anabaptists; GOLD=Important events for Catholicism; ORANGE=Catholics "martyred"; RED=Evangelicals martyred; GRAY=Other martyred; Disclaimer: some dates may vary
PINK=Marriage issues; PURPLE= Crusades or massacres; TURQUOISE=Martyrology info; BLUE=Part Protestant areas; AQUA=U.S. Const; LT GREEN=Disputed areas; LIME=Bible issues; GREEN=Major dates. (Page 79)

Thomas P. Johnston
Geographic History
Page 80

Date	Germany-Austria-Scandinavia	Switzerland	France-Alsace	British Isles	Italy, Spain, Low Lands
1484	The people in attendance at the burning of a heretic were said to receive a "customary" indulgence for being in attendance!	sermon will be preached in defence of the faith, and that they will hand over a certain heretic to secular justice; and that all should come and be present, being granted the customary Indulgences" [Eleventh method] "Of One who has Confessed to Heresy, is Relapsed, and is also Impenitent" [burned in like manner to 10th] [Twelfth method] "Of One Taken and Convicted, but Denying Everything" [if impenitent, burned alive; if penitent, imprisoned for life]			
1484		[Thirteenth method] "Of One who is Convicted but who hath Fled or who Contumaciously Absents himself" [condemned as a heretic, i.e. burned alive] "The Fourteenth method of finally concluding a process on behalf of the Faith is used when the person accused of heresy, after a careful discussion of the circumstances of the process with reference to the informant in consultation with learned lawyers, is found to be accused of that heresy only by another witch who has been or is to be burned. And this can happen in thirteen ways in thirteen cases."			
1484		**Sentence to Be Read Against a Non-Penitent Heretic [as part of Tenth method]**			
1484		"We, N., by the mercy of God Bishop of such a city, or Judge in the territories of such Prince, seeing that you, N., of such a place in such a Diocese, have been accused before us by public report and the information of credible persons (naming them) of heresy, and that you have for many years persisted in those heresies to the great hurt of your immortal soul; and since we, whose duty it is to exterminate the plague of heresy, wishing to be more certainly informed of this matter and to see whether you walked in darkness or the light, have diligently inquired into the said accusation, summoning and duly examining you, we find that you are indeed infected with the said heresy.			
1484		"But since it is the chief desire of our hearts to plant the Holy Catholic Faith in the hearts of our people, and to eradicate the pest of heresy, we have used diverse and various suitable methods, both by ourselves and by others, to persuade you to renounce your said errors and heresies in which you had stood, were standing, and even now defiantly and obstinately stand with stubborn heart. But since the Enemy of the human race is present in your heart, wrapping you up and entangling you in the said errors, and you have refused and yet refuse to abjure the said heresies, choosing rather the death of your soul in hell and of your body in this world than to renounce the said heresies and return to the bosom of the Church and cleanse your soul, and since you are determined to remain in your sin:			
1484		"Therefore inasmuch as you are bound by the chain of excommunication from the Holy Church, and are justly cut off from the number of the Lord's flock, and are deprived of the benefits of the Church, the Church can do no more for you, having done all that was possible. We the said Bishop and Judges on behalf of the Faith, sitting in tribunal as Judges judging, and having before us the Holy Gospels that our judgement may proceed as from the countenance of god and our eyes see with equity, and having before our eyes only God and the truth of the Holy Faith and the extirpation of the plague of heresy, on this day and at this hour and place assigned to you for the hearing of your final sentence, we give it as our judgement and sentence that you are indeed an impenitent heretic, and as truly such to be delivered and abandoned to the secular Court: wherefore by this sentence we cast you away as an impenitent heretic from our ecclesiastical Court, and deliver or abandon you to the power of the secular Court: praying the said Court to moderate or temper its sentence of death against you. This sentence was given, etc.			
1485					**Inquisitor of Como** (Burbia, near Milan, Spain) ordered 41 "witches" shaved and burned alive (**Malleus**, Part 3, Intro)
1486			F. Lambert d'Avignon born	J. Eck born (1486-1543)	**Papal Bull gave Archdeacon of Cremona** authority to extirpate the Piedmont [Waldensian] "heretics"b2
1487			Bull of **Pope Innocent VIII** for the extirpation of the "Waldenses, and all other Hereticks whatsoever," given to **Albertus de Capitaneis**, for the Catholic bishops of Evreux, Lyons, and Vienna, "that the Catholick Faith in our times be propagated, and the evil of Heresie be rooted out from the borders of our Faithfull;" … "We therefore having determined to use all our		

1487					endeavors, and to imploy all our care, as we are bound by the duty of our Pastoral charge, to root up and extirpate such a detestable Sect, and the foresaid execrable Errors, that they may not spread further, and that the hearts of believers may not be damnably perverted from the *Catholick* Church; and to repress such rash undertakings; & having special confidence in the
1487					Lord concerning your Learning, your ripeness in counsel, your zeal in the faith, and your experience in the management of affairs; and in like manner hoping that you will truly and faithfully execute the things which we shall think good to commit unto you for extirpating such errours; we have thought good to constitute you at this time, **for the Cause of God and the**
1487					**Faith**, the Nuntio Commissioner of us, and of the Apostolic See, within the Dominions of our beloved Son *Charls* Duke of Savoy, and the *Delphinat*, and the Cities and Diocess of *Vienna*, and *Sedun*, and the adjacent Provinces, Cities, Lands and places whatsoever, to the end that you should cause the same Inquisitor to be received and admitted to the free exercise of his
1487					Office, and that you should induce the followers of the most wicked Sect of the *Waldenses*, and all others polluted with any other Heretical pravity whatsoever, to abjure their Errours, and to obey the Commandments of the same Inquisitor, and give way to your seasonable remedies. And that you may do this so much the more easily, by how much the greater Power
1487	No need to absolve from fealty (as in 1215 and 1243) as all European rulers were "Catholics", and thus needed				and Authority is given you by us, to wit, a Power, that by your self, or by some other person or persons, you may admonish and require most instantly all Archbishops, and Bishops seated in … and command them by vertue of Holy obedience, that together with our Venerable Brethren …, to execute the Office which is injoyned you with the forenamed Inquisitor, a man
1487	only to be constrained to use the sword against their "Heretical" citizens				no doubt endued with Learning and fervent Zeal for the salvation of souls, they do assist you in the premises; and together with you be able and willing *to proceed to the execution thereof against the forenamed Waldenses, and all other Hereticks whatsoever, to rise up in Arms against them, and by joint communication of processes, to tread them under foot, as*
1487					*venemous Adders*, and to procure diligently that the people committed to their charge do persist in the confession of the true Faith, and be confirmed therein… And to injoyn that all the moveable and immoveable goods of the Hereticks may be lawfully seized and given away by any body whatsoever, and to make a booty of all goods which the Hereticks bring, or cause to
1487					be brought unto the territories of Catholicks, or carry, or cause to be carried out of the same … and that they abstain from all commerce with the aforesaid Hereticks: And to declare, that neither they nor any others, who by any contract or otherwise are in any sort bound unto them to perform or pay anything, are henceforth at all obliged, or by the same authority can be
1487	The absolution of all contracts or debts with heretics; abstinence from all commerce with heretics; and				compelled thereunto…" m2
1487	freedom to pillage all the belongings of the heretics!				
1488	T. **Muntzer** born in Stolberg, Saxony-Anhalt				**M. Coverdale** born in Yorkshire

COLOR GUIDE: YELLOW=Roman Catholic areas; TAN=Bad years for Anabaptists; GOLD=Important events for Catholicism; ORANGE=Catholics "martyred"; RED=Evangelicals martyred; GRAY=Other martyred; Disclaimer: some dates may vary
PINK=Marriage issues; PURPLE=Crusades or massacres; TURQUOISE=Martyrology info; BLUE=Part Protestant areas; AQUA=U.S. Const; LIME=Bible issues; GREEN=Major dates.
LT GREEN=Disputed areas;

Thomas P. Johnston
Geographic History
Page 82

Date	Germany-Austria-Scandinavia	Switzerland	France-Alsace	British Isles	Italy, Spain, Low Lands
1489				T. **Cranmer** born	
1490			G. **Farel** born in Gap, France	**Mother**[c] [unnamed 1490][b] of **Lady Yonge** burned at the stake in England	
1491	**Luke of Prague** was sent by the *Unitas Fratrum* (of **Moravian Brethren**) to Greece and Constantinople for information on the Eastern churches[S3]		J. **Langlois** burned at the stake in Paris		I. **Loyola** born in Spain
1491					
1492 Spanish Inquisition 1492	**Luke of Prague**, a Brethren theologian and author of over 150 works, met Jews in Constantinople, who were fleeing the Spanish inquisition, he seems to have won one of them to Christ[m6]			More at Oxford	["In 1492 **Columbus** sailed the ocean blue"] The **Spanish inquisition** of **Torquemada**, promulgated against **Jews**, **Mohammedans**, and **Saracens**; it was extended to all who did not have allegiance to the Catholic church, including **Waldenses** and **Albigenses**[b]
1492					
1492					All **Jews** who would not accept baptism into the Church of Rome were expelled from Spain[l4]
1493			H. **Picard** burned at the stake in Paris		**Pope Alexander VI** promulgated *Inter caetera* (4 May 1493) allowing the kingdom of Castille to colonize in the "New World"
1494				W. **Tyndale** born	

1496											**Menno Simons** born in Friesland[m]
1497	**Luke of Prague** sent by the Moravian Brethren to meet with the French and Italian **Waldenses**[3]										All Jews who would not accept baptism into the Church of Rome were expelled from Portugal[4]
1498											**J. Savanarola**[c] [strangled and] burned at the stake in Florence, Italy
1499											**P. Scriptorus**[b] taught against transubstantiation, was driven into banishment ↓
1500										More became friend of **Erasmus** ↗	
1501	**Luther** entered University of Erfurt										
1502		**Zwingli** taught at St. Martin School, Basel					**Lambert**[y] (at 15 yrs) entered monastery of Observant Franciscans				
1502											
1503											**Erasmus** published first edition of *Enchiridion*
1503	**Hubmaier** at Univ. of Friedberg (under **J Eck**); received B.A.										**Hubmaier** became student of J. Eck ↙

COLOR GUIDE: YELLOW=Roman Catholic areas; TAN=Bad years for Anabaptists; GOLD=Important events for Catholicism; ORANGE=Catholics "martyred"; RED=Evangelicals martyred; GRAY=Other martyred; Disclaimer: some dates may vary
PINK=Marriage issues; PURPLE=Crusades or massacres; BLUE=Part Protestant areas; AQUA=U.S. Const; TURQUOISE=Martyrology info; LIME=Bible issues; GREEN=Major dates. (Page 83)
LT GREEN=Disputed areas;

Thomas P. Johnston Geographic History Page 84

Date	Germany-Austria-Scandinavia	Switzerland	France-Alsace	British Isles	Italy, Spain, Low Lands
1504	**Hussites**b made to confess Catholicism to the King of Bohemia, those refusing were put to death				**Scriptorus**b died in exile
1505	**Luther** received M.A from Erfurt.; entered Augustinian Monastery			**J. Knox** born	
1505				**J. Rogers** born in Deritend, Aston	
1506		**Zwingli** ordained, began ministry in Glarus	**R. Olivétan**, cousin of **Calvin**, born in Noyon		**Francis Xavier**, co-founder of Jesuit order, missionary to the East, was born
1506					
1507	**Waldenses**b made to confess Catholicism to King Uladislaus of Bohemia, and if not were exterminated				
1509	**N. Rust**b taught in Mecklenburg: (1) That letters of indulgence were nothing but subtle deceptions to rob the plain and simple people of their money; (2) That the pope does not have as much power as people suppose; (3) That the popes, cardinals, bishops, and prelates were leading lascivious lives, etc. (4) That saints ought not be invoked; **Rust** was compelled to flee to Wismar, and then elsewhere; his fate is unknown		**J. Calvin** born in Noyon, France	**T. Norys**c burned in Norwich, England; **Erasmus** wrote *In Praise of Folly* at home of **More**	Approximate birth of **P. Carnesecchi**, Secretary to **Pope Clement VII**b5
1509				**W. Tyndale** studied in Cambridge under **Erasmus**, translated his *Enchiridion* into English	
1509					
1509	**Waldenses**b inquisited in the area of Mecklenberg, near Mooren				

1510	B. Liblinensis[b] taught: (1) That it is impossible that the whole world should obey a single man, as is the pope; (2) That the popes themselves were not of one mind; for one prohibits that which another has instituted to be observed; (3) That therefore it is sufficient to believe in Christ, and to obey Him alone; the fate of Liblinensis is unknown					Priest Thomas[c] and T. de Bongay[c] burned in Norwich, England					
1510	Luke of Prague (author of over 150 treatises) wrote "On the Renewal of the Church"m6										
1510	Hubmaier ordained, became rector at Univ of Friedberg →										
1511		Pierre Viret born in Orbe, Canton de Vaud v2									
1512	J. Picus[b], J. Hilton[b], and others spoke against the papal abuses of the time; their fate is unknown			"Farel began his studies in Paris" v2	Lefevre published Paul on justification by faith	Tyndale earned B.A at Cambridge			Hubmaier changed universities to study under Eck at Ingolstadt ←		
1512	Luther awarded Doctor of Theology	Hubmaier attended Univ of Ingolstadt (under J. Eck), where he received Licentiate and Doctorate				Pop d'Aye[c] burned in Norwich					
1512						N. Peake[c] burned in Ypswich with his dog					
1513				The Frenchman, W. Budaeus[b] wrote: (1) The popes and bishops originate war between princes and potentiates; while they by rights ought to advise							

COLOR GUIDE: YELLOW=Roman Catholic areas; TAN=Bad years for Anabaptists; GOLD=Important events for Catholicism; ORANGE=Catholics "martyred"; RED=Evangelicals martyred; GRAY=Other martyred; Disclaimer: some dates may vary
PINK=Marriage issues; PURPLE=Crusades or massacres; TURQUOISE=Martyrology info; BLUE=Part Protestant areas; AQUA=U.S. Const; LT GREEN=Disputed areas; LIME=Bible issues; GREEN=Major dates.
(Page 85)

Date	Germany-Austria-Scandinavia		Switzerland		France-Alsace		British Isles		Italy, Spain, Low Lands	
1513					and help to peace; (2) They fill the world with pride, avarice, gluttony, drinking, lasciviousness, by their works; they are to their hearers the					
1513					cause for eternal damnation whoredom, adultery, surpassing in these vile deeds the laity; (3) They are Epicures, who do not care for eternal					
1514					life, as they show		**Tyndale** earned M.A. at Cambridge	**Coverdale** became a priest in Norwich upon		
1514						**Lefevre** accused of heresy and defended before the Sorbonne		graduating from Cambridge		
1515	**Luther** (reading **Lefevre**?) realiz-ed meaning of Romans 1:16-17						**R. Hunt**[C] burned in London			
1516	**Luther** published first edition of a German Theology	**Hubmaier** named chaplain at cathedral in Regensburg; joined	**Zwingli** began ministry in Eindsiedeln					**More** wrote Book One of *Utopia*, which undermined Lollardie		
1516	**Johann Tetzel** sold indulgences in **Luther**'s area	crusade against Jewish community in Regensburg								
1517 95 Theses	**Luther** (~34 yrs old) nailed his 95 Theses on the Cathedral door in Wittenberg, Germany; thereby									
of Luther 1517	marking the initial spark of the Magisterial [local government approved and protected by the military] Protestant Reformation									
1518		**Hubmaier** attended Diet in Augsburg to	**Zwingli** opposed **Samson**'s sale of indulgences;					**More** became King's Counselor	**Pope Leo X** responded to **Luther**'s objections to indulgences in a decree, "Cum postquam" (9 Nov 1518; DS 1447-1449), affirming	

1518		ministered in Zurich				that the Pope held the keys of the Kingdom of Heaven, and could dispense the from the overabundant merits of Christ and
1518						the saints, by means of indulgences, the temporal punishment of the living and the dead in purgatory (DS 1448); he
1518						then decreed that this needed to be taught by all, under threat of excommunication (martyrdom) (DS 1449)
1519	Luther involved in Leipzig Disputation against J. Eck	Hubmaier joined in expelling Jews from Regensburg; miracle on site of	Zwingli became the "people's priest" at the Great Church			J. Eck disputed against Luther at Leipzig Disputation
1519	Luther wrote *Two Kinds of Righteousness*	synagogue led to the building of Beauteous Mary [zur schönen	(*Grossmunster*) in Zurich; he began his *lectio continua* in			
1519		Maria]; **Hubmaier** was its first Chaplain; **Papal Bull** declared that	Matthew; Zwingli's ministry during the plague in 1519 endeared			
1519		persons visiting Beauteous Mary would reduce their time in purgatory	him to the people			
1519		by 100 days				
1519				J. Crespin born in Arras, France	Marguerite de Valois, sister of King Francis I, converted	
1520	Luther published *To the Christian Nobility, The Freedom of the*	J. Bugenhagius (aka. Pomeranus) of Wittenberg wrote a little book treating				Pope Leo X issued a Bull, *Exsurge Domine*, calling Luther to
1520	*Christian* and *The Pagan Servitude of the Church* (a.k.a.	Unborn Infants, stating that men had erred for twelve centuries		Farel taught in Paris	through Lutheran tracts; provided some protection for Lefevre and	retract his 95 Theses, which Bull Luther publicly burned, among the

COLOR GUIDE: <mark>YELLOW</mark>=Roman Catholic areas; <mark>TAN</mark>=Bad years for Anabaptists; <mark>GOLD</mark>=Important events for Catholicism; <mark>ORANGE</mark>=Catholics "martyred"; <mark>RED</mark>=Evangelicals martyred; <mark>GRAY</mark>=Other martyred; Disclaimer: some dates may vary <mark>PINK</mark>=Marriage issues; <mark>PURPLE</mark>=Crusades or massacres; <mark>TURQUOISE</mark>=Martyrology info; <mark>BLUE</mark>=Part Protestant areas; <mark>AQUA</mark>=U.S. Const; <mark>LT GREEN</mark>=Disputed areas; <mark>LIME</mark>=Bible issues; <mark>GREEN</mark>=Major dates. (Page 87)

Thomas P. Johnston

Geographic History

Page 88

Date	Germany-Austria-Scandinavia	Switzerland	France-Alsace	British Isles	Italy, Spain, Low Lands	
1520	*Babylonian Captivity of the Church*); **Luther** burned bull of excommunication		Olivétan, cousin of J. Calvin, converted to evangelical faith1		listed errors of Luther in the Bull is No. 33, "That the heretics were burned is contrary to the will of the Spirit" (DS 1483)	
1520						
1521	**Luther** appeared at Diet of Worms; stated "Here I stand, I can do no other, God help me"	**Hubmaier** accepted pastorate in	**Lambert** reading **Luther** (and the Bible) in his monastery in	**Briçonnet** stopped **Farel** from preaching in Meaux; **Calvin**	**More** became Under-Treasurer of England	**Pope Leo X** issued Bull excommunicating, calling **Luther's** extirpation **Emperor Charles** promulgated a law by which Lutheranism [and	**Loyola** wounded in battle
1521		Waldshut; read **Oecolampadius** on Luther	Avignon, became intrigued with Reformation principles ↘	attended University of Paris, where he earned B.A. and M.A. May 21: **Calvin** began receiving wages from chapel in Gesinep		Zwinglianism]b was made illegalc	Inquisitor-Gen. **Adrian Boeyens** banned Lutheran writings ↙
1521	**T. Muntzer** visited Zatec, Bohemia, the Taborite-						
1521	Waldensian Center, on his way to Prague m6						
1522 Inquisitor General as Pope 1522	**Luther** published NT, with its famous Preface	**Hubmaier** attended evangelical meetings at the house of **Hans Blabhaus** in Regensberg	**Lambert** preached in Geneva, Lausanne, Freiburg; preached against Catholic superstitions in Zurich, **Zwingli** interrupted	**Lambert**y (35 yrs old) began reading Luther, fled the Franciscan monastery (May) by volunteering for an official trip; entered Switzerland via Lyons ↙	**Tyndale** accused of the heresy of **Lutheranism**, moved to London, and then to Hamburg	Inquisitor-General **Adrian Boeyens** elected **Pope Adrian VI**	**Loyola** "converted" to the cause of the Roman church; began writing his *Spiritual Exercises*
1522	Statues and images of the saints burned in Wittenberg						
1522	**H. Sypphen**c burned at the stake in Altdorf,	While **Lambert**y preached on prayer to Mary and the saints in					
1522	Bavaria, Germany; many others secretly drowned in the	"Bruder, du irrst" [Brother, you err],	**Lambert**y, in Eisenach, waiting to meet Luther in Wittenberg, wrote	*Gospel Tracts Used in the Conversion of Marguerite de Valois* "But there was especially one soul, in the court of **Francis I**, who seemed prepared for the evangelical influence of the doctor from Étaples and the Bishop of Meaux. **Marguerite**, uncertain and unsure, in the midst of the			

Year	Event 1	Event 2	Event 3	Event 4	Event 5	Event 6
1522	Rhine in Halle, Germany	"139 Propositions" by which he was willing to debate anyone on issues	corrupt society that surrounded her, sought something firm, and she found it in the Gospel. She turned herself to this new wind that was reinvigorating the world, and she inhaled with delight the emanations from heaven. She learned from several of the ladies in her court what was being taught by			
1522	Anabaptist's began from Saxony, from one named **Nicolas Stork**, having a militant millenarianism[c]	related to the Reformation, no adversary came forward ↙	**Lambert**[Y] removing his cowl and discarding his Rosary ↖	the new doctors; their writings were communicated to her, their small books, called in the language of the times 'tracts'; they spoke to her of the primitive church, the pure Word of God, worship in spirit and in truth, Christian liberty that removes the yoke of the superstitions and traditions of men to attach itself uniquely to God.' Soon this princess met **Lefèvre, Farel**, and **Roussel**; their zeal, their piety, their beliefs, everything in them struck her; but it was especially the **Bishop of Meaux** [Briçonnet], long acquaintance of hers, who became her guide in the path of faith."[a]		
1522	**Luke of Prague** sent by Moravian Brethren to meet with Luther in Wittenberg[S3]					
1523	**Lambert d'Avignon**[Y] met with **Luther** in Wittenberg; published "Reasons for Leaving the Minor Orders", and	**Hubmaier** attended second disputation; result was that town council voted: "Nothing is to be established or to be taught except what can be proved by	**Zwingli** authored "67 Theses" for First Zurich disputation; result was that town council voted: "Nothing is to be established or to be taught except what can be proved by	The hermit **J. Vallière**[w] burned at the stake in Paris (may have rejected the virgin birth)	**Lefèvre**[p] New Testament published	**Tyndale** traveled to London to ask permission to translate the Bible from Bishop of London, **Cuthbert**	**Coverdale** entered the Augustinian Monastery in Cambridge, where he befriended R. Barnes
1523	A treatise on the Franciscan Rule, with a foreword of **Luther**	joining Lutheran sect; Waldshut accepted reforms →	the testimony of the gospel doctrine and the authority of	**L. de Berquin**[w] tried for heresy (e.g. for translating Erasmus' *Enchiridion* into French)[w]	**Lefèvre** became Grand-Vicar[p] of Meaux **Briçonnet**[p], Bishop of Meaux, recanted his Lutheranism, and turned over **J. Leclerc**[p] to show the sincerity of his recantation	**Tunstall**; Tunstall was uninterested, so Tyndale was housed for six months at the house of London Alderman H. **Monmouth**[w2]	
1523	**Lambert d'Avignon**[Y] (36 yrs old) was first Reformer married ↙↓		sacred Scriptures by themselves" (S. M. Jackson [1922])	Evangelist **Farel**[p] in Gap, France ↙	**J. Leclerk**[cr] (of Meaux) branded, tortured, and his body burned,		**Loyola** went on pilgrimage to Jerusalem; completed writing his spiritual exercises
1523	**Luther** wrote "Neues Lid" on the	Bohemian-Moravian Old	**Hubmaier** conducted mass in German and abolished laws on	After a crucifix was torn down, **Zwingli** called for a second	seeming to follow the pattern described in 2 Macc 7:1-23		(Nov 19): **Giuliano Medici** elected **Pope Clement VII**; brought P. **Carnesecchi** to become his secretary, giving him the title of **Papal Protonotary**, presenting him
1523	martyrdom of **Voez** and **H. Koch**[b] and **L. Meister**[b]	Waldensian				**Augustinians H. Voez**[c] and **J. Esch**[c] burned in Bruxelles for the Lutheran heresy	

COLOR GUIDE: YELLOW=Roman Catholic areas; TAN=Bad years for Anabaptists; GOLD=Important events for Catholicism; ORANGE=Catholics "martyred"; RED=Evangelicals martyred; GRAY=Other martyred; Disclaimer: some dates may vary
PINK=Marriage issues; PURPLE= Crusades or massacres; TURQUOISE=Martyrology info; BLUE=Part Protestant areas; AQUA=U.S. Const; LIME=Bible issues; LT GREEN=Disputed areas; GREEN=Major dates.

(Page 89)

Geographic History

Date	Germany-Austria-Scandinavia	Switzerland	France-Alsace	British Isles	Italy, Spain, Low Lands
1523	put to death in Augsburg	fasting and Celibacy ↙ disputation on images and the Mass			with the revenues of two Abbeys[b5]
1524, "Peasants' Revolt"	July 1524: Innsbrook officials ordered an attack on Waldshut, because they would not turn over **Hubmaier**; Aug 1524:	**C. Tauber**[b] arrested and burned alive in Vienna, Austria	**Zurich** accepted reforms, and removed images, closed monasteries	**Farel**[p] disputed against Romanism in Basel, Switz; went to Montbeliard and Strasbourg	**Lambert**[y] visited Metz (for 8 days), during the time of the arrest of **Castellan** was troubling the city	**Tyndale** fled England, moved to Hamburg, Germany, a free city; he also visited **Luther** in Wittenberg	**Menno Simons** was ordained to the Catholic priesthood in March 1524, probably in Utrecht, and served as priest for 7 years in Pingjum[m]
1524	**Ferdinand** also ordered an attack on Waldshut; "Peasant's Revolt"	**Hubmaier** wrote "18 Theses" and "On Heretics and Those Who Burn Them"	**City Council of Zurich** (& **Zwingli**) published a city ordinance against **Anabaptists**[b]	**Lambert** published his "16 Propositions"		Freedom of conscience was removed from Zurich by **Zwingli** on the issue of believer's baptism
1524	blamed on Anabaptists [who were exercising freedom of conscience… what of Rome's instigation of the attack? Or worse yet, its absolution of fealty from heretics? (see 1073, 1207, 1215, 1243, 1415, 1487)]	**Münzer** published "Against the Unspiritual, Soft-living Flesh at Wittenberg"		**Lambert** had to flee the city for Strasbourg ↙		From the indulgence book, *Taxation of the Roman Ministry*.[p] "Absolution for a priest who lives with a concubine is taxed at seven *carlins*." "The absolution for all acts of impurity, of whatever nature they may be, committed by a [religious] clerk, be it with a nun, in the cloister or elsewhere, or with his/her parents or relatives, or with a spiritual daughter, or with another woman, whomever that may be; being that the absolution be requested not simply by the clerk, or by he himself or his concubines, with the exemption of being able to keep his orders [religious position] and of holding its benefits, and with no claim of forfeiture, costs only thirty-six *tournois* and nine *ducats*."
1524	**Lambert d'Avignon** wrote on marriage in a commentary on Song of Solomon: *In Cantica Cantica-rum*	**H. Zutphaniensis**[b] horribly put to death by the Ditmarish Peasants	**Zwingli** (~40 yrs old) married **Ana Reinhart** [whom he had known since 1522?]			49th of **Zwingli**'s *67 Theses*: "I know of no greater scandal than the prohibition of lawful marriage to priests, while they are permitted for money to have concubines. Shame! (*Pfui der Schande!*) [from Schaff, *Creeds of Christendom*]

Thomas P. Johnston — Page 90

1524	*Salomonis* (Strasbourg, 1524; Nurnberg, 1525), also publishing								
1524	against the pollution of celibacy (1524)								
1525	**Luther** published "**Bondage of the Will**"	**Hubmaier** and 60 others baptized by **W. Reublin** in Waldshut;	**Anabaptists** were officially organized 21 Jan 1525 when they	**Lambert**y wrote **Frederick the Wise** of the martyrdom of	**J. Castellan**c degraded of the priesthood and burned alive,	**Tyndale** began the printing of his NT in Cologne, Germany ←	**Tyndale NTs** were smuggled into England in cotton bales		
1525		**Peter Quentels** of Cologne printed the **Tyndale NT**, but when	On Easter 1525, Zurich officially abolished the Mass, instituting the Lord's Supper "in remembrance" of	Castellan, published a tract called "Le martyre de Jehan	Metz, France (12 Jan), after nine months in prison	**Tyndale** used **Luther's** order of canonical books, his notes, and his introductory material			
1525		authorities forbade the printing, he moved to Worms, where it was	the Lord Jesus' atoning death	Chastelain"; **Lambert**w also wrote of the martyrdom of **J.**		**Sample note from Tyndale NT on Matt 16:17-19** "Peter in the greke sygnieth a stone in englysshe. This confession is the		**J. Pistorius de Worden**c burned in The Hague, Holland	
1525		printed in two sizesw2	Zwingli leaned against infant baptism; Zwingli arrested	**Leclerk** in the Preface of his commentary on Micah	he fled to Strasbourg	rocke. Nowe is simon bariona, or simon inoas sonne, called Peter, because of his confession. whosoever then this wyse			
1525	**Luther** (~42 yrs old) married **Katherine von Bora**	**Hubmaier** (~41 yrs old) married **Elsbeth Huglin**e	**Hubmaier** when he fled to Zurich; **Hubmaier** released after he		The German **W. Schuch**cp of St. Hippolite, burned	confesseth of Christe, the same is called Peter. nowe this confession come too all that are true christen. Then ys every christen man &			
1525	**Luther** wrote "Stab, Smite, Slay" against Peasant's Revolt	Waldshut, "Peasants Revolt" overthrown	read a recantation of believer's baptism		at the stake in Nancy, France; **J. Pavanes**crw burned at the	woman peter. Rede bede, austen & hierom, of the maner of lowsinge & bynding and note how hierom checketh the presumcion of the			
1525		Former Bavarian priest, **L. Keyser**, studied the	Anabaptist **Wolfgang Ulimar** +10	**Marguerite of Navarre**p assisted Bible	stake at Place de Grève, Paris; the **Hermit of Livry**p also burned at the	pharises in his tyme, which yet had nott so monstrous interpretacions as oure new goddess have feyned. Rede Erasmus annotations. Hyt was		Neither did **Luther** give Anabaptists freedom of conscience, calling for their destruction (especially against those that took up arms to defend their freedom of	
1525	writings of **Zwingli** and **Luther**; **Keyser** then traveled to	the stake in Vienna, Austria	others burned in Waldsee	colporteurs, especially into Southern France	stake, parvis Notre Dame, Paris	not for nought that Christ bad beware of the leven of the pharises. noo thynge is so swete that they make not sowre with their tradicions.		conscience); hence the strong anti-military and anti-war sentiments of the Mennonites; protected by the U.S. Constitution	

COLOR GUIDE: YELLOW=Roman Catholic areas; TAN=Bad years for Anabaptists; GOLD=Important events for Catholicism; ORANGE=Catholics "martyred"; RED=Evangelicals martyred; GRAY=Other martyred; Disclaimer: some dates may vary
PINK=Marriage issues; PURPLE= Crusades or massacres; TURQUOISE=Martyrology info; BLUE=Part Protestant areas; AQUA=U.S. Const; LT GREEN=Disputed areas; LIME=Bible issues; GREEN=Major dates. (Page 91)

Thomas P. Johnston | Geographic History | Page 92

Date	Germany-Austria-Scandinavia	Switzerland	France-Alsace		British Isles	Italy, Spain, Low Lands
1525	Anabaptist **Melchior Veit** [Vet?][b] burned at Wittenberg and there took the Lord's Supper; he returned to Bavaria and joined the **Anabaptists**[b]	**20 Anabaptists**[b] left to die in tower in Zurich	The fate of **M. Saulnier**[w] who was imprisoned with **Pavanes** is uncertain	Disciples of **Lefevre** begin translating Bible from the originals: **Farel, G. Roussel, M. d'Arande, S. Robert and Vadasta**[l]	The evangelion, that joyfull tidynges, ys nowe bitterer then the olde lawe, Christes burthen is hevier then the yoke of moses, out condicion and estate ys ten tymes more grevious then was ever the iewes. The pharises have so levened Christes swete bread.w2	
1525	**Pastor**[c] from Brisgau drowned for marrying in Prague	Zwingli attended Baden Disputation				**M. Nicolas**[c] was arrested for bounty of 30 gold Carolins, sentenced, placed in a sack and drowned at Antwerpt, Brussels
1525	**Lambert**[y] attended **Diet of Spier**, as did Philip of Hess and	Zurich council passed edict that made adult baptism punishable by drowning				
1525	200 Hessians; Spier affirmed "whose region, his religion"	**Hubmaier** baptized Hans Denck and others; wrote *Twelve Articles on the Christian Faith*; fled to Moravia				
1525	The *Reformatio Eccelsiarum Hassiae* prohibited refusal to baptize infants, as well as rebaptisms	**Archduke Ferdinand** began to unleash persecution	**Calvin** began studies at Univ of Orleans, earned B.A. and Licentiate in Arts	Poet **C. Marot**, valet for **Francis I** won to the Reformation[l]	**J. Rogers** graduated from Cambridge with a B.A.	
1526	**Tyndale** completed printing his English NT in Worms	**20 Anabaptists** killed in Wurttenberg province	**G. Joubert**[w] burned alive in Paris for holding Lutheran doctrine	**G. Roussel** completed translation of the Pentateuch from the Hebrew[l]	**Tyndale**'s English NT continued to be printed in Worms, Germany and smuggled into England.w2	**Menno Simons** began reading the Bible for the first time, two years after his ordination to the priesthood, in order to validate the doctrine of transubstantiation[m]
1526			**L. de Berquin**[w] tried for heresy for the second time	Feb 5th Act of Parliament of France made it illegal to own or to sell Bibles in France	**Coverdale** assisted in the trial of **R. Barnes**, who was accused of the Lutheran heresy	Papal Letter of **Clement VII**, *Cum ad Zero* (7 Dec 1526) published for purposes of inquisition
1526						Inquisition was established in the Spanish New World by **Emperor Charles V**l4
1527	In Bavaria, former priest and Anabaptist **L. Keiser**[bc] placed	**Archduke Ferdinand** crowned king of Bohemia	5 Jan: **Felix Manz** [1526][b] became the first Anabaptist to be	**Farel** preached near Bern, Switzerland	"**Viret** enters Paris and commences studies for the	Anabaptists **J. Walen**[b] and **two others**[b] roasted by a fire in Haarlem

1527	in the fire and rolled out; pushed back in and rolled out the other side;	**Leonhard von Liechtenstein** turned **Hubmaier**	condemned to death by drowning in Zurich		priesthood at Montaigu College"v2					An old woman, the Anabaptist widow **Weynken**b, daughter		
1527	finally his body was cut to pieces and returned to the fire	over to Emperor Ferdinand		In August 1527, **Michael Sattler**, and other Swiss Brethren gathered in Schleitheim, Switzerland, and	**Viret** began a three year process resulting in his					of Claes, strangled and burned at The Hague 20 Nov 1527 [includes the		
1527	Former monk, the Anabaptist **M. Sattler**b was burned in	**G. Carpenter**c burned at the stake in Bavaria, Germany		authored "Seven Articles" as a Confession. This document became known as the "**Schleitheim Confession**" and became a focal	conversion to the Protestant faithv2					emotional dialogue she suffered up to her death]b		
1527	Rotterburg, other brethren received the sword, sisters were drowned	**G. Blaurock**c and another burned in Tyrol		document for the [ana]Baptist movement.								
1527	Anabaptist **T. Herrmann**b and 67 othersb were	**G. Wagner**b burned alive in Munich on 8 Feb 1527										
1527	martyred at Kitzbuehl											
1527	**Luther** wrote → against the martyrdom of L. Keyser	←**Eck** wrote in favor of the martyrdom of L. Keyser										
1528	P. Flistedec and A. Clarebachc burned at the	**B. Hubmaier**bt burned at the stake in Vienna		25 Lutheransp arrested in Nonay, brought to Vienna, seve-	**P Bart**w (E. de la Court) burned at the stake in Rouen [there is a	**Lefevre** completed OT translation from Latin Vulgate;		**Coverdale** fled to Antwerp to avoid persecution in England →		**M. Henry**c burned at the stake in Tournay, Flanders	**Loyola** began his studies in Paris (until 1535)	
1528	stake in Cologne, Germany	[or Bruenn, Moravia]b and 2 others (**Thomas**b and **Dominicus**b);		ral died in prison, others paid fines and were released	question if he converted to Judaism]	retiring to Nérac, to the residence of **Marguerite de Navarre**				**Menno Simons** chose to believe the Bible over the teachings of the	On the Continent (Antwerp), **Coverdale** began	
1528	Former barefoot friar, turned Anabaptist, **L.**	**Hubmaier's wife**b drowned in Danube		Bern officially adopted the Reformationv2 Ten [Reformation] Theses of Bernr2 [written by B. Haller and F. Kolb] 1. The holy catholic church, whose sole head is Christ,		**D. de Rieux**c slowly burned to death over a fire in Meaux, France				Catholic church, finding assistance in **Luther's writings**m	to translate Bible into English	

COLOR GUIDE: YELLOW=Roman Catholic areas; TAN=Bad years for Anabaptists; GOLD=Important events for Catholicism; ORANGE=Catholics "martyred"; RED=Evangelicals martyred; GRAY=Other martyred; Disclaimer: some dates may vary PINK=Marriage issues; PURPLE= Crusades or massacres; TURQUOISE=Martyrology info; BLUE=Part Protestant areas; AQUA=U.S. Const; LIME=Bible issues; LT GREEN=Disputed areas; GREEN=Major dates. (Page 93)

Thomas P. Johnston — Geographic History — Page 94

Date	Germany-Austria-Scandinavia	Switzerland	France-Alsace	British Isles	Italy, Spain, Low Lands
1528	**Schiemer [Schnoener]b and about 70 others martyred in**	has been begotten from the word of God, in which it also continues, nor does it listen to the voice of any stranger. 2. The Church of Christ establishes no laws or statutes	[first known French use of *l"Estrapade*, a device by which a		
1528	**H. Schlaefferb and L. Frickb executed** with a sword in Schwatz Rottenburg on the 14 Jan 1528	beyond the Word of God. Thus the traditions of men, which are called by us precepts of the Church, bind our consciences only insofar as they are founded or have been commanded in the Word of God.	person was raised and lowered over the flames]w		
1528	**H. Feyerer [Feiererjb and 5 Anabaptist brethrenb and 2 sistersb burned**	3. Christ alone is our wisdom, righteousness, redemption, and satisfaction for the sins of the whole world. Therefore, whoever recognizes either merit by which one may be readied for blessedness, or any	Franciscan **Renierp** executed by the Archbishop of Vienna		
1528	**brethrenb and 3 sistersb burned alive in Munich** alive at Znaym, Moravia	other satisfaction for sin, denies Christ. 4. That the body and blood of Christ are received essentially and corporeally in the bread of the Eucharist cannot be proven in any way from sacred Scripture.			
1528	Anabaptist **L. Schneiderb** beheaded in Augsburg **W. Ulmanb +10 Anabaptistsb burned in Walzen**	5. The Mass, as it is used today, in which Christ is offered to God the father for the sins of the living and	**Olivétan** studied Hebrew and Greek in Strasbourg		
1528	Anabaptist **H. Pretleb burned alive** **18 Anabaptistsb burned alive in Salzburg**	the dead, is contrary to sacred Scripture, is blasphemy against the most holy sacrifice, passion, and death of Christ and, by reason of abuses of such, detestable before God.	**Little Hans of Stotzingenb** beheaded in Zabern, Alsace		
1528	**Vilgardb and Casparb of Schoeneck** beheaded near **9 Anabaptist brethrenb and 3 sistersb executed**	6. Just as Christ alone has died for us, so He ought to be called upon as sole Mediator and Advocate between God the Father and us believers. Thus all other mediators and advocates who are called upon			
1528	by the sword in Bruck, on the Mur, in Steyermark Brixen	beyond the bounds of this world [and] above the foundation of the Word of God, are renounced. 7. Outside of this world, corrections or purgations of fire is not revealed in the Scripture. Thus all homage to			
1528	Anabaptist **John Bairb** of Lichtenfels, was arrested in 1528 and imprisoned for 23 years in the Tower of Bamberg, in Franconia, dying in prison in 1551	the dead, for example vigils, funeral rites of the seventh and thirtieth anniversary, lamps, candles and such are vain. 8. To fashion images in order to stand before them for			
1528	**Luther** in a letter to **John, the Elector of Saxony**: "No one—whether noble, burgher, peasant, or of whatever rank he may be, except the	worship is contrary to the Word of God comprehended in the books of the Old and New Testament. Thus wherever they have so dishonored themselves, as it is a danger, they should be abolished and not adored.			

1528	regular pastors … is permitted to preach and baptize, or to buy and read forbidden books; but that every one who learns of such doings shall	9. Holy marriage is forbidden to no order or condition of men in Scripture, but is commanded and permitted to every order of men as a means of avoiding fornication and impurity.				
1528	make them known to the magistrates of the place where they occur, in order that these persons may be brought to prison and justice."v	10. Because open fornication excommunicates according to Scripture, it follows that fornication or impure celibacy are to be condemned by reason of scandal [in] no other order of men more than in the priesthood.				
1528	Death of Luke of Prague m6					
1528		[Note: Sebastian Franck wrote that "**far more than two thousand**"				
1528		Anabaptists were put to death by popedom; in				
1528		Ensisheim alone about 600 were slain]b				
1529	Luther attended Marburg Colloquy, disagreed with Zwingli on Lord's Supper	Zwingli participated in First Cappel war	L. de Berquincprw burned at the stake in Paris after his third accusation of heresy	Bishop Briçonnetp of Meaux, after he had recanted Lutheranism for the third time, was executed for heresy	More became Lord Chancellor of England	
1529	Luther wrote the hymn "Ein' Feste Burg" (a.k.a. "A Mighty Fortress Is Our God")	Zwingli attended Marburg Colloquy			More wrote a scathing attack on Tyndale's NT, likening Tyndale	Tyndale's translation of five words especially infuriated Rome: (1) Translating Greek πρεσβύτερος
1529	The 1529 Diet of Speyer made a decree against Anabaptists: "All Anabaptists and rebaptized persons, male or female, of mature age, shall				to the "great arch-heretic **Wycliffe**" who translated the Bible into English and "purposefully corrupted the holy	(Latin *senior*, *presbuteri*, or *senes*, depending on context), as "elder," rather than "Priest";
1529	be judged and brought from natural life to death, by fire, or sword or otherwise, as may befit the persons, without preceding trial by spiritual				text", More stated that Tyndale's NT	(2) Translating Greek ἐκκλησία

COLOR GUIDE: YELLOW=Roman Catholic areas; TAN=Bad years for Anabaptists; GOLD=Important events for Catholicism; ORANGE=Catholics "martyred"; RED=Evangelicals martyred; GRAY=Other martyred; Disclaimer: some dates may vary
PINK=Marriage issues; PURPLE=Crusades or massacres; TURQUOISE=Martyrology info; BLUE=Part Protestant areas; AQUA=U.S. Const; LT GREEN=Disputed areas; LIME=Bible issues; GREEN=Major dates. (Page 95)

Thomas P. Johnston
Geographic History
Page 96

Date	Germany-Austria-Scandinavia	Switzerland	France-Alsace	British Isles	Italy, Spain, Low Lands
1529	judges…. Such persons as of themselves, or after instruction, at once confess their error, and are willing to undergo penance and			"was not worthy to be called Christ's New Testament, but either	
1529	chastisement therefor, and pray for clemency, these may be pardoned by their government as may befit their standing, conduct, youth, and general			Tyndale's own testament or the testament of his master Antichrist";	
1529	circumstances. We will also that all of their children according to Christian order, usage, and rite shall be baptized in their youth. Whoever shall			More continued: "to study to find errors in Tyndale's book were like	(Latin *ecclesia*), as "congregation", rather than "Church"; "concregacion" is found 83 times in Tyndale's NT; (3) Translating Greek μετανοέω (Latin *paenitentiam*
1529	despise this, and will not do it, in the belief that there should be no baptism of children, shall, if he persists in that course, be held to be an Anabaptist,			studying to find water in the sea"w2	*agite*), as "repent", rather than "do penance" or
1529	and shall be subjected to the above named constitution."v				"penitence" (4) Translating Greek ὁμολογέω (Latin
1529	Anabaptist **Vigil Plattner** [Plaitner]b put to death by sword in Bavaria	**4 brethren**b and **4 sisters**b (named in van Bracht), martyred on 16 Nov in Ful, Elschland		*confiteamur*), as [ac]knowledge, rather than "confess" or "[do] confession" (5) Translating Greek ἀγάπη (Latin *caritas*),	
1529	Anabaptist **Louis Hetzer**bt (after long imprisonment) + 2	Anabaptist hymn writer **Hans [John]**b **Hut**b was tortured and burned in Augsburg, after his death, he was		as love, not Charity (e.g. "acts of charity")	
1529	**others**b put to death by sword at Constance	In Basel, **3 of 9 rebaptized Anabaptists** were banished; the other 6 apostacizedb			
1529	**E. Binder** +2 burned in Salzburg	condemned to death by fireb			

1529	C. Prader[b] + several others[b] shut up in a house and burned in Salzburg						
1529	Anabaptists **Anna Maler**[b] and **Ursula**[b] drowned						
1529	Nine Anabaptist[b] men and several sisters[b] were condemned of Anabaptism at Altzey; the men died by the sword						
1529	**D. Kropf**[b] + 2 brethren[b] and 4 sisters[b] martyred in Bairisch-Graitz, in Steyermark; men by the sword and women drowned						
1529	**H. Langenmantel**[b] and **manservant**[b] put to death by sword, and **maidservant**[b] drowned, at Weissenhom						
1529	Seven Anabaptist brethren[b] (incl. a 14 year old lad who had been confined for a year) "executed for the evangelical truth"[b] at Gmuend in Swabia						
1529	Eight Anabaptists executed in Vill						
1529					Anna of Freiburg[b] drowned in Freiburg, and then her body was burned		
1529	Two brethren[b] and 2 sisters[b] martyred						
1529	About 350 Anabaptists[b] executed in Alzey; others maimed and tortured						
1529	**P. of Langenlonsheim** was beheaded in Creitze						

COLOR GUIDE: YELLOW=Roman Catholic areas; TAN=Bad years for Anabaptists; GOLD=Important events for Catholicism; ORANGE=Catholics "martyred"; RED=Evangelicals martyred; GRAY=Other martyred; Disclaimer: some dates may vary
PINK=Marriage issues; PURPLE= Crusades or massacres; TURQUOISE=Martyrology info; BLUE=Part Protestant areas; LT GREEN=Disputed areas; AQUA=U.S. Const; LIME=Bible issues; GREEN=Major dates. (Page 97)

Geographic History — Page 98

Date	Germany-Austria-Scandinavia	Switzerland	France-Alsace	British Isles	Italy, Spain, Low Lands
1529	Anabaptist itinerant evangelist G. Blaurock[b] was evangelizing and planting churches in Switzerland and Tyrol for 2-3 years; H. van der Reve[b] seems to have				
1529	assisted with new churhes; both Blaurorck and van der Reve, and their companions were arrested in Gusodaum and burned alive near Clausen in Etzlandt				
1529	Excerpts from the final writings of Blaurock and van der Reve exemplify their evangelistic fervor: "The enemy fights with me in the field in which I now am; he would fain drive me from the field. But Thou, O Lord, givest me the victory. … O God,				
1529	how soon didst Thou hear me, thou speedily camest with Thy help and turnedst back mine enemies; therefore, I will sing praises to Thy name in my heart, and forever spread abroad the grace which has come to me"[b] "He now causes His divine Word to be published and instructs men, that				
1529	they should turn from their sinful life, believe in Christ, be baptized upon faith, and obey the Gospel. … O Father, through grace Thou didst choose us, and didst not despise to put us into Thy work; grant that, when the evening comes, we may receive the hire with rejoicing."[b]				
1529	Many Anabaptists were put to death in the Gusodein district, in Clausen, Brixen, Stertzing, Balzen, Neumark, Katren, Terlen, Gundersweg; and in the valley of the Inn, at Inst. Petersberg, Stejen in the Spruckthal, Schwatz, Rattenburg, Kufstein, and Kitzbuehl[b]				
1529	Eventually Jacob Huter gathered many Tyrol Anabaptists and they migrated to Moravia[b]				
1529	Judas' arose, who betrayed the Anabaptists to priests and judges, men as Prabeiger, G. Frueder, P. Lantz, and Pranger sought out the brethren and for money turned them over in large numbers[b]				
1529	Anabaptist G. Baumann[b] beheaded in Wurttemberg	Anabaptist W. Brandhuber[b], Hans [Niedermair][b] ← Brandhuber wrote "that in everything				

Year	(Purple)	(Green)	(Blue)	(Yellow)	(Lt Green)	(Red)	(Gold/Orange)	(Orange/Tan)
1529							Mittermaier[b] and 70 others[b] martyred in Linz,	which is not contrary to God, we should be obedient
1529							above the Enns; Peter Niedermair was later released after 3 years	and subject to the authorities"[b]
1529							imprisonment[b]	
1530		Farel led revival and reform in Neuchatel[p]		Lefevre published French Bible authorized by King Francis I			Anabaptist G. Grunwald[b] burned alive at Kufstein on the	Luther (or truly Melancthon) wrote the Augsburg
1530		"Farel commences preaching in Orbe, but is		Tyndale completed the translation of and published the		England; T. Bilney[c] burned at the stake Bishop Thomas	Inn; Alda[b] was executed several days later at the same place	Confession in preparation for a diet called by Emperor Charles
1530		violently driven out of the city by the Catholic opposition"v2				Thomas Hytten[c] burned at the stake, Maidstone, More of Norwich, presiding	Anabaptist G. Steinmetz[b] was beheaded at Portzen, Germany	V, s3; it was signed by numerous leaders, who in 1531
1530				Pentateuch (Antwerp: Johann Hoochstraten)	Bishop Tunstall and Cardinal Wolsey opposed			formed the Smalcald League of Protestant regions
1530					the Tyndale Bible, confiscating, buying and burning that	23 year old Patrick Hamilton[c]		Lambert d'Avignon died (in Marbourg?)
1530					Bibles at St. Paul's cross"w2	martyred in Scotland		
1531		"Having renounced Roman Catholicism,	Melchoir Hofmann began to preach Anabaptist doctrines in Strasbourg, initiating the Melchiorites[m]				Menno Simons was transferred to be priest to his home village of	Cornelius wrote: "In Tyrol and Görz, the number of executions [of Anabaptists] in the year 1531 already reached one thousand; in Einsisheim, six hundred. At Linz, seventy-three were killed in six weeks. Duke
1531		Viret flees Paris and returns to Orbe"v2				A taylor, S. F. Snijder[m], martyred for rebaptism in Leewarden, 20th March, in → Friesland; the reason for his	Witmarsum, Friesland[m]	William, of Bavaria, surpassing all others, issued the fearful decree to behead those who recanted, to burn those who refused to recant. Throughout the greater part of upper Germany the persecutions raged like wild

G. Morel estimated that there were 800,000 persons professing the faith of the Waldenses

Former Lutheran, now itinerant Anabaptist preacher, Melchior Hofmann baptized Jan Volkerts Trypmaker in Strasbourg ↘

Itinerant Anabaptist preacher, J. V. Trypmaker, baptized Sicke Freerks Snijder in Emden, East Friesland[m] ↗

(Page 99)

COLOR GUIDE: YELLOW=Roman Catholic areas; TAN=Bad years for Anabaptists; GOLD=Important events for Catholicism; ORANGE=Catholics "martyred"; GRAY=Other martyred; Disclaimer: some dates may vary
PINK=Marriage issues; PURPLE=Crusades or massacres; TURQUOISE=Martyrology info; BLUE=Part Protestant areas; AQUA=U.S. Const; RED=Evangelicals martyred; LT GREEN=Disputed areas; LIME=Bible issues; GREEN=Major dates.

Thomas P. Johnston — Geographic History — Page 100

Date	Germany-Austria-Scandinavia	Switzerland	France-Alsace	British Isles	Italy, Spain, Low Lands	
1531	chase. The blood of these poor people flowed like water; so that they cried to the Lord for help. But hundreds of them, of all ages and both sexes, suffered the pangs of torture without a murmur, despised to buy their lives by	"Farel persuades Viret to begin preaching"v2				death impacted Menno Simonsm
1531	by recantation, and went to the place of execution joyful and singing Psalms"v	"May 6, Viret, 20 years old, becomes pastor and preaches				At Rome: the Spanish nobleman, Juán de Valdés
1531	Luther published his Commentary on Galatians	Anabaptist W. Mairb and 2 othersb executed by the sword in	Zwingli participated in Second Cappel			brought the influence of the Reformation to South Italy; he led
1531	Anabaptists M. Mater "the painter"b, W. Eslingerb,	Walsburg [Wolfsberg], Kaernthen	his first sermon at hometown Orbe"v2			a circle of friends, including Carnesecchi, later to be influenced by
1531	Painb, Melchiorb and 3 others (including a 16 year old servant)b	Anabaptist G. Zaunringeradb died by sword in	war; died in battle in October			the doctrine of Justification by Faithb5
1531	executed by sword at Gmunden	Franconia, near Bamberg	"Viret administers his first Christian baptism in Orbe"v2 ↙			
1531					David Joris, a Flemish born Lutheran, was influenced by	
1531					Melchior Hofmann, and became a Melchioritem	
1532 Swiss Ref-orm-ers & Wald-en-sian Meet in Chan-fo-rans 1532	Schmakald League formed and Peace of Nuremberg	"Viret officiates at his first Christian wedding in Orbe"v2	Farel attended general synod of Waldensian churches in	Calvin composed the treatise "De Clementia"p	Cranmer appointed Archbishop of Canterbury	In Assersouw, Anabaptist H. J. Kraenb and Maryb, his wife, and two the
	At Stertzing in Etschland, six Anabaptists (L. Gruber, H. Beck,	"Viret journeys to Grandson to carry the	Chanforans; the Waldenses decided to underwrite a	J. de Caturcecr burned at the stake in Languedoc for saying "May Christ rule in our hearts" instead of "Drink to the King"	J. Rogers became rector of Holy Trinity and reader at St. Paul's, London	G. Baynamc and a Bucherc burned at the stake in London for denying purgatory	othersb: Mary was drowned in Haarlem, the others in Gravenhage were
	L. Schumacher, P. Plaver, Peter, and H. Taller)b were tortured on	recaptured, tortured, finally had his left side opened and had	Reformation to that village"v2	French translation of the Bible to be done by Alpine		W. Thracec exhumed and burned at the	chained to stakes with fires placed around them until they roasted to death
	the rack and executed Also in Sterling, Anabaptist C.	boiling oil put in, then was burned alive in Glabbeck of Juelich	Passover, March 31, Viret offers communion to seventy-seven	evangelist Olivétanp ↘	Olivétan charged with translating from the original languages what	stake in Toddington	R. Bayfieldc, monk from Bury, burned for
		Feb 18, 1532 (Munster, the first formal preaching					

1532	Feichter[b] and several others were tortured and executed	of the Reformation by Rothmann; it spread quickly[s3]	Farel arrived in Geneva, taught French refugees[p]	was to become the French Geneva Bible[p] ↙			translating books of Tyndale	
1532			believers, including both Viret's parents"v2				William Allen, later an ardent Romanist and treasonous antagonist to Queen Elizabeth's reign, born in Lancashire[s3]	
1532			"June 4, Viret travels to Payerne to preach. He is forbidden access to the churches, and preaches instead in the taverns"v2					
1532								
1533		Feb 15: the Reformation took hold so quickly in Munster that Rome's Bishop had to flee the city; the free city began to attract Anabaptists[s3]	"While returning home one evening Viret is stabbed by a Catholic priest in Payerne"v2 →	Olivétan went to Geneva	Lutheran church in Paris numbered about 400 people[p]	J. Pointet[c], physician from Savoye, guilty of recommending marriage for monks and priests due to prominence of venereal diseases, burned alive in Paris	J. Rogers went to Antwerp as chaplain to the English merchants; was converted to Protestantism under the influence of W. Tyndale and M.Coverdale	Cranmer annulled marriage of Henry VIII and Catherine of Aragon
1533	Fest[b] was executed Anabaptist new mother Christina			"January, Viret accepts a pastoral call to Neuchatel [Switzerland]v2	300 Anti-Mass posters [by Antoine Marcourt]W were placed in around Paris (and 5 other cities); one was placed in King's bedroom at the Louvre (Lutherans were blamed)c[p] ← [text] [aftermath] ↗	A. Canus[cr] burned alive in Paris		Anabaptist S. Snyder[b] arrested in Leeuwaerden, Friesland, where he was executed with a sword
1533	Haring[b] died by the sword in Kitzbuehl					M. Hofmann imprisoned in Strasbourg[m]; Matthys "hijacked" the Anabaptist	Rogers married Antwerp native Adriana de Weyden	
1533	[Or 1534] "True articles on the horrible, great and unbearable abuses of the Papal Mass, invented directly against the 'holy scene' of our Lord, only Mediator and only Savior Jesus Christ" (translated from: www.bethel-fr.com)							J. Frith[c] burned at the stake in London, captured and tried by T. More due to unbelief in transubstantiation
1533	"I invoke the heavens and earth as witness to the Truth, against this pompous and haughty Papal mass, by which the world (if God does not soon remedy) is and will be totally ruined, marred, lost and desolate: when in [it] our Lord is so outrageously blasphemed and the people seduced and							
1533	blinded, that which we must not suffer nor endure.... "1) To all faithful Christians it is and must be very certain that... Jesus Christ, as the great Bishop and eternal Pastor ordained by God, [gave] his body, his soul, his life and his blood for our sanctification, in a very perfect sacrifice: which cannot be nor should be ever repeated by							

COLOR GUIDE: **YELLOW**=Roman Catholic areas; **TAN**=Bad years for Anabaptists; **GOLD**=Important events for Catholicism; **ORANGE**=Catholics "martyred"; **RED**=Evangelicals martyred; **GRAY**=Other martyred; Disclaimer: some dates may vary
PINK=Marriage issues; **PURPLE**= Crusades or massacres; **TURQUOISE**=Martyrology info; **BLUE**=Part Protestant areas; **AQUA**=U.S. Const; **LT GREEN**=Disputed areas; **LIME**=Bible issues; **GREEN**=Major dates. (Page 101)

Thomas P. Johnston • Geographic History • Page 102

Date	Germany-Austria-Scandinavia	Switzerland	France-Alsace	British Isles	Italy, Spain, Low Lands
1533		any visible sacrifice… and nevertheless the earth is… filled with miserable sacrificers, who, as if they were our redeemers, put themselves in the place of Jesus Christ or make themselves [his] companions, saying that they are offering to God a sacrifice that is pleasant and pleasing… for the salvation both of the living as well as the deceased: which thing they do	movement; went to Munster		
1533		[openly] against every truth of the Holy Scriptures… (Epistle to the Hebrews, ch. 7, 9, 10)… "2) In this unfortunate mass, one has virtually provoked the world to a universal public idolatry, when falsely one is given to hear that in the species of the bread and of the wine Jesus Christ is corporally and truly contained and hidden, and… personally in flesh and bone, as great and perfectly as if in the present he were alive. That which			
1533		our Holy Scriptures, and our faith, does not teach us, but… the contrary. For Jesus Christ after the resurrection rose up to heaven, and is seated at the [right] of God the almighty Father and from there will come to judge the living and the dead… By which it follows well, that if his body is in heaven, at this same time, then it is not on earth.…			
1533		3) The blind sacrificers… in their frenzy also said and taught that after having breathed or spoken over the bread, which they take in their hands and over the wine, which they place in a chalice, therein abides neither bread nor wine, but… by transubstantiation, Jesus Christ is behind the *accidens* of the bread and the wine hidden and surrounded… Wherein did they invent this ghastly word "transubstantiation"? Saint Paul, Saint Matthew, Saint			
1533		Mark, Saint Luke and the ancient Fathers never spoke such: but when they mention the holy scene, they [openly] and simply speak of the bread and the wine…			
1533		"4) The fruit of the mass is truly contrary to the fruit of the holy scene of Jesus Christ, which is not too [astonishing], for between Christ and Belial there is nothing in common. The fruit of the holy scene of Jesus			
1533		Christ is to publicly make a protest of one's faith and in sure confidence of one's salvation have memory of the death and passion of Jesus Christ, through which we are redeemed from damnation and perdition. Also remembering the great love and tenderness by which he so loved us that he gave his life for us… Also, in partaking together of one bread and one drink, we are admonished to love and great unity in which all by one			
1533		spirit must live and die in Jesus Christ. But the fruit of the mass is quite other… By her all knowledge of Jesus Christ is erased, the preaching of the Gospel is rejected and prevented, time is spent with ringings, howlings, chants, ceremonies, luminaries, incense, disguises and every manner of monkey business [lit. *singerie*], through which the poor world like sheep or miserable lambs not cared for and [duped] by these ravaging wolves are			
1533		eaten, gnawed on, and devoured…. "They kill, they burn, they destroy, they murder like robbers anyone who contradicts [them]… Truth threatens them, Truth follows them and overtakes them, Truth terrifies them. By which [soon] they will be destroyed. [so may it be!] Amen."			
1534 Major events in Germany, Fran-	Luther published entire Bible (including apocrypha) in German	Rothmann preached Anabaptist doctrines in Munster; the people soon rejected their government;	Olivétan completed French Bible translation as commissioned by Waldensians (incl. Etienne de la Forge); later	"Jan. 4. Viret, by order of the Council of Bern, joins Farel in Geneva"v2	Calvin presided over Mass three times at the Angouleme chapter	Placards Revenge January: Six Lutherans[r], incl. the paralytic B. Milon[cr] burned over a slow fire, N. Valeton[c], J.	1 Nov 1534 English Senate abolished authority of Pope in England, transferred it to the King Henry VIII, in a	A. Hewet[c] burned at the stake in London for agreeing with Frith	At the request of Charles, duke of Savoy, P. Berfour of Roccapiata sent an army of 500 men into the Piedmont valley of Italy, "val Lucerna" to	Anabaptist W. Wiggers[b] of Harsinghorn near Schagen in North Holland, was beheaded for the faith

ce and England		**Matthys** arrived and announced that the Kingdom of God had come,				destroy all that they found, as they were all deemed **Waldensian** heretics			
1534	**J. Rogers** joined Luther in Wittenberg to study the Scriptures; was ordained to the ministry	and that believers must now defend it[m]	"Jan. 29. **Dispute of Geneva** in which **Guy Furbity** opposed **Farel** and **Viret**"v2	revised to become French "**Geneva Bible**"p	**N. Volcyr** wrote a tract on the death of **J. Castellan**	**du Bourg**[C], **H. Poille**[C], Bible colporteur **E. de la Forge**[Cr], and female school-teacher **Catelle**[C], all burned in six Paris plazas,	document titled the "**Act of Supremacy**"; hence, Anglican church was founded	The Upper House of Convocation of Canterbury petitioned **King Henry VIII** for a new translation of the Bible, which eventually		
1534		**Matthys**[m] was killed in a sortie against the beseiging army;	"Feb. 22. **Viret** preaches and performs a		(*Traité nouveau de la desecration et execution actuelle de Jehan Castellan* [Paris, 1534])w	following a long procession, while the **Archbishop of Paris** was	became the "**Great Bible**" (1539); delays due to	**W. Tyndale** revised his entire NT; some have felt that this		
1534		**Jan of Leyden** took his place as king of Munster[m]	Christian baptism in the house of Monsieur de Baudichon. His			offering the "sacrifice of the Mass" to **Francis I, King of France**	disapproval to print in Paris, etc[w2]	revision was his crowning achievement[w2]		
1534			sermons are so well attended that there was not not room enough in			burned alive in Essarts; **Nicolas**[C], **J. de Pois**[C], and **E.**				
1534			the hall to receive the people"v2			**Bourlet**[C] martyred in Arras	**Aftermath of Placards Incident** Total condemned to death-102; total executions-27[T]	**More** arrested and imprisoned for not accepting edict of Senate ↙		
1534			"Mar 1. Bernese authorities give **Farel** and **Viret** the Church at			August 15: Jesuit **Francis Xavier** took vows of poverty, chastity, and obedience at Montmartre in Paris,				
1534			Rive in which to preach the Reformation"v2			also vowing to convert the Muslims in Middle East				
1535		**Munster** was overthrown by an army mustered by the **Catholic**		**Geneva Disputation** called; Catholic party boycotted;	**Sorbonne** sought Calvin; **Marguerite de Valois** protected	**J. Cornon**[C] burned at the stake in Bresse; **P. Gaudet**[C]	**T. More** and **J. Fischer**, Bishop of Rochester,	**Emperor Charles V** issued to the Lowlands A decree against Anabaptists: "In order to guard against and remedy the errors which many sectarians and authors of contempt, with their adherents,		
1535		**Bishop of Munster**[m]; the entire population was massacred,		Geneva voted to prohibit Catholicism[p]	him, he fled to Switzerland[p]	burned at the stake in Savoy	beheaded for treason; three Chartreux monks strangled and	have dared for some time to sow and spread in our territories, against our holy Christian faith, sacraments, and the commandments of our mother the holy church, we have at different times ordained, and caused to be executed many		

COLOR GUIDE YELLOW=Roman Catholic areas; TAN=Bad years for Anabaptists; GOLD=Important events for Catholicism; ORANGE=Catholics "martyred"; RED=Evangelicals martyred; GRAY=Other martyred; Disclaimer: some dates may vary PINK=Marriage issues; TURQUOISE=Martyrology info; BLUE=Part Protestant areas; AQUA=U.S. Const; LIME=Bible issues; GREEN=Major dates. PURPLE= Crusades or massacres; LT GREEN=Disputed areas; (Page 103)

Thomas P. Johnston
Page 104

Geographic History

Date	Germany-Austria-Scandinavia	Switzerland	France-Alsace	British Isles	British Isles	Italy, Spain, Low Lands
1535	The U.S. Constitution affirms self-rule in its words	Calvin settled in Basel?		stretched for treason	decrees … that the chief promulgators and sectarians may be punished and corrected as an example to others. And since it has come to our knowledge, that notwithstanding our aforesaid decrees, many and various sectarians, even some
1535	"For the people, by the people"			Tyndale revised his NT a third time, but not significantlyw2	who call themselves Anabaptists, have proceeded, and still daily proceed, to spread, sow, and secretly preach their aforesaid abuses and errors, in order to allure a great number of men and women to their false doctrine and
1535	government was crushed by another "Holy Crusade" (à la Deut 13)			Coverdale's Bible translation was completed and sent to England; it	reprobate sect, to seduce them and to rebaptize some, to the great reproach and disregard of the sacrament of holy baptism, and of our edicts, statutes and ordinances; therefore we, intending to guard against and remedy this,
1535				was dedicated to King Henry VIII, who gave it to his advisors for their	summon and command you, that, immediately upon receipt of this, you cause it to be proclaimed within every place and border of your dominions, that all those, or such as shall be found polluted by the accursed sect of the Anabaptists, of
1535	Jan of Batenburg kept the Munsterite ideals alive; his			advise; they found it fraught with problems, but could not point	whatever rank or condition they may be, their chief leaders, adherents, and abettors, shall incur the loss of life and property, and be brought to the most extreme punishment, without delay: namely those who remain obstinant and
1535	followers were called Batenburgersm			one out; so King Henry decreed that Coverdale's translation be	remain in their evil belief and purpose, or who have seduced to their sect and rebaptized any; also those who have been called prophets, apostles or bishops—these shall be punished with fire. All other persons who have been
1535	Heretics were denied the right of "life, liberty, and property" (see John Locke, "A Letter Concerning Toleration" [1689]), which was			acceptedw2	rebaptized, or who secretly and with premeditation have habored any of the aforesaid Anabaptists, and who renounce their evil purpose and belief, and are truly sorry and penitent for it, shall be executed with the sword, and the
1535	brought into the Bill of Rights of the U.S. Constitution as the God-given right for all men to pursue "life, liberty, and happiness"				women buried in a pit. "And in order to better detect these Anabaptists, their adherents and accomplices, we expressly command all subjects, to make known and report them to the officer of the
1535					place where they reside or shall be found…. "Moreover, we prohibit all our subjects from asking for mercy, forgiveness, or reconciliation for the aforesaid Anabaptists, or from presenting any petition for this purpose,
1535					on pain of summary punishment; for because of their evil doctrine, we will not have or permit that any Anabaptists shall have any mercy shown to them, but that they shall be punished, as an example unto others, without any

1535										dissimulation, favor or delay…" [from Brussels, 10 June 1535]b
1535										**300 Munsterites** (including the brother of **Menno Simons**) laid hold of an old monastery (Oude Kloster) outside the city of Bolsward and entrenched itself there; government forces besieged the cloister and killed 130 of them; the remaining
1535										were executed on April 7thm; **Menno Simons** felt personally responsible for their blood, as he had not dared to part from the Church of Rome up to that time….
1535										The "Old Cloisterites" genocide (above) led to the final "conversion" of **Menno Simons** to turn from the ease and safety of the Church of Rome, with all its heretical teachings;
1535										he dared to openly attack the evils of the Catholic church; this went on for 9 months in his parish of Witmarsumm
1535							**P. Koster**b, ordained Anabaptist teacher, arrested in Amsterdam,			Anabaptists **S. Jans**b, **H. G. van Campen**b, **S. Benedictus**b, and two women (**Femmetgen**b and
1535							sentenced to death by the sword, which took place in 1535			**Welmut**b) were apprehended in Hoorn, West Friesland; the men were beheaded and the woman drowned
1535								**Anabaptist A. Claessen**b beheaded in Leeuwaerden, Friesland		
1535						**Tyndale** arrested in Antwerp, held in a castle near Brussels ↗	**Twelve Germans**c burned in London; fivec			
							burned at the stake in Edinburgh			
					M. Gonincr strangled and drowned in Grenoble				**Menno Simons** definitively broke from the Catholic church, leaving his post at Witmarsum in Jan 1536; he spent the year in hiding, leaving traces of his
					Lefevre died at the castle in Nérac					whereabouts (Witmarsum to Leeuwarden, back to Witmarsum and to Groningen) in the records of the martyrs who were later punished for sheltering him
				Farel convinced-threatened **Calvin** to stay in Genevap						
1536	**David Joris** was disowned by the **Obbenite** Anabaptists,	**Anabaptists J. Kels**b of Kufestein, **M. Seifensieder**b of								
1536	founded a sect called the **Davidians**m	Wald, and **H. Oberacker**b of Eschtland were betrayed and								

COLOR GUIDE: YELLOW=Roman Catholic areas; TAN=Bad years for Anabaptists; GOLD=Important events for Catholicism; ORANGE=Catholics "martyred"; RED=Evangelicals martyred; GRAY=Other martyred; Disclaimer: some dates may vary PINK=Marriage issues; PURPLE=Crusades or massacres; BLUE=Part Protestant areas; AQUA=U.S. Const; LIME=Bible issues; GREEN=Disputed areas; LT GREEN=Part Protestant areas; TURQUOISE=Martyrology info; GREEN=Major dates. (Page 105)

Thomas P. Johnston

Geographic History

Date	Germany-Austria-Scandinavia	Switzerland	France-Alsace	British Isles	Italy, Spain, Low Lands	
1536					Seven Anabaptists from Gofedaum in Etschland were arrested in Vienna, where they were burned alive	Anabaptists P. Gerrits[b], P. Joris[b], P. Leydecker[b], and
1536					Johanna Mels[b] were tortured and put to death on the rack in Zierichzee, then burned	arrested and put to death; "Thus they were put to death mightily admonishing the people to repent"[b] (H. Beck, W. Schneider, C.
1536		Calvin wrote the first edition his Institutes of the Christian Religion		G. Cowbridge[c] burned at the stake at Oxford	Tyndale[c] betrayed to Antwerp authorities,	
1536		dedicated to King Francis I of France[p]		Rogers began work to complete Tyndale's translation of OT	condemned for heresy, strangled, and burned at the stake in Brussels	Alzeiter, B. Gesel, Wolfert, H. Maurer, and P. Kranewitter)[b]
1536				T. Cromwell interceded on → Tyndale's behalf	Erasmus died	After the death of Clement VII, Carnesecchi and others gathered around the principles of the Reformation in
1536				Anne Boleyn[c], her brother, Lord of Rocheford[c], and others put to death	Indian student burned for heresy in Mexico[4]	Florence, Italy, influenced by Juán de Valdés and Ochino,
1536					Inquisition [re]introduced in Portugal[4]	whom Valdés had led to salvation[b5]
1537	After a first imprisonment and release,		Poet C. Marot, who assisted with the	The completed Tyndale Bible of Latimer, Bishop of Worcester	Menno Simons married Gertrude[m]	
1537	Anabaptists S. Glasmacher[b] and H. Gruenfelder[b] were arrested at Imst. in the uppervalley of the Anabaptist G. Vasser[b] went to Pechstall, Austria, to evangelize and		poetry of the book of Psalms, for the French Geneva	John Rogers was issued a series of injunctions stating that every church clerk published in Paris and Antwerp under the	Menno Simons was ordained an Anabaptist elder by Obbe Philips (who himself left the brotherhood in 1541) in	

1537	Inn, and were executed by sword	plant a church; a deceiver betrayed him; he was arrested, tortured, and executed by sword		Bible, recanted his faith in order to return to France as a poet for the court of **King Francis I**			pseudonym **Thomas Matthew**; **Rogers'** notes were largely borrowed from the French **Lefevre** and **Olivétan** versionsw2	should own a copy of the entire Bible or at least the New Testament in both Latin and Englishw2		the province of Groningen sometime in early 1537, at that time they were known as "**Obbenites**"m
1537									In Cassel of Flanders, the Anabaptist **P. de Keurs**b was arrested for separating himself from "this wicked world", he was imprisoned and martyred	
1537	Anabaptist minister **H Peiz**b was arrested with some of his **fellow** **H. Bartel**b were	Anabaptists **H. Wucherer**b and **H. Bartel**b were								
1537	**believers**b; they died in prison	arrested in Bavaria, were repeatedly tortured on the rack, and burned alive									
1537										
1538	Anabaptist **M. Wideman**b [or **Beck**] was arrested	Anabaptist **L. Lochmair**b (a former priest) and **O. Greizinger**b	Geneva expelled **Farel** and **Calvin**p	[from 1538 on, it became more common in France for heretics to be burned hanging over a fire, using an Espadrade, instead of being attached to a stake]			In December 1538, a decree was published in England "against the believers baptized according to the ordinance of Christ"b	**J. Nicholson** (called **Lambert**)c burned at the stake in London [not Winchester]h		Anabaptist teacher **P. Vandruyen**b and **M. Stevens**b, **J. Block**b, and
1538	in Ricten in Allgau; he was beheaded and burned	(with a large sum upon his head) were apprehended and	**Olivétan**p disappeared while travelling to Rome; the bait						**Adrian**b were strangled and burned in Vucht near	
1538	Anabaptist **M. of Vilgraten**b and **C. Schumacher**b arrested in	brought to Brixen in Tyrol; **Greizinger**b was severely tortured	was to discuss questions of Hebrew translation; he was never heard from again; he was thought to have been poisoned →					**Henry VIII** commissioned **Coverdale** to prepare the "Great Bible" translation into English, which was printed in	**Olivétan**p disappeared while travelling to Rome; was thought poisonedp and left to die in Ferrara, Italy ←	Herzogenbusch (9th Sept); 11th Sept, **Paul's wife**b was strangled,
1538	Michelsberg in Priesterthal; executed with sword	to tell of those who had harbored him; he was put on the rack				**Coverdale** began to oversee the printing of the "Great Bible" for Henry VIII in Paris, until the				alone with **two other women**b and **J. van Capelle**b 4th Sept,
1538	Anabaptist **H. Seyel**b of Mur and **Hans**b of	multiple times but gave no information, he was burned alive				French Inquisitor-General forbade the printers		France ←		a **young man**b was beheaded

(Page 107)

COLOR GUIDE: YELLOW=Roman Catholic areas; TAN=Bad years for Anabaptists; GOLD=Important events for Catholicism; ORANGE=Catholics "martyred"; RED=Evangelicals martyred; GRAY=Other martyred; Disclaimer: some dates may vary
PINK=Marriage issues; PURPLE= Crusades or massacres; TURQUOISE=Martyrology info; BLUE=Part Protestant areas; AQUA=U.S. Const; LIME=Bible issues; LT GREEN=Disputed areas; GREEN=Major dates.

Thomas P. Johnston — Geographic History — Page 108

Date	Germany-Austria-Scandinavia	Switzerland	France-Alsace		British Isles	Italy, Spain, Low Lands
1538	**Wels** were arrested in Sandweid of Kaernthen; they were executed by sword				27 English **Anabaptists** fled to the Netherlands to flee persecution[b] →	Anabaptist **Walter of Stoelwijk**[b] arrested in Vilvoorden, Brabant; he was held prisoner until 1541 (see below)
1538	on Oct 31st, **Lochmair**[b] was beheaded Nov 2nd					27 English **Anabaptist**[b] put to death in the Netherlands
1539	In Tyrol, **Apollonia**[b], wife of L. Seyle, arrested as an Anabaptist, brought to Brixen, where she was tested and drowned		**J. Vindocin**[r], former priest, burned at the stake in Agen	Law of the [Catholic] "**Six Articles**" brought to English Parliament, led to a persecution of Protestants	Cromwell ordered "**Great Bible**" placed in English churches	**Anna of Rotterdam** was put to death for her testimony of Christ in the same city on Jan 24th; she left a testimony for her son, Isaiah
1539	**King Ferdinand** sent his Marshall from Vienna to arrest 150 Anabaptist men and women in Steinborn, Austria, on Dec 6th; they		**L. Courtet**[c] burned at the stake in Savoy			The 31 English **Anabaptists**[b] (16 men and 15 women) who fled persecution were arrested in Delft and put to death the same year
1539	were brought to the castle of Falkenstein, where they were questioned and kept for some time →		**Robert Estienne** became the King's printer in Paris; printing primarily Latin Bibles			**T. Reynerts**[b], an Anabaptist from Friesland, was arrested and killed on a wheel on 8 Jan 1539 because he had sheltered **Menno Simons**; Simons had
1539	→				31 English **Anabaptists** fled to Delft, Holland to flee persecution[b] →	**A. Jacobs**[b], his wife[b], and son[b] were arrested, brought to Monickendam, tortured, and drowned
1539	→					also baptized him
1539	→					Wanted posters of **Anabaptist** leaders were posted on doors, gates, and other public places in West Friesland, promising large sums of money for delivering them into the hands of officers and executioners[b]
1539	→					**Menno Simons** wrote the 250 page *Foundation of*
1539	→					Anabaptists **A. Jacobs**[b], his wife[b] and eldest

1539		→							son[b] arrested and brought to Monickendam; they were drowned
1539		→							with stones tied to their necks
1540		Anabaptist H. Simeraver[b] arrested in	Calvin (~31 yrs old) married Idelette de Bure	Crespin received doctorate and was approved as a Lawyer to the	Etienne Brun[c] burned at the stake in Dauphin; C. le Peintre[c]				Paul III established Loyola's Society of Jesus (Jesuits), "The Church Militant," by Papal Bull
1540		Ninety Anabaptist men were sentenced to go to the sea; they		Parliament of France; witnessed → burning of	burned at the stake in Paris	Coverdale fled to Tubingen, Germany ←			
1540		were driven through the country, where they shared the		Claude le Peintre[c]				4 theologians[c] martyred at Louvain	
1540		Gospel as they went; 75 men were able to escape and return to Moravia, the			M Ory[r] established as Inquisitor General of France				
1540		rest were placed to row in the Galleys; their fate is unknown[b]		C. Marot presented the first 30 Psalms to					
1540		Coverdale arrived in Tubingen, Germany, ended		Francis I, who then gave them to Charles V; he paid Marot					
1540		up serving as a Lutheran pastor →		and encouraged him to continue[l]					
1540			Farel and Calvin returned to Geneva						
1541	At the Disputation of Worms, Eck called attention to				Pastor A. de la Voye[r] strangled (or neck broken)		English Parliament passed Law (1541) of Six	R. Mekins[c], 15 year old brought before Bishop Bonner of	J. Marlar[c] decapitated and Marguerite Boulard[c]	Loyola elected first secretary general of Jesuits
1541	the changes Melancthon had inserted into the Augsburg				and burned in Bordeaux		Articles that its citizens must believe: (1) Transubstan-	London, who delivered him up to be martyred; Jean[c], Gilles[c] (a Bruxelles	buried alive in Douais; J. Jusberg[c] decapitated in	Anabaptist Walter of Stoelwijk[b] was

COLOR GUIDE: YELLOW=Roman Catholic areas; TAN=Bad years for Anabaptists; GOLD=Important events for Catholicism; ORANGE=Catholics "martyred"; RED=Evangelicals martyred; GRAY=Other martyred; Disclaimer: some dates may vary
PINK=Marriage issues; PURPLE=Crusades or massacres; TURQUOISE=Martyrology info; BLUE=Part Protestant areas; AQUA=U.S. Const; LIME=Bible issues; GREEN=Major dates. (Page 109)

Thomas P. Johnston — Geographic History — Page 110

Date	Germany-Austria-Scandinavia	Switzerland	France-Alsace	British Isles	Italy, Spain, Low Lands	
1541	**Confession**, making it too favorable to **Calvinistic** views³		tiation; (2) Use of Host only; (3) Celibacy of Priests; (4) Binding nature of vows of chastity; (5) Private masses at church only; (6) Necessity of confessions^c	German) and **Lancelot**^c burned in London at 5 a.m.; R. Spencer^c and A. Hewet^c burned	In an attempt to extirpate Anabaptism from Friesland, money was put on **Simons** head (100 Carl [gold] Guilders), as well as a pardon from **Queen Mary**, Regent of the Netherlands^m	burned alive after 3 years in prison. **Anabaptist** leader, **Obbe Philips**, laid down his office as bishop and left the "**brotherhood**"^m
1541					Anabaptists D. P. Krood^b, P. Trijnes^b, C. Roders^b, and P. C. Jans^b of Wormer in Waterlandt were arrested and brought to Enchuysen, where they were executed [year unknown]	**Simons** shifted his ministry to Amsterdam^m. **Menno Simons** authored the 160 page *The True Christian Faith*^m
1541						
1542 Inquisition re-established by Pope Paul III 1542	**Dirk Philips** became the [Mennonite] **Anabaptist** bishop [traveling pastor] in the area of Danzig^m	*Ecclesiastical Ordinances* made law in Geneva	**Constantin**^c, O. Bouncer^c, J. Challes^c, G. Fonques^c, all burned for heresy in Rouen [It became habitual in France that tongues were cut out before burning, lest martyrs preach to the crowds as they were burning, cf. 2 Macc 7:4]	Knox converted to reformation. J. Morton^c and T. Bernard^c burned in Lincoln; J. Porter^c died in prison in London for reading from the Apostle Paul in the Bible at church	Anabaptists J. Egtwercken^b, C. Meliss^b, W^b. and A. Mellis^b, H. Walings^b, T. Amkers^b, C. Luyts^b, C. Dirks^b, C. Claess^b, and J. D. G. van der Busch^b from Krommeniersdijck, Waterlandt, were executed	G. Tielemans^c martyred in Bruxelles; Remy^c decapitated, and his wife, **Matthinette du Buiset**^c, was buried alive in Douais
1542			C. Marot's translation of the Psalms was		Jacob^b and his wife Seli^b, arrested in Wormer; they were	**Pope Paul III** published bull to

1542	Anabaptist H. Huber[b] [or Schumacher] imprisoned in Wasrburg, Bavaria; was burned alive	Anabaptist L. Bernkop[b] was arrested in Salzburg; built a fire near him to roast him and burned him alive (cf. 2 Macc 7:5)			deemed suspect, an arrest warrant went out for him by the Parliament of Paris; he fled to Geneval ↙		brought to Amsterdam, where they were burned alive		convene Council at the Alpine city of Trent
1542			Menno Simons and Dirk Philips ordained Roelof			Gillis of Aachen became the [Mennonite]	Dec 7, 1542, Charles V placed a bounty of 100 gold Guilders on the head of Simons, forbidding people to shelter him or to read his books[m]		Pope Paul III's *Licet ab Initio* (21 July 1542)w3 reinstituted the "Congregation for Pontifical Inquisition" [of
1542			Martens [aka. Adam Pastor] as a bishop; Pastor was later excommunicated in 1547[m]			Anabaptist bishop [traveling pastor] in the Rhineland[m]			which apparently no document exists outside of Rome's closed archives]h3
1543	In Emden, East Friesland, Countess Anna set up a Zwinglian	Coverdale served as a Lutheran pastor and schoolmaster until 1547		Calvin authored his tract "*Advertisement ... on the invention of the holy bodies and reliques...*"	[it became common practice to burn Bible colporteurs with their Bibles and books tied around their necks]	Secretary to the Cardinal of Paris, F. Bribard[c] burned in Paris; and Priest J. de Bec[c] burned in Troye	A. Peerson[c], R. Testwood[c], and J. Marbeck[c] burned at the stake at Windsor due to Six Articles	In West Friesland, Remission of crimes was promised for any murderers or thieves, a pardon of the Emperor, as well as 100 Carl Guilders	
1543	Protestant church under the leadership of John a Lasco[m]							for anyone who would turn over Menno Simons[b]	
1543	Menno Simons settled his ministry in northwest Germany, away			C. Marot left Geneva, presumably not	Poet Clement Marot[c], suspected of being Lutheran fled to Geneva;	The University of Paris published 25 Articles of the		Menno Simons moved his ministry into northwest Germany[m] ←	
1543	from the severe edicts of Holy Roman Emperor Charles V[m]				getting along with Calvin; he died in Turin; of Marot it is said, "the 50	he later helped with editing the	Faith by which Evangelical heretics were to be tried			
1543					Psalms of Marot"l	Geneva Bible	burned at St. Paul's Cross in London w2			

COLOR GUIDE: YELLOW=Roman Catholic areas; TAN=Bad years for Anabaptists; GOLD=Important events for Catholicism; ORANGE=Catholics "martyred"; RED=Evangelicals martyred; GRAY=Other martyred; Disclaimer: some dates may vary
PINK=Marriage issues; PURPLE= Crusades or massacres; TURQUOISE=Martyrology info; BLUE=Part Protestant areas; AQUA=U.S. Const; LIME=Bible issues; GREEN=Major dates.
(Page 111)

Thomas P. Johnston — Geographic History — Page 112

Date	Germany-Austria-Scandinavia	Switzerland	France-Alsace	British Isles	Italy, Spain, Low Lands
1544	In East Friesland, three "Anabaptist" groups existed: **Bratenburgers**, **Davidians** (followers of **David Joris**), and **Menists** (later **Mennonites**)m	[**Husson** was tied by the hands and feet behind his back and hoisted up by a large pulley above a fire; the device was called an *espadrade*]	**G. Husson**c gave Gospel booklets before parliament of Rouen, went to do likewise in Dieppe, was found, arrested, tongue cut out, and hung over a fire		In Amsterdam, Anabaptists **L. Lamberts**bm (87 years old) and **J. Claeszoon**bm [**Claess** or **Claassen**, an ordained Anabaptist minister], both baptized by Menno Simons, were martyred [on Jan 19m]; **Claess'** crime was printing and distributing books of Menno Simons, and teaching strange opinions and sectarianismb	Converted on a business trip to Germany, **F. de St Romain**c wrote letters to Spain and tracts in Spanish, was immediately arrested arriving at Anvers, found guilty of being "parfait Lutherien," partially burned, removed, not recanting, built up the fire again, in Spain
1544		**Calvin** authored his tract "*The Excuse of the Nicodemites*" **Calvin** also authored a book against the *Communal Anabaptists*, for the pastors of the churches in Neuchatel, titled: *Brief Instruction to Arm all the Good Faithful against the Errors of the Communal Sect of the Anabaptists* (trans from French by this author); he responded to the following points: 1) Infant baptism; 2) Excommunication; 3) Right to bear arms; 4) Power of princes; and 5) Making vows; To these he added the following: 6) Incarnation of Jesus; 7) Life and condition of the	**King Francis I** signed an arrest warrant for certain **Waldensians** and **Lutherans** who lived in Merindol and Cabrières		Anabaptists **Maria van Beckum**b and **Ursula**b (her brother's wife) arrested in the province of Utrecht and brought to Deventer; burned alive one at a time on 13 Nov at Delden
1544	Jan 28-31, 1544, **Menno Simons** met with **John a Lasco** to discuss matters of theology, they disagreed on the incarnation, the calling of ministers, and baptismm				In Rotterdam, an Anabaptist meeting was betrayed to the Papists; they were arrested and tortured to cause them to apostacize; the **men**b were beheaded; and the **women**b were thrown from a boat to die under the ice
1544	**Menno Simons** fled to Cologne, Germany, where Archbishop **Herman von Wied** was transforming the bishopric into a Lutheran Principalitym	Ex-Munsterite, **David Joris**, left the "Anabaptist" sect he founded called **Davidians**, moved to Basel, joined the Reformed church, and changed his name to **John of Bruges**m			Belgium Inquisitor **Jacques Mason** died (68 yrs old)
1544	**Lasco** published **Simons'** confession and used it against him, although tolerating "**Menists**"m				

1544				souls of the dead before the day of the last resurrection			
1545	At Vienna, Anabaptist Oswald[b] of Jamnists; after 1.5		**Crespin** condemned for heresy, forced to flee to Strasbourg	Since the **Waldensian** and **Lutheran** sects were reproved		**Council of Trent** began [strategically located between Rome and Wittenberg, in an area controlled by Austria]	→
1545	At Ried in Bavaria, Anabaptist H. Blietel[b] was betrayed for money and arrested; **Hans** was sentenced to be burned alive on		**P. Brully** (aka Paul Mioce)[C] and **J. Chobard**[C] burned at the	and contrary to the Catholic faith, and since many of their people		**Roch**[C], an artist, mutilated one of his statues of Mary, for this	→
1545	St. John's day; he preached and sang while on the fire; one of those		stake for heresy in Lorraine	lived in Merindol and Cabrières, on the 16th of April everyone in the		**A. Estallufret, J. de Bucq**[C], **N. van Poule**[C], and **M.**	→
1545						**Huerblocq**[C], "blasphemy" he was burned at the stake in Belgium	→
1545	who watched said that he would tell the church in Bavaria of his end		In Metz, where **Farel**[C] had preached, **Adam**[C] beaten to	two towns were massacred, over **850 killed**[C], historian H.		**Marie** (aka Marion) **de la Pierre**[C] and **wife of J. de Bucq**[C]	→
1545			death with sticks and trampled by a police horse, also **Three**[C]	Martin estimated **4 to 5 thousand killed**[r]; some refugees fled to Geneva	**Death Sentence Pronounced against Quirinus Pieters of Groeningen** → [from Amsterdam Secretary's Archives]	buried alive in Belgium	→
1545			forced in the river, stoned, and drowned		"Whereas Quirinus Pieters, a native of Groeningen, has embraced the unbelief and heresy of the	In Friesland, Anabaptist **Francis**[b] of Bolsweert was	→
1545					Anabaptists, having been rebaptized about six years ago, by Menno Simons, a teacher of the aforesaid sect, and whereas he holds	burned alive on Palm Sunday eve	→
1545			**Bible bookseller** in Avignon beaten and		pernicious views concerning the sacraments of the holy church, and, moreover, has induced others, into such unbelief and errors, persuading	(having been baptized by **Menno Simons** in Friesland), was	→
1545			burned with two Bibles at his neck (one in front and in back)		them into it, directly contrary to the holy Christian faith, the ordinances of the holy church, and the decrees of his Imperial Majesty, our gracious	arrested because he "has induced others into such unbelief and	→
1545						errors, pesuading them in it, directly contrary to the holy Christian	→
1545						faith", burned alive for heresy on April 16	→

COLOR GUIDE: YELLOW=Roman Catholic areas; TAN=Bad years for Anabaptists; GOLD=Important events for Catholicism; ORANGE=Catholics "martyred"; RED=Evangelicals martyred; GRAY=Other martyred; Disclaimer: some dates may vary
PINK=Marriage issues; PURPLE= Crusades or massacres; TURQUOISE=Martyrology info; BLUE=Part Protestant areas; AQUA=U.S. Const; LT GREEN=Disputed areas; LIME=Bible issues; GREEN=Major dates.

(Page 113)

Thomas P. Johnston Geographic History Page 114

Date	Germany-Austria-Scandinavia	Switzerland	France-Alsace	British Isles	Italy, Spain, Low Lands
1545				lord; and whereas he obstinately continues in the aforesaid unbelief, therefore, my lords the judges, having heard the demand made by	→
1545				my lord the bailif concerning the aforesaid Quirinus Pieters, as also his answer and confession, and having fully considered the	→
1545				circumstances of said matter, sentence the aforesaid Quirinus Pieters to be burned by the executioner; and furthermore,	→
1545				declare his property confiscated for the benefit of the exchequer of his Imperial Majesty. Pronounced this sixteenth day of April, A.D. 1545, in	→
1545				the presence of the entire bench of judges, except Sir Henry Dirks, Burgomaster"b	→
1546	Luther (~63 yrs old) died in Eisleben	C. Senarclens wrote *Historia vera de morte sancti uiri Ioannis*	The Fourteen from Meaux (P. Leclerk, E. Mangin,	Interrogation of Dirk Pieters → Amsterdam, Holland "Q. The apostles certainly went forth to teach; where did they go teach?	The Spanish J. Diaz c (aka Ensinas), turned over by
1546	From Kaufbeuren, Kofler b was arrested at Ips and beheaded four Anabaptist families (H. Stauctach b, A.	*Diazii Hispani* (Basle, 1546)w about the martyrdom of	M. Caillon, J. Bouchebec, J. Brissebar, H. Butinot,	"A. Whithersoever they came, they went into the synagogues, and preached the Gospel of Christ." "Q. We have heard that you also	his brother, burned in Rome b, likewise his brother
1546	Keyn b, B. Beck b, and L. Schneider b) arrested in	J. Diaz ↙	F. Leclerk, T. Honnore, J. Baudouin, J. Flesche,	teach wherever you go? "A. O Lord, what should I preach; we may read the Gospel together. "Q. Where did you read it together?	François c was killed in a querelle over the Gospel
1546	Austria, while fleeing to Moravia, they were brought to Vienna; their		J. Picquery, P. Picquery, J.Mateflon, and P. Petit) c plus a	"A. At the dyke. "Q. With whom did you read it? "A. This I do not know. "Q. How should you not know with	J. Eck died
1546	wives [and children?] were released; the four men were		P. Chapot c, strangled and burned at the stake for bringing Bibles into Paris	whom you read it? "A. How should I know it, sometimes with this one, sometimes with another.	April 8, 1546, the Council of Trent published its "Decree Concerning
1546	Matschilder, his wife, and H. Gurtzham arrested; they		man named Couberon c who was encouraging them were		

1546	beheaded at daybreak on Nov 22nd in order to avoid a sensation;	were imprisoned for 3 years until an amnesty in 1549[b]		E. Poulliot[C] burned at the stake in Paris	burned alive in Paris, one, M. Piquery, was hung because of		Canonical Scriptures", in which it stated, "it receives and venerates with a
1546	all four were beheaded	The Lutheran Princes were defeated by the			his youthfulness		feeling of piety and reverence all the books both of the Old and New
1546	**Menno Simons** fled to Holstein, Germany, on the	Catholics in the Smalcald War; this forced **Menno Simons** to flee to		"Q. Have you any books of Menno Simons and of David Joris?" "A. No, I have no books in the house, except a Bible and a Testament, and a little book on the faith."[b]			Testaments, since one God is the author of both; also the traditions,
1546	Baltic, where he remained to the end of his life (1561); he	Cologne and Archbishop **H. von Wied**[m] ←				A book published in London on the martyrdom of Anne Askewe:	whether they relate to faith or to morals, as having been dictated either orally
1546	became the **Anabaptist bishop** [traveling pastor] of				Roger[C] burned at the stake in London; **Anne Askew**[C], **N. Beleniam**[C], **J. Adams**[C], and **J. Lascelles**[C] burned at the	"The first examinacyon Anne Askew, Lately martyred	by Christ or by the Holy Ghost, and preserved in the Catholic Church in
1546	northern Germany; Holstein was under the				stake in London	in Smythfelde"	unbroken succession." In its list of OT books are found the Apocryphal
1546	rulership of the King of Denmark[m]			books rejected by Luther, Calvin, and in Thomas Cranmer's 1553 42 Articles of the Church of England (later revised as the 39 Articles).			
1546	At **Lubeck** the [Mennonite] **Anabaptist bishops** met to			In its "Decree Concerning the Edition and Use of the Sacred Books," **Trent** condemned the publishing of Scriptures or teachings not in accord with the Catholic church, refering to the 4th Lateran Council's anathema [extirpation by death] (1215). The session ended giving bishops a blank check to enforce and punish heretics and schismatics as they deemed best: "Furthermore, wishing to repress that boldness whereby the words and sentences of the Holy			
1546	discuss the doctrinal position of **N. Blesdijk**[m]			Scriptures are turned and twisted to all kinds of profane usages, namely, to things scurrilous, fabulous, vain, to flatteries, detractions, superstitions, godless and diabolical incantations, divinations, the casting of lots and defamatory libels, to put an end to such irreverence and contempt, and that no one may in the future dare use in any manner the words of Holy Scripture for these and similar purposes, it is commanded and enjoined that all people of this kind be restrained by the bishops as violators and profaners of the word of God, with the penalties of the law and other penalties that they may deem fit to impose."			
1546				June 17, 1546, **Trent** published its "Decree Concerning Original Sin" in which they affirmed that infant baptism washed away the guilt of original sin. Several anathemas directly concerned so-called "Anabaptists" in Decree 3, "If anyone asserts that this sin of Adam, which in its origin is one, and by propagation, not by imitation, transfused into all, which is in each one as something that is his own, is taken away either by the forces of human nature or by a			(Page 115)

COLOR GUIDE: YELLOW=Roman Catholic areas; TAN=Bad years for Anabaptists; GOLD=Important events for Catholicism; ORANGE=Catholics "martyred"; RED=Evangelicals martyred; GRAY=Other martyred; Disclaimer: some dates may vary PINK=Marriage issues; PURPLE=Crusades or massacres; TURQUOISE=Martyrology info; BLUE=Part Protestant areas; AQUA=U.S. Const; LT GREEN=Disputed areas; LIME=Bible issues; GREEN=Major dates.

Geographic History

Date	Germany-Austria-Scandinavia	Switzerland	France-Alsace	British Isles	Italy, Spain, Low Lands
1546					remedy other than the merit of the one mediator, our Lord Jesus Christ, who has reconciled us to God in his own blood, made unto us justice, sanctification and redemption; or if he denies that that merit of Jesus Christ is applied both to adults and to infants by the sacrament of baptism rightly administered in the form of the Church, let him be anathema."
1546					Decree 4, "If anyone denies that infants, newly born from their mothers' wombs, are to be baptized, even though they be born of baptized parents, or says that they are indeed baptized for the remission of sins, but that they derive nothing of original sin from Adam which must be expiated by the laver of regeneration for the attainment of eternal life, whence it follows that in them the form of baptism for the remission of sins is to be understood not as true but as false, let him be anathema"
1545					Decree 5, "If anyone denies that by the grace of our Lord Jesus Christ which is conferred in baptism, the guilt of original sin is remitted, or says that the whole of that which belongs to the essence of sin is not taken away, but says that it is only canceled or not imputed, let him be anathema. For in those who are born again God hates
1546					nothing, because there is no condemnation to those who are truly buried together with Christ by baptism unto death, who walk not according to the flesh, but, putting off the old man and putting on the new one who is created according to God, are made innocent, immaculate, pure, guiltless and beloved of God, joint heirs with Christ; so that there is nothing whatever to hinder their entrance into heaven. But this holy council
1546					perceives and confesses that in the one baptized there remains concupiscence or an inclination to sin, which, since it is left for us to wrestle with, cannot injure those who do not acquiesce but resist manfully by the grace of Jesus Christ; indeed, he who shall have striven lawfully shall be crowned. This concupiscence, which the Apostle sometimes calls sin, the holy council declares the Catholic Church has never understood to be called sin in the
1546					sense that it is truly and properly sin in those born again, but in the sense that it is of sin and inclines to sin. But if anyone is of the contrary opinion, let him be anathema" (source www.forerunner.com)
1547	Emperor Charles V sought to unify all of Germany through the Diet of Augsburg, continuing the policy of the Diet of Spier (1526)s3		J. Taffigon[c] & his wife J. Sejournam[c], S. Mareschal[c] & his wife, J. Bailly[c], G. Michaut[c], J. Boulereau[c] & J. Bretenay[c] burned at the stake in Langres	J. l'Anglois[c] burned in Sense	→Trent M. Miquelot[c] (Destoubequin) burned alive in Tournais
1547	[Mennonite] Anabaptist bishops met semi-annually at		L. du Pre[c] burned alive in Paris	Upon the death of King Henry VIII, his son Edward VI became King (1547-1553); he moved England in a more definitive Protestant direction	Jan 13, 1547, the Council of Trent published its "Decree Concerning Justification": of which "the instrumental cause is the sacrament of
1547			J. Brugière[c] burned alive at Issoire	"It is estimated that some forty versions of Tyndale's, Coverdale's, Matthew's, the Great Bible, and even	In Ilst, Friesland, a pregnant Anabaptist woman named Richst Heynes[b] was arrested and imprisoned in Leeuwaerden, after three weeks she
1547	Emden to discuss matters of doctrine and discipline[m]		Under Henry II, King of France (1547-1559), was instituted a special courtroom to deal with	Taverner's were issued in Edward's seven-year reign (1547-1553)w2	bore a son, who had the marks of her chains; she baptism, which is the sacrament of faith" (Chap 7). Chap 9 being "Against

1547	Anabaptist bishop **Adam Pastor** was excommunicated due to false teaching on the divinity of Christ[m]	heretics, "La Chambre Ardente" (1547-1559), as a result 600 **Huguenots** were arrested from 1547-1550[r]	was cruelly tortured so that she would betray her husband; finally she was placed in a bag, and drowned	the Vain Confidence of the Heretics" who believe that "that absolution and justification are effected by this faith alone." ⤶
1547				
1547		**Council of Trent, Canons Concerning Justification: Cannon 9**, stated "If anyone says that the sinner is justified by faith alone, meaning that nothing else is required to cooperate in order to obtain the grace of justification, and that it is not in any way necessary that he be prepared and disposed by the action of his own will, let him be anathema."		
1547		**"Canon 11**. If anyone says that men are justified either by the sole imputation of the justice of Christ or by the sole remission of sins, to the exclusion of the grace and the charity which is poured forth in their hearts by the Holy Ghost, and remains in them, or also that the grace by which we are justified is only the good will of God, let him be anathema."		
1547		**"Canon 12.** If anyone says that justifying faith is nothing else than confidence in divine mercy, which remits sins for Christ's sake, or that it is this confidence alone that justifies us, let him be anathema."		
1547		**"Canon 13.** If anyone says that in order to obtain the remission of sins it is necessary for every man to believe with certainty and without any hesitation arising from his own weakness and indisposition that his sins are forgiven him, let him be anathema.		
1547		**"Canon 14.** If anyone says that man is absolved from his sins and justified because he firmly believes that he is absolved and justified, or that no one is truly justified except him who believes himself justified, and that by this faith alone absolution and justification are effected, let him be anathema."		
1547		**"Canon 15.** If anyone says that a man who is born again and justified is bound ex fide to believe that he is certainly in the number of the predestined, let him be anathema."		
1547		**"Canon 16.** If anyone says that he will for certain, with an absolute and infallible certainty, have that great gift of perseverance even to the end, unless he shall have learned this by a special revelation, let him be anathema."		
1547		**"Canon 17.** If anyone says that the grace of justification is shared by those only who are predestined to life, but that all others who are called are called indeed but receive not grace, as if they are by divine power predestined to evil, let him be anathema."		
1547		Canon 18. If anyone says that the commandments of God are, even for one that is justified and constituted in grace, impossible to observe, let him be anathema."		
1547		March 3, 1547, **Trent's "Decree Concerning the Sacrament"** with 13 **"Canons on the Sacraments in General"**, 14 **"Canons on Baptism"**, 3 **"Canons on Confirmation"**. The following are some peccadilloes: **On the Sacraments in General:**		
1547		**"Canon 1**. If anyone says that the sacraments of the New Law were not all instituted by our Lord Jesus Christ, or		

COLOR GUIDE: YELLOW=Roman Catholic areas; GOLD=Important events for Catholicism; ORANGE=Catholics "martyred"; RED=Evangelicals martyred; GRAY=Other martyred; Disclaimer: some dates may vary PINK=Marriage issues; PURPLE= Crusades or massacres; TAN=Bad years for Anabaptists; TURQUOISE=Martyrology info; BLUE=Part Protestant areas; AQUA=U.S. Const; LT GREEN=Disputed areas; LIME=Bible issues; GREEN=Major dates. (Page 117)

Thomas P. Johnston
Geographic History
Page 118

Geographic History

Date	Germany-Austria-Scandinavia	Switzerland	France-Alsace	British Isles	Italy, Spain, Low Lands
1547					that there are more or less than seven, namely, baptism, confirmation, Eucharist, penance, extreme unction, order and matrimony, or that any one of these seven is not truly and intrinsically a sacrament, let him be anathema." "**Canon 4.** If anyone says that the sacraments of the New Law are not necessary for salvation but are superfluous, and that without them or without the desire of them men obtain from God through faith alone the grace of
1547					justification,[2] though all are not necessary for each one, let him be anathema." "**Canon 5.** If anyone says that these sacraments have been instituted for the nourishment of faith alone, let him be anathema."
1547					"**Canon 6.** If anyone says that the sacraments of the New Law do not contain the grace which they signify, or that they do not confer that grace on those who place no obstacles in its way,[3] as though they were only outward signs of grace or justice received through faith and certain marks of Christian profession, whereby among men believers are distinguished from unbelievers, let him be anathema."
1547					"**Canon 8.** If anyone says that by the sacraments of the New Law grace is not conferred *ex opere operato*, but that faith alone in the divine promise is sufficient to obtain grace, let him be anathema."
1547					"**Canon 13.** If anyone says that the received and approved rites of the Catholic Church, accustomed to be used in the administration of the sacraments, may be despised or omitted by the ministers without sin and at their pleasure, or may be changed by any pastor of the churches to other new ones, let him be anathema." On Baptism: "**Canon 3.** If anyone says that in the Roman Church, which is the mother and mistress of all churches, there is not the true doctrine concerning the sacrament of baptism,[11] let him be anathema."
1547					"**Canon 7.** If anyone says that those baptized are by baptism made debtors only to faith alone, but not to the observance of the whole law of Christ, let him be anathema."
1547					"**Canon 8.** If anyone says that those baptized are free from all the precepts of holy Church, whether written or unwritten, so that they are not bound to observe them unless they should wish to submit to them of their own accord, let him be anathema."
1547					"**Canon 13.** If anyone says that children, because they have not the act of believing, are not after having received baptism to be numbered among the faithful, and that for this reason are to be rebaptized when they have reached the years of discretion;[14] or that it is better that the baptism of such be omitted than that, while not believing by their own act, they should be baptized in the faith of the Church alone, let him be anathema."
1547					"**Canon 14.** If anyone says that those who have been thus baptized when children are, when they have grown up, to be questioned whether they will ratify what their sponsors promised in their name when they were baptized, and in case they answer in the negative, are to be left to their own will; neither are they to be compelled in the meantime to a Christian life by any penalty other than exclusion from the reception of the Eucharist and the other
1547					sacraments, until they repent, let him be anathema" (source www.forerunner.com).
1548	J. Rogers returned to England →	Coverdale returned to England →	Crespin arrived in Geneva	Crespin fled from France for Geneva ↓	S. Nivet[c] of Meaux martyred in Paris	J. Rogers returned to England (from Germany)	In Ostende, the Anabaptist C. Lecks[b] was arrested, →

Year	(blue)	(yellow)	(yellow)	(orange/red)	(lt green)	(green)	(orange/red)	(gold)
1548			Bible Printer, R. Estienne, went from Lausanne to Zurichl3	Bible printer, R. Estienne, left Paris for Lausannel3 ←	O. Blondel^C burned at the stake in Tours for warning someone of their impious and superstitious speech		examined, and sentenced to be strangled and burned	→
1549			Calvin's wife, Idelette died (they were married about 9 years) [PURPLE]	Investigation of King Henry II into atrocities of Menier in the massacres at Merindol and Cabrières; no decision was rendered, which led to more killings →	H. Burre^C burned in Dijon	Knox in England	Cranmer authored Book of Common Prayer	In Ostland, Elizabeth^b, wife of Menno M. Nicholas^C, Augustin^C and his wife,	→
1549					E. Peloquin^C to have tongue cut out and to be burned over a small fire in Paris			Simons, taken from her home on 15th Jan, where they Marion^C martyred in Belgium	→
1549					a Tailor^{Cr} for the King in Paris (who gazed at the King as he burned)			found a Latin Testament; long interrogation; drowned in a bag on March 27th In Amsterdam: six Anabaptist men and two women burned alive on March 20th. P. Janz^b,	→
1549					A widow, Anne Audebert,^C was captured as she sought to flee to Geneva, tried in Paris, burned alive in Orleans			T. Questinex^b, J. Pennewaertz^b,	Council of Trent Continued
1549					Menier executed Gaultery^C in Digne and B. Audouin^C in Aix-en-Provence, and several others^C also			At Leeuwarden Anabaptists Eelken^b beheaded, and G. Jans^b, E. Jans^b, L. Michiels^b, Barbara	
1549					To celebrate the return of King Henry II into Paris, two former priests, F. Venot^C and L. Galimar^C, burned alive after the King's dinner in front of the Notre Dame^r			Fije^b strangled and burned Thielemans^b and Truyken Boens^b	→
1549								In Amsterdam, Anabaptists J. Claess^b (tortured on Oct 22nd) and his wife Cecilia Jerony-mus^b burned alive on Nov 9th	→
1550			Bible printer, R. Estienne, settled in Geneva13	C. Thierry^C burned at the stake in Orleans	J. Rogers received the crown livings of St. Margaret Moyses		Second French "Authorized Bible", called	→
1550			Bible), second French "Authorized Bible" published, called	J. Godeau^C and G. Beraudin^C burned alive in Chambery	Common man A. Wallace^C burned in Scotland before	In London, Anabaptists J. Kneb^b (or Buchner) and		Louvain [Belgium] published ↓ Fanino^C hung and burned Ferrare, Italy	→
								F. Negri wrote *De Fannii Faventini* (1550)w	

COLOR GUIDE: YELLOW=Roman Catholic areas; TAN=Bad years for Anabaptists; GOLD=Important events for Catholicism; ORANGE=Catholics "martyred"; RED=Evangelicals martyred; GRAY=Other martyred; Disclaimer: some dates may vary PINK=Marriage issues; PURPLE= Crusades or massacres; TURQUOISE=Martyrology info; BLUE=Part Protestant areas; AQUA=U.S. Const; LIME=Bible issues; LT GREEN=Disputed areas; GREEN=Major dates. (Page 119)

Thomas P. Johnston — Geographic History — Page 120

Date	Germany-Austria-Scandinavia	Switzerland	France-Alsace	British Isles	Italy, Spain, Low Lands	
1550			the Louvain Bible; hoped to replace Lefevre's Bible and	a great crowd of impressive folk	Anabaptist Hymnwriter,	→
1550			(especially) the Swiss Olivétan Version	Anna Cantiana**b** burned alive; Knel was burned on May 2nd	Loyola completed draft of the Constitutions for the Jesuit order	H. van Overdam**b** and H. Keeskooper**b** were arrested with	→
1550					At Lier in Brabant, in January, four Anabaptists,	many others at a meeting in the woods; they were betrayed by a	→
1550					Govert**b**, Gillis**b**, Mariken (a 75 year old	false brother; van Overdam had written a letter to the lords of Ghent;	→
1550					woman)**b**, and Anneken**b**, burned alive	they were burned alive	→
1550					At Leyden, Willem**b**, Martigen**b**-Dieuwert-	At Limmick in Jueelick, T. van Haustelraed**b**,	→
1550					gen**b**, and Maritgen**b** confessing, tortured,	"very diligent with the talent that the Lord had committed to him,	→
1550					refusing to apostacize killed as heretics	to bring many to the knowledge of the truth, and to strengthen those	→
1550					At Remunde, of Guelder-land, T. van Lindt**b**,	who had received the truth, in the same"**b**, after severe contests,	→
1550					arrested for his evangelism, was tormented	was condemned to be burned alive	→

Bible colporteur M. Moreau**c** burned alive in Troyes (1550)

1550											Near Sittert, R. Ramaeckers[b] burned alive and burned alive in Borren, near Millen,	→
1550											At Wislen, G. van Kempen[b] burned alive. P. Palmen[b], burned alive. Eleven[b], then seven[b]	→
1550											At Antwerp, A. van Asselroye[b] burned alive. executed with sword in Millen and Borren	→
1550											At Bamberg, two young girls[b] put to death. Three[b] (incl one Jan) burned in Antwerp	→
1550											At Leeuwaerden, 15 year old J. Dosie[b] killed	→
1550								September 25, 1550 Decree of Charles V, especially against Anabaptists[b] (renewed thrice by his son, Philip II in 1556, 1560, and 1564), also cited in 1569 by William I, Prince of Orange, in defense of his adversaries				Another decree of Charles V to increase inquisition in the Netherlands, given on April 29th in Brussells[b] (particularly carried out through inquisitors in the cities of Brabant)	→
1550												→
1550											Anabaptist R. Dircks[b] examined by torture on July 9, was burned alive in Amsterdam on Aug 16	→
1551					C. Monier[c] slowly roasted over a fire in Lyon (see below)	18 year old T. de St. Paul[c] burned alive in Paris for quietly correcting someone for their vulgarities			Coverdale named Bishop of Exeter	J. Rogers named vicar of St. Sepulchre's and reader of St. Paul's	Gilot Vivier[c], his brother-in-law M. Lefevre[c], his father, J. Lefevre[c], and Gilot's wife,	→
1551	Anabaptist John Bair[b] of Lichtenfels, died in prison after 23 years in a dark dungeon of the tower of Bamberg				M. Secenat[c], a former priest, burned at the stake in Nimes						Hanon Lefevre[c], from Valenciennes (in the Low Lands) burned at the stake, Hanon was pregnant at her arrest, so she was	→

COLOR GUIDE: YELLOW=Roman Catholic areas; TAN=Bad years for Anabaptists; GOLD=Important events for Catholicism; ORANGE=Catholics "martyred"; RED=Evangelicals martyred; GRAY=Other martyred; Disclaimer: some dates may vary
PINK=Marriage issues; PURPLE=Crusades or massacres; TURQUOISE=Martyrology info; BLUE=Part Protestant areas; AQUA=U.S. Const; LT GREEN=Disputed areas; LIME=Bible issues; GREEN=Major dates. (Page 121)

Thomas P. Johnston
Geographic History
Page 122

Date	Germany-Austria-Scandinavia	Switzerland	France-Alsace	British Isles	Italy, Spain, Low Lands	
1551		Confession of "Anabaptist" **Jan the Old Clothes Buyer**[b] Antwerp, Brabant, 1551 Q. "What do you think of infant baptism?"	Edict of Chateaubriand (from the "Chambre Ardente") listed **46 articles** describing heresy	22 year old colporteur **J. Joery**[cr] and his young		kept in prison until she gave birth, then she was burned alive	→
1551		A. "I do not think it to be anything but a human institution" Q. "By what then will you prove or maintain your baptism?" A. "Mark 16" Q. "What are your views concerning the sacraments?"		**servant**[c] burned alive in Toulouse (Bibles around their necks)		**Michelle de Caignoncle**[c] was burned alive with **Gilot** and the others ↑	→
1551		A. "I have nothing to say of the sacraments of men, but the Supper, as Christ held it with His apostles, I approve and esteem; for I think that there are many who do not know what sacrament means." Q. "What do you think of the Roman church?"	**M. Claude Monier, d'Auvergne** "Claude Monier, an educated man, native of St. Amand of Talande, also of La Chaire, three leagues from Issoere in Auvergne [county]: after having been instructed for some time in the public schools of this town, and in			An Anabaptist **Smith**[b], arrested at Komen, Flanders, and beheaded in prison, as if he had recanted	→
1551		A. "Nothing, but I esteem the Christian church, which is the church of Christ." Q. "What do you hold concerning the host which the priest holds in his hand? Do you not believe that our Lord is in it with flesh and blood?"	Clermont, capital city of Auvergne, having been taught from his youth a special fear of God and the knowledge of His Holy Word, became hated and suspect by the haters of the same, so much so that he lost his charge as a teacher. So he left in the direction of Auvergne and other villages			Ghent, Flanders: Anabaptists **Gillis**[b] and **Elizabeth**[b] burned alive for heresy	→
1551		A. "No; for it is written, Acts 1, that He shall come again in like manner as He ascended into heaven." Q. "What do you think of the pope?" A. "That he is the antichrist." 1 Thess 2:3	around the same, publicly preaching the Word of God, up until the time that he was persecuted, and constrained to retire to the land of the Gospel [Switzerland], and the Reformed Church by the Word of God. After which he retired to Lausanne, city in the jurisdiction of the Lords of Bern, and			Ghent, Flanders: Anabaptists **Joris**[b], **Wouter**[b], **Grietgen**[b], and **Naentgen**[b] condemned, left in	→
1551		Q. "What do you think of the mass, ceremonies, and confession observed in the church?" A. "Nothing, since the tree from which they spring is good for nothing." Q. "Where were you baptized?"	studied there for some time. Since finding himself in Lyon, he had the charge of several children, who he instructed in the Holy Letters: so much so that in a little time he became known of several faithful, who rejoiced in his holy conversation: for he was gifted with a tender spirit, peaceable and			prison for another 8 months, finally executed by being hung over a fire and burned alive	→
1551		A. "My lords, if you know it, why do you yet ask me?" The bailiff then said, "I adjure you by your baptism, that you tell us where you were baptized?" Matt 26:63. A. "My baptism I hold to be good and right; but your adjuration I do not	meek, according to the testimony given him by several faithful witnesses, who were familiar with his good life, and the pure doctrine that he announced to each one who he was able to encounter there: as is also manifestly noted by the fruit of his life and [as] the true mark that follows			Ghent, Flanders: **Catharine**[b] was burned alive 8 days later	→
1551		regard." They then read to me the names and surnames of all that had been baptized with me and said, "Assuerus has confessed it to us." I then said, "It is true."	the said doctrine. For it soon came about, on a Sunday the fifth of July 1551, having been in the home of his friend to give him advice to hold himself away from the Provost [of the town] who had come to take him: after having guided the friend and done the action of a true Christian:			Antwerp, Brabant: **J. Segers**[b], his wife **Lijsken Dircks**[b], and **Big Henry**[b] arrested for heresy;	→
1551		Q. "Who baptized you?" A. "It does not behoove me to tell." Q. "We shall make you tell." A. "My flesh is before you; do with it as you please."	returning from his trip, there came upon him the Provost suspicious to take Monier, and brought him as a prisoner to the *Official* [prison], after which he was questioned on several things. Thus it would be that God would give him the grace that while being a prisoner he wrote part of the judicial acts			both men burned alive on Sept 2nd; Since **Lijsken** was pregnant, was placed in a bag and drowned in the Scheldt	→
1551			and interrogations held against him, we have here his letter containing his entire confession, in the strength to which it was put into writing for the faithful, as follows… [4 pages of folio type]"[c]			Antwerp, Brabant: **P. Bruynen**[b], **Jan, Pleunis**[b], and **Jan**[b] (the old clothes buyer), and **another brother**[b] Anabaptist **Willem**[b] a	→

Year	(Blue: Marriage/Protestant)	(Yellow: Roman Catholic)	(Lt Green: Bible issues)	(Red: Evangelicals martyred)	(Orange: Catholics martyred / Gold: Major events)
1551					cabinet maker in Weesz, of Cleves, beheaded in Cleves (one of his judges, **C. Meselaer** ↓, abstained)
1551					**C. Meselaer**[b] judge of **Willem** (above), resigned his office,
1551					became a brother, and died (unclear how), with **W. Rauens**[b]
1552	The Protestant **Maurice of Saxony** finally secured religious freedom in some German states by the **Treaty of Passau** (31 July 1552) s3	**Calvin** and **P. Viret** (pastor in Geneva) wrote to the Lausanne Five while they were in prison, as well as **D. Peloquin**; some letters describe the conversion of a thief in prison named **Jean Chambon** who later went to Geneva →	The Anglican *Book of Common Prayer* was revised, prescribing even more Protestant styles of worship	The "Five of Lyon"[r] **M. Alba**[c], **P. Escrivain**[c], **Bernard Seguin**[c], **C. Favre**[c], and **P. Navihère**[c] arrested on their third day in Lyon, imprisoned, judged guilty of heresy, strangled and burned at the stake; **P. Bergier**[c], **D. Peloquin**[c], former priest, returning to Geneva with his sister, degraded and burned alive at Ville-Franche; **H. Gravier**[c] martyred in Bourg-en-Bresse; **R. Poyet**[c] (illegitimate son of the Chancellor of France, **Guillaume Poyet**) burned at the stake in Anjou having signed the confession of **B. Seguin**, was strangled in Lyon	**G. de Hamelle**[c] burned at the stake in Tournay; **C. Volcart**[c], **Humbert**[c], **Philebert**[c], and **P. Roux**[c] were burned at the stake in Flanders; **G. da Milano** wrote of Fanino's martyrdom (*Passione de fanino martyr*); Young Englishman, **G. Gardiner**[cf], who took a consecrated hoste from the Cardinal and stepped on it (before the King), was tortured, then burned over a fire in Lisbon, Portugal; **Edward Seymour**[c], the Duke of Somerset beheaded
1552				In 1552, **King Henry II of France** established 28 Presidential [heresy] courts, there were and are no records of the resulting executions from these courts specifically set up to deal with heretics m7	
1552	An example of the torture of **Cornelliss** (→) "Saturday morning they came before eight o'clock, and took me to the torture chamber, where the executioner was. They then asked me whether I had not changed my mind, and would answer their questions. I began to admonish them. They said: 'We have not come here to be taught by you; but we ask you whether you will answer our questions.' But this I did not intend to do.		**Cornelliss** (↘) warned of the need for knowing as little as possible: "They then laid before me the letters I had sent them, and also the hymn; they readily saw that it was the same handwriting; but I did not confess it. I thought to myself: 'There is plenty of time yet for it; for I will have to tell		**Maria of Monjou**[b] imprisoned a year, tortured for 3 days to recant, went to her drowning singing
1552					In Guelich: **Barbel**,[b] drowned
1552	The executioner then stripped me, and bound my hands behind my back. There was a windlass there, and tying a block to my feet, they drew me up and left me hanging. While thus suspended they interrogated me,		them something anyway, when they torture me." For the matter concerned myself; hence I did not keep it secret, when I was tortured;		At Blankenberg: **W. of Bierck**,[b] **C. of Geistens**,[b] **C.** At Leyden: **Mariken**[b] and **Anneken**[b] put to death

COLOR GUIDE: YELLOW=Roman Catholic areas; TAN=Bad years for Anabaptists; GOLD=Important events for Catholicism; ORANGE=Catholics "martyred"; GRAY=Other martyred; Disclaimer: some dates may vary
PINK=Marriage issues; PURPLE=Crusades or massacres; TURQUOISE=Martyrology info; BLUE=Part Protestant areas; AQUA=U.S. Const; LIME=Bible issues; GREEN=Major dates. (Page 123)
RED=Evangelicals martyred; LT GREEN=Disputed areas;

Header note: Council of Trent Continued

Thomas P. Johnston — Geographic History — Page 124

Date	Germany-Austria-Scandinavia	Switzerland	France-Alsace	British Isles	Italy, Spain, Low Lands	
1552	but I did not answer. They then let me down, and the bailiff asked me where I had worked since I left Flanders. At Delft, I replied. Thereupon they asked me still other questions, and as I refused to answer them,				At Komen, Flanders: **W. van Robaeys**[b] tortured, killed	→
1552	they drew me up again, and untied the block. The executioner then placed a piece of wood or iron between my legs, which had been bound together, and stood on it. Being let down again, I was asked by the				At Amsterdam: six burned alive Aug 6: **L. Jans**,[b] **M. Hermans**,[b] At Leyden: **H. Dirks**, **D. Jans**, and **A. Corneliss**	→
1552	bailiff, whether I and six of my friends had not been in Leyden at a certain time, which he specified. I did not confess it. Again the executioner drew me up, they having blindfolded my eyes, and they took rods and				were sentenced to death, **Corneliss** was **P. Thymans**,[b] **R. Egberts**,[b] **H. Anthoniss**,[b] **C. Gerbrants**[b]	→
1552	scourged me. After I was let down the bailiff said: 'Tell it, or I shall tell you?' I would not accuse any one. They drew me up again, pulled my beard and hair, and beat and scourged my back; but as my eyes were				arrested for evangelizing the jailer	→
1552	blindfolded, I could not see who did it. They might have asked: 'Who smote you?' Luke 22:46. This continued until I had been beaten with seven or eight rods. When they let me down, and I did not answer for a long time,				In Ghent: **P. van Olman**[b] [or van **Werwijck**] put	→
1552	they, fearing that I should faint away, poured water over me, which they had also done while I was suspended. I sat down, and as I did not speak for a long time, the bailiff said: 'You will not tell it; I will tell you: you slept at				to death at the Castle of Kuhlenbergh: a lad, **Cornelis**,[b]	→
1552	**Stephen Claes**'."[b]				imprisoned for 3 years; finally burned alive	→
1553	[beginning with **N. Nail** became common in France to tie	Reformed Pastors **Calvin**, **Viret**, and **Farel** correspond with	**N. Nail**[Cr] arrested with Bibles from Geneva burned	**Cranmer** authored *42 Articles of the Church of England*	At Amsterdam (Jan 16): **H. Jans of**	→
1553	sticks in the mouth of the condemned so that they could	the Five of Lyon, **M. Dymonet**, **R. Lefevre**, and others while they	**M. Dymonet**[Cr] martyred for heresy in Lyon	**King Edward** died; **Queen Mary Tudor** I took the throne ↓ →	**Sollem**[b] burned alive, his property being	→
1553			**L. de Marsac**[C] and his cousin[C] and **E. Gravot**[C] burned at	**Jane Gray**[C] and her husband, **Guilford Dudley**[C],	Arrested at Diexmuyde, Flanders: **W. van Capelle**[b] put to death	→
1553	not speak to the crowd while being burned]	are imprisoned in Lyon; also seek the help of the Lords of Berne	the stake for heresy in Lyon	beheaded by **Queen Mary**		
1553			**G. Neel**[Cr], former Augustin monk, burned at the stake in Evreux	**J. Rogers** was placed on house arrest in London	At Leeuwaer-den, Friesland: two young maidens: the lame **Tijs**[b] confiscated for the benefit of the Emperor	→

1553	Knox in Frankfort for a short time	Execution of the Socinian **Servetus** (who had a price on his head from the Roman Catholic Inquisition) in Geneva	**S. Laloé**C martyred in Dijon, **J. Sylvestre**, was his executioner, converted as a result and moved to Geneva	**E. le Roy**C and **P. Denocheau**C executed in Chartres	**Coverdale** lost his post as Bishop of Exeter, so he went into exile to Denmark, where his brother-in-law was chaplain to the king	**J. Knox** went to Frankfurt, to pastor an English speaking church	At Amsterdam (Jan 16): **Felistis Jans**	and the bedridden **Beerentge**b were drowned	→
1553				**P. Serre**cr, former priest, burned at the stake in Toulouse			**of Vreden**,b Westfalia, burned alive	At Kortrijck: **J. Kindt**b burned	→
1553		Knox moved to Geneva to pastor the first English Puritan church	**D. Peloguin**C burned at the stake in Villefranche				At Bergen op Zoom, Brabant: arrested for not bowing to an image, **Simon the shopkeeper**b was burned alive	at the stake [his testimony is quite compelling]	→
1553								In Vuren, Flanders: struck an unnamed **man**b seven times and sawed off his head	→
1553							At Leeuwarden: **P. Witses**,b strangled at the stake		→
1553							Rome, 15 Sept 1553: a train of prisoners holding candles follow six Cardinals to the tribunal, all recant save two **Mollio**,w3 a Bolognese professor, and **Tisserano**w3; after a word from **Mollio**, where he threw down and extinguished his candle, both were immediately executed at Campo del Flor		→
1553									→
1553									→
1554 Protestant	**J. Crespin** shocked by the martyrdom of the **Lausanne Five**, and desirous that their deaths not be forgotten		**P. Panier**C, former member of parliament of Bourgogne, decapitated in Dole of Bourgogne	**G. Dalençon**cr, Bible colporteur, betrayed, martyred with a repentant dyer of cloth C in Montpelier	January 1554, **J. Rogers** sent in Newgate prison by **Bonner**, the new Bishop of London; he was there with **J. Hooper**,	**John Foxe** published a Latin Book of Martyrs, *"Commentarii Rerum in Ecclesia Gestarum. Liber*	**O. Cateline**C, converted in England, burned alive in his Hometown of Gand, Belgium	In Ghent, Flanders: **David**b and **Levina**b burned alive; David was also stabbed with a pitchfork	→
Martyrologies									

COLOR GUIDE: YELLOW=Roman Catholic areas; TAN=Bad years for Anabaptists; GOLD=Important events for Catholicism; ORANGE=Catholics "martyred"; RED=Evangelicals martyred; GRAY=Other martyred; PINK=Marriage issues; PURPLE= Crusades or massacres; TURQUOISE=Martyrology info; BLUE=Part Protestant areas; AQUA=U.S. Const; LT GREEN=Disputed areas; LIME=Bible issues; GREEN=Bible issues;

Disclaimer: some dates may vary (Page 125) Major dates.

Thomas P. Johnston — Geographic History — Page 126

Date	Germany-Austria-Scandinavia	Switzerland	France-Alsace	British Isles	Italy, Spain, Low Lands
begin to be written and widely published		began writing his *History of the True Witnesses to the Truth of the Gospel, Who with Their Blood Signed, from John Hus to the Present Time* (Geneva, 1554)	J. Filleul[C] and J. Leveillé[C] hung and burned alive in Paris for travelling to Geneva	*primus"* (Strasbourg: Rihel)	At Ghent, Flanders: **W. van Louvain**[b] put to death →
			R. Le Fevre[C] arrested in Lyons, burned at the stake in Paris	L. Saunders, J. Bradford, and others	T. Calbergue[C] burned alive in Tournay for owning a Geneva songbook, and for writing spiritual songs →
1554			P. de la Vau[C] burned alive in Nimes	J. Day published a martyrology of Lady Jane in London, "*An epistle of ladye Jane… Also another epistle to her sister, with the words she spake on the scaffold*"	Council of Trent Continued
1554			D. Le Vayr[C], former priest, from Normandy, colporteur of Geneva Bibles, raised from the fire three times before being burned alive in Rouen	As persecution intensified under Mary I, Puritan believers went underground; they were called "**Marian Separatists**" as they separated the Church of England while Mary was queen	J. Malo[C] executed in Mons
1554			F. Gamba[C] burned at the stake at Bresse in Lombardie	Knox fled to Geneva	
1554				Queen of England [Bloody] Mary I Tudor began executing Protestants (1555-1558) ↓	
1555		Four martyrologies published in Strasbourg: L. Rabus in German: *Historien der heyligen ausserwölten Gottes Zeügen…*; two in French by J. Crespin, *Receuil de plusieurs personnes* and *Histoire memorable de la persecution de Merindol et Cabrieres*, and J. Sleidan in Latin, *De statu religionis et republicae, Carolo Quinto Caesare Commentarii*	G. de Dongnon[C], former priest, burned at the stake in Limoges	Feb 4th in London J. Rogers[C], the first heretic burned alive under reign of Queen Mary, he was a former priest, was married, ordained in Wittenberg, and returned to England to preach the Gospel, became a professor of theology under Ridley (later burned Oct 16th); Bishop J. Hooper[C] burned in Gloucester; H. Gudaker[C], primate of Ireland poisoned; 5th Feb, Minister and Lawyer R. Taylor[C] thrown in the fire at Aldham Common; 8th Feb, L. Saunders[C], minister in London, burned at the stake in Coventry; 26th Feb, Bishop R. Ferror[C] burned at	27th March J. Lawrence[C], R. White[C], and W. Dighel[C] at Gloucester, W. Pygat[C] at Braintree, J. →
1555			The Chambery Five (J. Vernou[C], A. Laborie[C], J. Trigalet[C], G. Tauran[C], and B. Bataille[C]) at first sentenced to rowing for the King's ships, changed to beheading in Chambery,	Alcock[C] died of sickness in a London prison, his body was thrown on a manure pile 24th April,	Witcoq[C] beheaded in Mons Waldrue Carlier[C] buried alive in Mons for allowing Bible reading in her home; J. Porceau[C] martyred in Mons →
1555		More correspondence available between the		Pastor G. Marsh[C] burned at the stake at Westchester, and W. Flower[C] burned at Westminster for whistling during mass; 31st May, Minister J. Cardmaker[C] burned at the stake in	Paul IV gave special powers to Jesuits to make war on the disciples of Jesus (named after the 1326 so-called "Police of Jesus") →
1555					Portugal, called "**Police of Jesus**" →

1555				**Chambery Five**, John Calvin, Pierre Viret, and others included	Savoy, France	the stake at Carmarthen; 5th March, T. Thomkins[C] burned on hand prior to being burned at the stake in London, also T. Higby[C] at Horndon;	London with businessman J. Warren[C] **Feb-May 1555 English Martyrs** February: 5 ministers March: 8+2 persons April: 1+1 May: 1+1	→
1555				by Crespin →		T. Causton[C] burned at Raleigh; 15th W. Hunter[C] at Brentwood; 25th S. Knight[C] at Malden	In Antwerp, four put to death in the marketplace: Pieter[b] (with the lame foot), J. Droogh- schreerder,[b] H. Borduerwercker,[b] and F. Sweerdtveger[b]	→
1555				**Villegaignon** → asked the Geneva town	Vice Admiral of England, **Villegaignon**, set sail from Le	A convicted thief, **Toulee**, spoke against Rome and the Pope before his death, leading to a proclamation; in June 1555, the **Archbishop of Canterbury** published this proclamation:		→
1555				council for ministers of the Gospel; they sent P. Richier and	Havre, France, presumably in the hopes of establishing a	"Anyone not accepting the Holiness of the **Pope** was to be condemned as a heretic" (excommunication as defined by Aquinas [above] meant extirpation from the world by death)	Drowned in Scheldt (Antwerp), **Tanneken van der Leven**[b]	→
1555				G. Chartier who were accompanied by many from	Reformed colony in Brazil, with peace and tranquility for	Also martyred in July, J. Wade[C] burned in Dartford; D. Harman[C] in Lewes; J. Lander[C] in Oxford;	In Antwerp, put to death in marketplace: **Bartholomew**[b] (the potter)	→
1555				France, set sail from Honfleur, France	those who believe the Gospel from France ←	M. Bucer's[C] & P. Fagius'[C] bodies exhumed and burned as heretics in Cambridge, likewise the body of the wife of P. Martyr[C] at Oxford;	In Antwerp, put to death in the marketplace: **Rommeken**[b]	→
1555						9th June, T. Watts[C] at Chelmsford; 10th June, Count T. Hawkes[C] burned at the stake in Goggeshall for not wanting his son baptized in the method of the Papists; 11th June, N. Chamberlain[C], in Colchester, J. Simson[C] in Rochfort, and J. Erdley[C] at Rayleigh; 12th June,		→
1555						W. Butler[C], T. Osmond[C]; J. Bradford[C] and John Leaf[C] burned on a pile of wood in Smythfield near London; 11th July,	[Crespin wrote that in the first 2 years of Queen Mary's reign 800 Protestants (mainly leaders) were put to death]	→
1555						G. Ming[C], a minister of the Gospel, died in prison beforen martyrdom; 12th July, J. Bland[C], J. Francks[C], N. Scheterden[C], and	**June-July 1555 Engl Martyrs** June: 6 July: 12+1 died in prison	→
1555						H. Middleton[C] burned in Canterbury In August, G. Aileward[C] died in prison; J. Abs[C] burned Edmondsbury; J. Denleye[C] burned	6th of Sept burned in Canterbury, G. Bradbrige[C], J. Tuttye[C], A. Burward[C], G. Catner[C],	→
1555	Arrested in Bavaria, taken to Worms: publicly						In Dordrecht: placed in bag and drowned in Puttox Tower: **Digna Pieters**[b]	→

COLOR GUIDE: YELLOW=Roman Catholic areas; TAN=Bad years for Anabaptists; GOLD=Important events for Catholicism; ORANGE=Catholics "martyred"; RED=Evangelicals martyred; GRAY=Other martyred; Disclaimer: some dates may vary
PINK=Marriage issues; PURPLE= Crusades or massacres; TURQUOISE=Martyrology info; BLUE=Part Protestant areas; AQUA=U.S. Const; LT GREEN=Disputed areas; LIME=Bible issues; GREEN=Major dates. (Page 127)

Thomas P. Johnston — Geographic History — Page 128

Date	Germany-Austria-Scandinavia	Switzerland	France-Alsace	British Isles	Italy, Spain, Low Lands	
1555	beheaded Christian[b]			in Uxbridge; Elizabeth Warne[C] burned in Stadford; J. Neuman[C] burned in Safron; Six burned on the 13th Aug in Canterbury: R. Coker[C]	R. Steuter[C]; 11th James Leaf[C] died in prison in London, also were burned T. Hayward[C] and	In Rome: P. Algier[Cb] burned with oil, then burned to ashes [van Bracht dates his death at 1557]	→
1555				H. Lawrence[C], G. Hopper[C], G. Stere[C], and R. Wright[C], 14th of August, R. Citier[C] burned in Tautone; the 26th G. Tankerfield[C]	T. Gorway[C] at Litchfield; R. Smyth[C], G. Andrew[C], and G. Bing[C] died at the Tower of London ("Tower	B. LeBlas[C] burned at the stake in Tournay	→
1555			N. DuChesne[C] traveling from Lausanne to get	and G. Baumeford[C] in St. Albons, P. Patinghan[C] in Uxbridge, and R. Smyth[C] burned at Stanes; the 30th S. Harwood[C] and T. Fusse[C]	of Lollards"); 19th R. Glover[C] and C. Bungaye[C] burned at Coventry; 16th of Oct	Brothers F and N. Matthys[CC] Burned at the stake in Malines (Belgium)	→
1555			his wife, arrested in Gry for not lifting his hat before an	burned at Ware; the 31st J. Neuma[C] and J. Denleye[C] burned at Safronwalden and G. Harles[C] at Barnet; 2nd of Sept Rev.	J. Web[C], G. Painter[C] burned in Canterbury, Bishop of London N. Ridley[C] and bishop of	In Volewijk, near Amsterdam: six	→
1555			inquisitor, burned at the stake in Gry on October 8th	R. Samuel[C] burned in Ipswich; 3rd G. Alyn[C] at Walsingham T. Cosby[C] at Chetford, T. Cox[C] at Yexford	Worchester H. Latimer[C] burned at Oxford; also died in Oct, G. Wiseman[C] died in the Tower of	Brethren[b] arrested in a boat; all strangled at the stake and left 13 weeks in a frozen state	Council of Trent Continued
1555				Aug-Oct 1555 English Martyrs August: 14+1 died in prison September: 12 + 3 died in prison October: 2 bishops	London, J. Gorte[C] died in prison in Colchester		
1555							
1555			C. de la Canesiere[C], arrested in Lyon on his way to	J. Philpot[C], church doctor, burned at the stake in London;	T. Cramner[C], Archbishop of Canterbury, author of 42	Laurent[C] and J. Fasseau[C] beheaded at Mons, Belgium	Pope Paul IV published *Index librorum prohibitorum* further delineating prohibited Bibles and other books
1555			Geneva, burned at the stake in Lyon on Feb 1	five men burned in London on Jan 27th, Pastor T. Whittle[C], B.	Articles, accused of treason, burned at the stake in Oxford;		→
1555			Former priest, P. de Rousseau burned similarly in Angers	B. Green[C], T. Brown[C], J. Tudson[C], J. Went[C], with 2	five burned in Canterbury: J. Lomas[C], Anne Albright[C]	A. de Lopphen[C] burned over slow fire and	→

1555					women, Agnes (Isabelle) Foster[C], Jeanne Lashford[C]	J. Sole[C], Jeanne Painter[C], Agnes Snoth[C]: burned at Bury, J.	J. de Lespedarme[C] also martyred in Ath, Belgium	→
1555						Abbes[C]		→
1556	**Of the Ordinances and Decrees Made for All Times and for General Observance, and Proclaimed Everywhere, from the 25th of September 1550, and Renewed and Confirmed by His Royal Majesty in the**	Crespin published two more editions of			Two women burned in London: Anne Potten[C], and the wife[C] of Micheal the shoemaker		Loyola died in Rome	→
1556	**Year 1556** (decree of Philip II, King of Spain) "We likewise forbid all lay persons, and others, to converse or dispute concerning the holy Scriptures,	his martyrology, including Book 3	30th April François de Mauny, Archbishop of	J. Bertrand[C], martyred in Blois	Minister at Pambram J.	Martyrs: March 24, Salisbury: Spicer[C], Maundrelle[C], Corbeley[C]: April 2, Cambridge: minister J. Hoillarde[C]; Rochester: Hirtpoole[C], and a widow Jeanne Beches[C]; April 10, in London:	R. Oguier[C] and his son Bauchedon[C] burned at the	→
1556	whether openly or secretly, especially in doubtful and difficult matters; or to teach, expound or interpret the holy Scriptures to others, unless they [who do so] be theologians and versed in divinity and spiritual law, and	The Ministers from Geneva and the boats, arriving in Brazil,	Bordeaux, officially prohibited the singing of the	Hullier[C] burned in Cambridge	2 ministers, G. Tymmes[C], R. Drakes[C], G. Ambroise[C], J. Cavel[C], T. Spurge[C], R. Spurge[C]; April 28, in Golchester: minister C. Lyster[C]; J. Mase[C], R. Nichol[C], J. Spencer[C], J. Hamon[C],	stake in Lisle, Flanders, eight days later his wife[C] and other	→
1556	approved by some notable university, or others authorized thereto by the ordinary [Bishop] of the place; be it well understood, however, that this is not to be regarded as relating to those who simply and exclusively	after much difficulty, were well received by Villegaignon;	Psalms at home, church, or in the streets, nor sale or owning of	Arnaud Monier[C] and Jean de	Former tailor turned travel-	S. Joyne[C]: May 5, in Glochester: 2 blind men, Thomas[C] and J. Uprise[C]; Croker[C] and the lame and aged H. Lauerok[C]; May 16, in London: a widow Catherine Hut[C], with two girls, Jean Horne[C] and	son, Martin[C], were burned at the stake	
1556	converse together on the aforesaid holy Scriptures, adducing thereto the expositions of the holy and approved doctors; but to those who, in order to seduce others, or to teach and instruct them in that which is	who asked the ministers to establish police and church order	Psalms or New Testaments in French[C]	Cazes[C] condemned to be	ling evangelist George	Elizabeth Thaeuel[C]: May 19 in Beccles: E. Polus[C], J. Denny[C], and a woman named Spencer[C]; May 31 in London: G. Leache[C] (died in prison); June 1 in Lewes: T. Harland[C], J. Osewarde[C], T. Rede[C],	Colporteur B. Hector[C], strangled and burned in	Council of Trent Continued
1556	forbidden, maintain and teach, contrary to the ordinances of our mother, the holy church, evil and false propositions and doctrines, which are notoriously considered heretics; or to preach, defend, allege or	according to the custom of Geneva		Priest J. Casabone[C], from Agenois,	Eagles[C], partially strangled, cut	T. Abington[C], and 2 preachers T. Hoode[C], T. Mylles[C]; June 23, in London: minister G. Aheral[C]; then June 25, J. Clement[C] + 2[C] who died in prison; June 27, in Alchester: a servant	Thurin, Italy (or 1555)m2	
1556	maintain, openly or secretly, any doctrines of the aforementioned authors. "On pain, that if any be found to have acted contrary to any of the above stated points, they shall be punished			arrested and burned at the stake for not teaching	into fourths in Cloches	(Lyon)[C]; in Stradforde: H. Adlington[C], R. Jacson[C], G. Holiwel[C], T. Bower[C], L. Parmen[C], L. Coyxe[C], H. Wie[C], J. Dorefal[C], J. Rothe[C], E. Hurst[C], G. Searles[C], Elizabeth Peper[C] and Agnes George[C];	In Beverwijk: tied to a ladder and drooped in the fire.	

COLOR GUIDE: YELLOW=Roman Catholic areas; TAN=Bad years for Anabaptists; GOLD=Important events for Catholicism; ORANGE=Catholics "martyred"; RED=Evangelicals martyred; GRAY=Other martyred; Disclaimer: some dates may vary
PINK=Marriage issues; PURPLE=Crusades or massacres; TURQUOISE=Martyrology info; BLUE=Part Protestant areas; AQUA=U.S. Const; LT GREEN=Disputed areas; LIME=Bible issues; GREEN=Major dates. (Page 129)

Thomas P. Johnston Geographic History Page 130

Date	Germany-Austria-Scandinavia	Switzerland	France-Alsace	British Isles	Italy, Spain, Low Lands	
1556	as seditious persons, and disturbers of our realm and the common peace, and be executed as such: "Namely, the men with the sword, and the women buried alive; that is, if they will not maintain or defend		according to the Church	-ter, head put on a stake	in London died in prison: T. Paret^c and M. Hunt^c; June 29 in Edmond-Burye: Spurdane^c, Fortune^c, and another^c July 1, in London: J. Carels^c died in prison; July 16, in Nuberie:	Augustine^b (the Baker)	→
1556	their errors; but if they persist in their errors, opinions, or heresies, they are to be executed with fire; and in every case all their property is declared confiscated, and forfeited to our benefit.				J. Guyne^c, Asken^c, and J. Palmer^c: July 18, in Grenestade: T. Dingat^c, J. Forman^c, mother Trie^c; Aug 1 in Darbie: a blind woman^c; Sept in Bristau: a weaver^c; Sept 24, in Amesfield: J. Hart^c, T.	In Flanders: three women burned alive: Francijntgen,^b	→
1556	"And as regards what we had ordained in our previous decrees and our last ordinances, that from the day they had acted contrary thereto, or had fallen into the aforesaid errors, they should be disqualified from				Rauendale^c, a shoemaker^c, a leathersmith^c, N. Holden^c; Sept 25, in Bristau: young man^c; in Newent, J. Horne^c and a woman^c; a the Canterbury castle: died of hunger: J. Clarke^c,	Grietgen,^b and Maeyken Doornaerts ^b	→
1556	disposing of property, and that all alienations, gifts, cessions, sales, conveyances, transfers, testaments, or last wills, made and executed by them from said day on, should be null, invalid and void.				D. Chettenden^c, G. Foster^c, and the wife of Polkins^c; early Oct in Northhampton: a shoemaker^c: Oct 18 at Canterbury castle: three	In Antwerp: publicly executed: J. de Kudse^b	→
1556	"Again (page 168): Since many, from our aforesaid countries, suspected of heresy, especially of the sect of the Anabaptists, change their place of abode, to infect the simple in places where their character is not known;				prisonners^c died	In Nimeguen: straneld and burned alive: G. Hasepoot^b	→
1556	we, in order to guard against this, will, ordain, and decree, that none of the inhabitants of our aforesaid Netherlands, of whatever state, quality or condition he be, shall be admitted or received into any city or village,					In Antwerp: publicly executed: C. Abraham^b	→
1556	of said countries, there to live, except he brings with him a certificate from the parish priest of the place where he last resided."					At Ghent: publicly executed: C. de Praet^b	→
1556	"Which certificate he shall be obliged to show and						→
1556	deliver into the hands of the principal officer of the city or village where he intends to live; on pain that those who do not bring such certificates shall not be admitted there to live."^b						→
	Personal Evangelism Methodology of Philbert Hamelin					
1557	"Many faithful spoke of him, how when he went along in the country, often he would spy out and find the field	In Brazil, Villegaignon turned on the	P. Hamelin^{cr}, fomer priest, converted at Saintes, France,	Burned at the stake in Dijon: A. Sepharon^c, P. Cene^c, Jacques,		In Bruges, Flanders: C. Conick^c (Le Roy) burned	Geneva mission trip to Sicily suffered 6-12 →
1557	workers at the hour of their break, as they are accustomed to do, at the foot of a tree, or in the shade of a haystack. There he would feign like he was resting with them, taking the opportunity by little methods and	Geneva ministers on the issue of transubstantiation, siding with a	imprisoned (in 1546), escaped death by denouncing, for	N. du Rousseau^c; N. Sartoire^c burned alive in		In Mons: A. Emphlitius^c (Merula) burned alive	martyrs^f every three years →

1557	easy speech, to teach them to fear God, and to pray both before and after the break, inasmuch as it was him [the Lord] who gave them all things for the love of His Son Jesus Christ. And after that, he would ask the poor				Cointac, a Sorbonne graduate, ended in some Geneva	12 years established printing press in Geneva, was	Chambery; midnight riot against a Protestant		In Moerkerke: A. Dierick[C] martyred	At Antwerp: Janneken Walraven[b] was burned alive	→
1557	peasants if they would like it if he prayed to God on their behalf. Some took great pleasure in this, and were edified, others were astonished, hearing things that they were not accustomed to hearing. Not a few would run				martyrs in Brazil →	married with children, then became colporteur, and	gathering on St James street, Paris: **one person Trampled**[r], 100-		At Haarlem (26 Apr): J. Simons[b] and C. Dirks[b]	Burned in Turin, J. Vavaillem2; burned in Val	Council of Trent Continued
1557	after him with hostile intent [Fr. "aucuns luy couroyent-sus"], because he would show them that they were on the way to damnation, if they did not believe in the Gospel. When he received their curses and outrage, he				**English Geneva NT** printed, a Bible divided into	was strangled (trumpets blaring) and burned in	120 arrested, leading to the death of some in jail, and the		strangled and burned	d'Oste, N. Sartoris m2	
1557	often had this warning in his mouth, My friends, you do not now know what you are doing, but one day your will understand, and I pray God to do such a grace on your behalf[c]				verses for the first time →	Bordeaux	burning of others the next year →	**English Geneva New Testament published in Geneva**		At Antwerp: M. Zaeywever,[b] J. Oudkleer-	
1557										kooper,[b] W. Droog- scheerder,[b] and V.[b] and	van Guelders,[b] Pieter[b] (the Miller), J. van Yperes,[b] and Maerten[b] (the	→
1557						A meeting of 50 [Mennonite] Anabaptist bishops met in Strasbourg to discuss "the ban"m				P.[b] de Backer publicly executed	Walloon) beheaded	→
1557											At Antwerp: Margriete,[b] wife of Jeronymus, Klaerken[b] and Janneken[b] of Dexteleer all drowned	→
1558			See → [Romyen would either be burned alive, or if he	in Cologne: Confession of the Anabaptist T. van Imbroeck[b]	Frances Civaux,[f] martyred in Dijon;	Arrested in Paris, G. Tardif[c], J. Caillou[c], and N. de Jenville[c].	Last martyrs under Queen Mary: deacon C. Simson[c], and shoemakers C. Devenysh[c] and H. Foxe[c], in Huntington, Lawton[c].			in Thurin [Italy]: G. Varagle[c]	→
1558			recanted strangled (then burned); they also announced	At Cologne (5 Mar): T. van Imbroeck[b] beheaded	B. Romyen[c] betrayed, body dislocated, then burned over a	burned at the stake in their hometowns; N. Clinet[cr]	dead in London prison: J. Mainerd[c], J. Harrison[c], Daye[c], and Agnes George[c]; in Norwich, R. Harris, J. Daws, the wives of			burned alive in Anvers: J. du Champ[c] and an	martyrs[c] (J. du Bordel[c], M. Vermeil[c], P. Bourdon[c]) from	→
1558			his death asking all good Christians to bring wood to the		fire in Marseille; G. Guerin[cr] martyred in Paris, recanted,	T. Gravelle[cr], and Philippe de Luns[f] (Gravelle)[c]	George[c] and three[c], dead in London prison, T. Tyler[c] and M. Wethers[c], executed were: H. Pond[c], M. Rycarbie[c],			Anabaptist[c] executed In Brussels:	in Brazil: news came of five	Geneva mission team

COLOR GUIDE: YELLOW=Roman Catholic areas; TAN=Bad years for Anabaptists; GOLD=Important events for Catholicism; ORANGE=Catholics "martyred"; RED=Evangelicals martyred; GRAY=Other martyred; Disclaimer: some dates may vary
PINK=Marriage issues; PURPLE=Crusades or massacres; TURQUOISE=Martyrology info; BLUE=Part Protestant areas; AQUA=U.S. Const; LIME=Bible issues; GREEN=Disputed areas; LT GREEN=Disputed areas; GREEN=Major dates.

(Page 131)

Thomas P. Johnston
Geographic History
Page 132

Date	Germany-Austria-Scandinavia	Switzerland	France-Alsace	British Isles	Italy, Spain, Low Lands	
1558			town marketplace in Marseille to burn a Lutheran]C then came to his senses, the crowd kindled the fire for him	J. Holidaie C, J. Flond C, R. Lavonder C, R. Holland C, and T. Sowthan C; in Norwich: T. Withed C; in Brainsford: J. Slade C	G. Verdickt C martyred	K. Schumaker, arrested, imprisoned, released b	→
1558			martyred in Paris; 5 or 6 days later martyred in Paris: N. le Cene C and P. Gabart C; also martyred in Paris, two students (tortured by water and fire): F. Rebezies Cr and F. Danville Cr; died of torture in	Pikes C + 3 others C; in Winchester: Bambridge C	In Rotterdam: 5 sentenced (Annetgen Antheunis, J. Hendricks, Stijntgen Jan, E. Nouts, P. van Eynoven), the failed execution of J. Hendricks led to a riot, in which all the prisoners were freed b	→
1558			seeing the martyrdom of Rebezies and Danville (→).	Mary Tudor died Nov 1558, two months after her father-in-law, emperor Charles V; the same week as Mary died, so did the Cardinal and Papal Legate		→
1558			Paris prison: R. du Seau C and J. Almaric C almost equivocated, he was burned alive in Paris	Reginald Pole (who had received absolution from the Pope for taking part in the Anglican church, and had persecuted many)	In Brussels: G. Jaspers b put to death	→
1558					At Kortrijck, Flanders: W. van Haverbeke b	At Kortrijck, Flanders: A. van Tomme b (the singer) burned	→
1558					At Kortrijck, Flanders: D. Verkampt b burned alive	At Kortrijck, Flanders: M. de Ledersnijder b burned alive	→
1558					At Antwerp: J. de Meiselaer b brought to the marketplace with a gag, put to death	At Antwerp: L. de Wever b beheaded in prison	→
1558					At Antwerp: F. Tiban b and Little Dirk b beheaded in prison	At Antwerp: H. Leeverkooper, b and A. b and D. b de Schilder beheaded	→
1558					At Gravenhage, Holland: W. Dirks, b M. Schoenmaecker, b and A. Pieters b put to death	At Honschoten, Flanders: W. van Honschoten b put to death and burned	→
1558						In Bruges: J. de Swarte, b H. van den Broecke, b and others b put to death	→

Year									
1558								At Antwerp: **H. van Duytsch**[b] beheaded in prison	At Antwerp: **S. Hendricks**,[b] **H. de Smit**,[b] **H. van Burculo**,[b] **P. in de Vettewarije**,[b] **A.**,[b] and **G.**,[b] **Passementwerker** publicly executed →
1558								At Antwerp: four sisters from Aix-la-Chapelle: **Grietgen**,[b] **Tanneken**,[b] **Lijntgen**,[b] and **Stijntgen**[b] were tied	At Antwerp: **Janneken**[b] and **Noel**[b] sentenced to death by drowning →
1558								crooked and drowned	At Dortrecht: **J. Wippe**[b] (Joosten's son), former →
1558							"He [Joris Wippe →] wrote several letters in prison, three of which have come into our possession.		burgomaster, drowned in a cask (of his letters ←) →
1558							He doubtless would have written more; but great watchfulness was exercised that he should		At Doornick: **A. van Hee**,[b] **J. Meeuwens**,[b] and **W.**,[b] **G.**,[b] and **E.**,[b] →
1558							have no ink, so that he wrote his last letter (to his children) with mulberry juice"[b]		**de Hoedemaeker**,[b] and **L. Doornick**[b] taken to a forest in Hainault and burned →
1558									At Winnick: **G. of Nonenberg**[b] and **P. Kramer**[b] beheaded standing →
1558									At Aix-la-Chapelle: **H. Smit**,[b] **H. Adams**,[b] **H. Beck**,[b] **M. Smit**,[b] **D.** In Leeuwarden: **J. d'Auchy** arrested and imprisoned ↓ →
1558									**Snijder**,[b] and **Seven**[b] others: publicly executed
1559			**Calvin** wrote the final edition of his *Institutes*	**J. Barbeville**[Cr] burned alive in a large fire in Paris; on the	**N. Ballon**[C], Bible colporteur, brought to the place of his	Elizabeth I became Queen of England; she was sympathetic to Protestantism; she enacted the "Elizabethan			"**Paul IV** ordered among the *Biblia prohibita* (prohibited books) a whole series of Latin Bibles. He added that all Bibles in the vulgar tongue could not be printed nor kept without permission of the Holy Office. This was in practicality a prohibition of reading the Bible in the vulgar tongue" (quoted from →
1559			An **Academy** is founded in	same day a thief was also hung in Paris; **P. Chevet**[C],	martyrdom with a ball in his mouth, strangled, then burned in Paris;	Settlement", comprising of an "Act of Supremacy" and an "Act of Uniformity"			→

COLOR GUIDE: YELLOW=Roman Catholic areas; TAN=Bad years for Anabaptists; GOLD=Important events for Catholicism; ORANGE=Catholics "martyred"; RED=Evangelicals martyred; GRAY=Other martyred; Disclaimer: some dates may vary PINK=Marriage issues; PURPLE=Crusades or massacres; TURQUOISE=Martyrology=Martyrology info; BLUE=Part Protestant areas; AQUA=U.S. Const; LT GREEN=Disputed areas; LIME=Bible issues; GREEN=Major dates. (Page 133)

Thomas P. Johnston • Geographic History • Page 134

Date	Germany-Austria-Scandinavia	Switzerland	France-Alsace	British Isles	Italy, Spain, Low Lands	→
1559		Geneva for the training of pastorsb4	more than 60 years old, invited to share the Gospel to a		*Dictionnaire de Théologie Catholique*, 15:738, col 2)s	→
1559		Bible printer, **R. Estienne**, died in the Fall 1959l3	Franciscan did so, was apprehended, cruelly murdered	Knox returned to Scotland from Geneva, leading to a war with **Mary of Guise** over religion in Scotland	May 1559, under **Ferdinand and Elizabeth**, in Valdolit, Spain, a specially built gallery (for royalty), stage, and grandstands	In Brussels: **A. Verdickt**C, brother of **G. Verdickt**	→
1559			the reign of **Francis II**; **Marguerite Le Riche**C,		for the judgment on 30 Lutheran heretics: the Augustinian doctor **F. de Cacalla**C, two of his brothers, a priest **F. de Bivero**C	above, was also taken and burned at the stake	→
1559			in Paris; **M. Marie**C, Bible colporteur from Geneva, hung		(iron in his mouth) and **J. de Bivero**C (to perpetual prison), two of his sisters **Blanche**C and **Constance**C, and the bones of	In Brussels: **B. le Hev**C quietly decapitated to avoid suspicion	→
1559			over a fire and burned in Paris; likewise a young carpenterC; in Sens; **P. Milet**C	Coverdale returned to England from Denmark	his mother, priest **A. Perez**C; Also **D. P. Sarmiento**C, his wife, **Mencia de Figueroa**C, **D. L. de Roxas**C,	**Marcgrave** (of Anvers) passed Law to catch those	→
1559			Bibles burned with him; colporteur **A. Daussi**C,	**W. Allen** left England for Douais, France, to establish an English school for training Catholic Priestss3 ↙	**Anne Henriques**C, **C. del Campo**C, **C. de Padilla**C, **A. de Huezuelo**C (iron in his mouth), **Catherine Romain**C,	who assembled unlawfully, with a financial reward	→
1559	U.S. Constitution assures freedom of peaceable assembly		following torture to extract information on collaborators, burned alive in Clermont		**F. Errem**C, **Catherine Ortega**C, **Isabella de Strada**C, **Jeanne Velasques**C, an ironworkerC, [a Portuguese	in Anvers: **Adrian**C, betrayed by his father, and **Henry**C were burned alive	→
1559			**M. Rousseau**C, **G. Le Court**C, and		Jew] **C. Vaes**C, **Jeanne de Sylva**C [wife of de Bivero above],	In Anvers: **C. Halewyn**C and **H. Janssen**C	→
1559			**P. Parmentier**C burned alive for having a Prayer meeting in Paris;		**Leonoro de Lisveros**C [wife of Huezuelo above], **Marina de Sajavedra**C,	strangled, half	→
1559			**J. Ysabeau**C burned alive in Tours		**A. Coiffier**C martyr in Danmartin; bookseller	**D. Quadra**C, **Marie de Rojas**C, **A. Dominique**C, [Englishman] burned, left on a wheel as a trophy to Marcgrave's brutality	→

Year	(Yellow)	(Blue)	(Purple/Blue/Green)	(Orange/Red)	→
1559	Part of **Jacques d'Auchy's** Confession: "I also confess that the higher powers are ordained of God, for the punishment of the evil, and the protection of the good; for they bear not the sword in vain; to which powers the Scriptures command us to be subject, and instruct us to pray for them, in order that, as Paul says, we may lead a peaceable and quiet life. Paul also calls the power a minister of God. Therefore since he is a minister of God, I would pray him that he would be pleased to be merciful to me, even as God is merciful. I hereby disclaim all fellowship with those who would resist the power with the sword and violence, which I regard as the doctrine of devils. Wisd 6:3; 1 Pet 2:13; Rom 13:1, 4; 1 Tim 2:2."[b]			alive (A. Huezuelo), 13 condemned to be strangled then burned, the rest to do perpetual penance in prison; 37 others	→
1559			The **Cardinal of Loraine**, the **Duke of Guise**, and the **Duke of Nemours**, conspired to keep the newly named **Huguenots** from appealing their case to the King; the **Huguenot** leaders were massacred	**J. Judet**[C] burned alive in Paris; **T. Moutarde**[C] burned alive in Valenciennes; **A. de Richieud**[C] beat to death and disemboweled in Draguignan.	In Leeuwarden: **J. d'Auchy**[b] was betrayed, imprisoned for 10 weeks before his first examination, examined over and over and over again, finally secretly killed in the night	→
1559			Death of **King Francois II** allowed some peace for Reformed Churches in France, as the Parliament of France called for an end to persecution until the determination of a Council on the issue[C]	The second "event" under Ferdinand and Elizabeth: from the church in Seville: **J. P. de Leon**[C] burned alive; **J. Gonzalue**[C] strangled and and burned alive with 5 women: **Isabel de Vaenia**[C], **Maria de Viroes**[C], **Cornelia**[C], **Marie de Bohorches**[C], and her sister **Joanne**[C], **Julien Hernandes**[C], **J. de Leon**[C], and escaped monk **Jean Hernandes**[C] (having been in Frankfort and Geneva); **Francisca de Chaves**[C] burned alive, medical doctor **C. de Losada**[C], **C. de Arellanio**[C]; herein Crespin had no further information on the hundreds imprisoned and condemned by these masters of inquisition, fear, and repression	In Leeuwarden: **Claesken**[b] and her **husband**[b] drowned, along with **Jacques d'Auchy** (above)	→
1559			**W. Allen** established an English school to train Catholic priests in Douais; this school had to move to Rheims in 1578, and became the center for the English Catholic **Douais-Rheims** translation of the Bible, produced to refute the many "false translations" found in the Protestant translations	At Kortrijck, Flanders: **J. de Groot**[b] and **M. van Halewijn**[b] put to death	→
1559				At Maestricht: a widow, **Trijnken Keuts**[b] was burned alive with a gag	→
1559	At Saltzburg: **W. Mair**[b] and **W. Hueber**[b] executed by sword and burned			In Jortrijck, Flanders: **K. van Tiegem**[b] burned by fire	→
1559				At Geervliet, S. Holland: **J. Jans Brant**[b] placed in a sack, stabbed, and dropped into a river	→

COLOR GUIDE: YELLOW=Roman Catholic areas; GOLD=Important events for Catholicism; ORANGE=Catholics "martyred"; RED=Evangelicals martyred; GRAY=Other martyred; Disclaimer: some dates may vary
PINK=Marriage issues; PURPLE= Crusades or massacres; TURQUOISE=Martyrology info; BLUE=Part Protestant areas; AQUA=U.S. Const; LT GREEN=Disputed areas; LIME=Bible issues; GREEN=Major dates. (Page 135)

Thomas P. Johnston — Page 136

Geographic History

Date	Germany-Austria-Scandinavia	Switzerland	France-Alsace	British Isles	Italy, Spain, Low Lands	
1559					At Antwerp: three women: **Fransken Vroevrouwe**,b **Naentgen Leerverkoopster**,b and **Pluentgen van der Goes**b drowned in a vat in the prison	At Antwerp: three women: **Betgen**,b **Neelken**,b and **Mariken**b **Franss** drowned	→
1559					At Antwerp: **A. Pan**b put to death by the sword; his **wife**b drowned after childbirth		→
1559					At Antwerp: six women: **Maeyken Kats**,b **Magdaleentken**,b **Aechtken**,b old **Maeyken**,b **Grietgen Bonaventuers**,b and **Maeyken de Korte**b: three drowned by night, the other drowned, and two put to death by the sword	At Ghent, Flanders: **H. de Vette**,b **P. Coerten**,b **K.**b and **Proentgen**b **Tanckreet**, **J. Spillebout**,b **A. Tanckreet**,b **Maeyken Floris**,b **A. van Cassel**,b **H.**b and **M.**b **de Smit**, **H.**b and **Maritgen**b **de Vette**, and **Tanneken de S.** Theseb ten of them were burned in a hut of straw, two pregnant women were beheaded after giving birth	→
1559					At Antwerp: **J. Bernaerts**b put to death		→
1559					At Maestricht: **J. Bosch**b (aka. **J. Bergh** or **J. Durps**) burned in a hut erected on a scaffold	At Waesten, Flanders: **H. Vermeersch** (aka. **H. van Maes**) executed	→
1559					At Antwerp (Nov 9): **A. Langeduib**,b **M. Pottebacker**b, **L. van der Leyen**b beheaded in prison		→

Year							
1560	Axiom 3 and 4 of the Jesuits, published in Cologne (1560)c: "3. That it is not-at-all for the political Magistrates to mix themselves with or gain knowledge of the doctrine that is proposed to the people: but that this solicitude is delegated to the priests. That upon issues of religion, the only duty of the Magistrates is, to execute the rebellious and contradictory of the Roman seat. "4. In confering the doctrine of the Church with the rules of the word of God, whoever finds them in discord, contradicts those of the Pope, ought to be exterminated from the midst of men, either by sword or by fire, so that peace and tranquility may be conserved. If so had occurred 40 years ago in the location of Luther and his sectarians, it would have been seen for a long time that there would have been a restitution of Ecclesiastical repose so desired."	Crespin published a Latin version of his martyrology			In Flanders, C. de Quekerec, J. Dienssartc, and Jeanne de Salomezc strangled, partially burned, cut into thirds and buried; J. Herwinc converted in London, arrested and burned alive in Flanders; Jean de Cruesc turned over to Inquisitor of Flanders, Renay, partially strangled and burned in Belle, buried by friends	In Rome, Italy, a pastor trained in and a Geneva Bourgeois, J. L. Pascalc, detained, tortured, found guilty of Lutheranism, strangled while preaching before his death, then burned before Pope Pius IV and a number of Cardinals	→
1560		English Geneva Bible completed and published		English Geneva Bible published			→
1560			Mary of Guise died (July)				→
1560			Knox drew up a Summary of Doctrine which was accepted by Parliament				→
1560						Decree of Pius IV "Desiring now to be able to for the greater salvation of those for whom this request was made, the council decreed that the entire affair be deferred to our very Holy Father, as he defers it by the present decree, according to his singular prudence, he himself will decide what he judges to be [both] useful for the Christian States and salvific for those who request the use of the chalice" (DS1760)	→
1560	At Neumarkt, Bavaria: N. Felbingerb (or Schlooser) and J. Leytnerb both beheaded						→
1560	Arrested near Rosenhaus, Bavaria, and taken to Innsbruck: J.				In Antwerp (?): A. Claes,b J. Tieleman,b and H. de Backerb drowned in a tub	In Antwerp: three women: Deaf Betgen,b Betgenb (of Ghent), and Lijsken Smitsb drowned in a tub	→
1560	Korbmacher,b G. Raeck,b and Eustace Kuterb all three beheaded		Joris' Reply to the Bailiff "A. D. 1560 there were brought before the court at Antwerp two pious Christians, named Joris and Joachim. As they were standing as sheep for the slaughter before the lords, the bailiff		At Antwerp: L. Plovier,b and Jennekenb and Maeykenb (of Aix-la-Chapelle) drowned		At Antwerp: W. de Kleermaeckerb strangled and burnt	→

COLOR GUIDE: YELLOW=Roman Catholic areas; TAN=Bad years for Anabaptists; GOLD=Important events for Catholicism; ORANGE=Catholics "martyred"; RED=Evangelicals martyred; GRAY=Other martyred; Disclaimer: some dates may vary
PINK=Marriage issues; PURPLE=Crusades or massacres; TURQUOISE=Martyrology info; BLUE=Part Protestant areas; AQUA=U.S. Const; LT GREEN=Disputed areas; LIME=Bible issues; GREEN=Major dates. (Page 137)

Thomas P. Johnston — Geographic History — Page 138

Date	Germany-Austria-Scandinavia	Switzerland	France-Alsace	British Isles	Italy, Spain, Low Lands	
1560					At Antwerp: **Joris**[b] and **Joachim**[b] killed by public burning	At Veer, Zealand: **J. Joosten**[b] gifted singer, severely tortured, burned in a hut of straw	→
1560			asked **Joris** whether he was rebaptized. He replied: "I am baptized according to the doctrine of Christ, as He commanded His apostles, saying: "Go, and preach to all nations. He that is believeth and is baptized, shall be saved." Matt 28:19; Mark 16:16. Hence they must first be taught and believe, and then be baptized in the name of the Father, the Son, and the Holy Ghost.""[b]		At Ghent: **Soetgen van den Houte**[b] and **Martha**[b] put to death		→
1560					At Ypres, Flanders: **L. van de Walle**[b] and **A. Schoonvelt**[b] publicly strangled and burned, as was **Kalleken Strings**[b]; **Maeyken Kocx**[b] publicly strangled and burned after she bore her child	At Honscote, Flanders: **Koolaert**[b] (the cooper) burned alive in Wijnoxberge	→
1560						At Antwerp: **J. Verbeeck**,[b] pastor, burned alive in a hut of hay	→
1560							→
1561	**Menno Simons** died of natural causes (!) in Wustenfelde, Holstein, Germany[m]	Crespin added Book 4 to his French martyrology			**J. de Lo**[c] burned alive in L'Isle; 27 year old **J. de Boschere**[c] secretly drowned and stabbed	**Mathurin**[c] and his wife[c], **J. de Carquignan**[c] from the valley of Luceme (Piedmont) burned alive	Council of Trent Continued
1561	**Orvel**[b], **Jan**[b], and **Pleunis**[b] apprehended in Cologne; questioned under torture; drowned in the Rhine	**Nicolas Colladon**, secretary for the Company of Pastors		**Queen Mary Stuart** arrived in Scotland and opposed reforms of Knox	in Anvers; **J. Keyser**[c] drowned and hung on a post, then buried; **P. Annood**[c] and **D.**		
1561	**J. Schut**[b] arrested in Vreden, Westphalia; executed by the sword	**Company of Pastors** (Geneva-trained Reformed student-pastors who travelled into France) reported that in 1561, 151 pastors were sent into France to evangelize, plant, and pastor	**Charles IX** called an Assembly of the royal court, cardinals and theologians of the Roman church (40-50 in all), with 12 Reformed pastors and 20 delegates (de Bèze as their spokesman) "to bring peace and unity in the kingdom"[c]		**Galland**[c] arrested on trip to England, tortured, burned, strangled, bodies placed on display on tall stakes in Dunkirk; **J. des Buissons**[c] decapitated in prison	Some **Waldenses** converted to Rome, others fled, the remainder were severely persecuted; e.g. Pastor Jean roasted	
1561			**Reformed pastor/ evangelist** went to Vaissy, Burgundy (near birthplace of Queen Mary) to plant a church, Oct 12th, which grew to 500-600 within a week, and needed to meet outside; 900 took communion on Dec 25th ↙				→
1561					at night; further persecution in L'Isle: **P. le Petit**[c], burned alive; **S. Guilmin**[c] and	in a fire; **60 died**; they sought to defend themselves; the **Duke of Savoy**	→

Year			
1561		Reformed churchesb4	sent in 4-5,000 troops to bring them under subjection of	→
1561			J. Denisᶜ (22 years old), burned alive; **S. Herme**ᶜ, burned alive; at Anvers, an assembly of 400-500 believers	→
1561			Rome; rapping, persecuting, and burning took place; **100+ died**	→
1561			meeting in the woods was broken up by **Le Drossard**; five were taken, four were released, **B. de Hoye**ᶜ (24 years old) was decapitated;	→
1561			J. de Lannoyᶜ lifted up and burned in Tournay	→
1561			June 5, 1561, treaty of the **Duke of Savoy** declared in favor of the "Waldensian"	→
1561			churches of the Piedmont, as they were unable to take their valley (lasted about 1 year)ᶜ	→
1561			9 Oct, **F. van Elstandt**ᵇ Janᵇ, **Hendrick**ᵇ, arrested in Arien for not **Bastiaen**ᵇ, bowing to a statue; **Mariken** 21 Oct, burned alive in **van Meenen**ᵇ,	→
1561			Arien, evening before **Beetken** St. Martin's Day, 12 **van Brugh**ᵇ, and Christians were **Lijntgen**ᵇ assembled for imprisoned in	→
1561			instruction: **A. Brael**ᵇ, Antwerp; burned **L. Hendricks**ᵇ, **Marijn** alive Aug 15 **Amare**ᵇ, **N. Amare**ᵇ, **H. Lisz**ᵇ,	→
1561			**A. de Meulenaer**ᵇ, In Ypres, **A. Keute**ᵇ, ᵇᵇ Flanders: the old **J. Hulle**ᵇ was arrested,	→

COLOR GUIDE YELLOW=Roman Catholic areas; TAN=Bad years for Anabaptists; GOLD=Important events for Catholicism; ORANGE=Catholics "martyred"; RED=Evangelicals martyred; GRAY=Other martyred; Disclaimer: some dates may vary
PINK=Marriage issues; PURPLE=Crusades or massacres; TURQUOISE=Martyrology info; BLUE=Part Protestant areas; AQUA=U.S. Const; LT GREEN=Disputed areas; LIME=Bible issues; GREEN=Major dates. (Page 139)

Thomas P. Johnston — Geographic History — Page 140

Date	Germany-Austria-Scandinavia	Switzerland	France-Alsace	British Isles	Italy, Spain, Low Lands	
1561					interrogated, and burned alive	→
1561					bbb	→
1561						→
1562 Huguenot Churches expelled from towns		1561 Assembly resulted in the 14 articles of the "Edict of January" [1562]c (written to trouble the Reformed churches) stipulating: -No services in any town -No carrying of weapons -No business meetings without presence of a royal delegate -Ministers must give an oath of loyalty before royal official -No preaching against the Mass and other ceremonies of the Church of Rome -Prohibition against unauthorized itinerant preaching [i.e. evangelism] -Prohibition against hiding a fugitive from the law [i.e. travelling evangelist]c	March 1, the **Duke of Guise** and 200 men ransacked the Vaissy church meeting, massacring 50-60c, 250 others stabbed and delimbed →	April 10, the **Cardinal of Guise, archibishop of Sens**, and his priests, led a procession to the place where the Huguenot church had met outside Sens (in obedience to the Edict); finding no one there, they returned to Sens to **murder dozens** and pillage the suspected Huguenots in town	22 May, **T. Watelet**c burned alive in Liege after 4 years of imprisonment;	Council of Trent Continued
1562				19 April, the **Prince of Condé** wrote the Queen Mother to ask her to bring order; apparently with no result [a possible foreshadowing of the St. Bartholomew massacre to come? Who was her confessor?]		In Honscot; 10 Oct **F. Varlut**c and **A. Dayke**c beheaded in **Florentin**c of Cologne hung in St. Nicolas; the the blind **A. Michel**c tortured, strangled, and burned in Tournay.	8 Oct, **C. Elinck**c secretly drowned
1562						15 Aug, **J. de Namur**c placed in a used resin barrel over a fire;	
1562					At Ghent, Flanders, four brethren: **P. van Maldegem**b, **P. van Male**b, **J. Bostijn**b, and **L. Allaerts**b executed.	Tournay; **A. Carron**c chased down in France with **Renaudine de Francville**c, **Renaudine** martyred, **Carron** burned in part while he was praying; **Barbe** and **Jacqueline**	→
1562			The **King of France** was accused of favoritism for the "Edict of January"c		At Ghent, **G. van Dale**b executed.	**de St. Amand**c drowned	→
1562			**Cardinal of Guise** had sought to take		House surrounded in Wervijck at night, arrested and brought to Kortrijck, **J. Strings**b,	At Ghent, Flanders, five women, including	

Year							
1562				part in the Augsburg Confession by dissimulation[c]		P.[b] and J. Potvliet[b] condemned to burn back in Werwijck	three sisters, Vijntgen[b], Goudeken[b], and	→
1562			F. du Calvet forsook his office as the Bishop of	At Rouen, A. Marlorat[c], minister and former Augustinian, N.		H. Eemkens[b], tailor, burned in Utrecht, on the scaffolds he repeated, "This is the	Janneken de Jonkheer[b], also Betgen van Maldegem[b] and	→
1562			Montauban to become a Huguenot Pastor, was married; 10 June arrested, 27	May 7, A. Vaze[c] and Cotton[c], Soccans[c], and the Lord of Mandreville[c] 15 year old nephew[c] decapitated or hung		narrow way!" – the executioner lit a pouch of gunpowder hanging on his breast,	Sijntgen van Gelder[b] executed	→
1562	No right of self-protection, as is provided in the 2nd Amendment of the U.S. Bill of Rights; rather, as in this case in France,		A triumvirate established themselves to exterminate the Reformed churches; Civil War erupted in France, as the Duke of Guise began to massacre Huguenots,	June condemned to be hung, strangled, and goods confiscated, which killed; others killed: J. Garin[c],	Civil war waged by the Duke of Guise continued	and he expired. ←	At Cologne, G. Friesen[b] and W. van Keppel,	→
1562	self-protection from planned genocide was/is considered an act of "Civil War"		Cahors, Carcassone, and elsewhere[c]	took place in Toulouse[c] G. Olivari[c], H. Pastouret[c] and L. Romillet[c]		In Hoschote, Flanders: a young girl named M. Aelmeers[b] burned	George they drowned, Wliiam the released	→
1562	**Execution of Heyndrick Eemkens (1562)**					alive for believers baptism	At Honschote, Flanders: seven persons, K.[b] and	→
1562	"When Heyndrick had ascended the scaffold, he began to speak to the people, saying, 'Good citizens, repent, and believe only the Gospel and not the traditions of men.' "When they led him to the lords, to hear his sentence, he again turned his face to the citizens and said that all the practices observed were only human traditions, and that whoever would not follow them had to be the reproach and offscouring of all men, yea, must suffer death Matt 15:6; 1 Cor 4:13.					In Bruges, Flanders: brother of M., N. van Aelmeers[b], burned alive	P. van der Velde[b], F.[b] and K. de Swarte[b], Jasper[b] the	→
1562	"The sentence having been read, many of the people, who pitied him, and did not want to see him die, went away. But Heyndrick Eemkens fell upon his knees and face, on the scaffold, to pour out his earnest prayer before the Lord. When the executioner saw him fall down, he drew his cloak from his shoulders, and pulled him up by his shirt, so that he could not finish his prayer.					In Kortrijk, Flanders: J. shoemaker, C. de Grendel[b] was arrested, imprisoned for a year, burned alive	shoemaker, C. de Wael[b], and M. Amare[b]: men and unmarried woman	→
1562	"Heyndrick then said to the people, 'Dear citizens, repent, for it is more than time. Live according to God's commandments and the words of the holy Gospel.' And he called again with a loud voice: 'This is the narrow way, and the strait gate'; and named the chapters where it was written, and many other Scriptures having the same bearing. He then stepped of his own accord, with a glad heart, upon the bench where he was to be strangled and burnt, and said again: 'This is the strait gate, press through it; through this pressed men of God, for he that fights steadfastly unto the end shall be saved; of this I have no doubt.' With great courage he put his body						burned alive; two wives drowned	→
1562	and neck to the stake, and said again with a joyful heart: 'Dear citizens, repent; believe the Gospel and not men; for this is the narrow way which the Christian must walk.' The executioner then took a chain, putting it around his body, and fastened a little bag of gunpowder to his neck, so that it hung over his breast. Heyndrick spoke boldly to the very last, but his words could not be understood very well, for the executioner took a cord, laid it around his							→

COLOR GUIDE: YELLOW=Roman Catholic areas; TAN=Bad years for Anabaptists; GOLD=Important events for Catholicism; ORANGE=Catholics "martyred"; RED=Evangelicals martyred; GRAY=Other martyred; Disclaimer: some dates may vary PINK=Marriage issues; PURPLE=Crusades or massacres; TURQUOISE=Martyrology info; BLUE=Part Protestant areas; AQUA=U.S. Const; LT GREEN=Disputed areas; LIME=Bible issues; GREEN=Major dates. (Page 141)

Thomas P. Johnston
Geographic History
Page 142

Date	Germany-Austria-Scandinavia	Switzerland	France-Alsace	British Isles	Italy, Spain, Low Lands
1562	neck, and twisted it tightly. Heyndrick closed his eyes, just as though he had fallen into a swoon, and he was not seen to move any more, save that he cast up his eyes to heaven once more, and then immediately lost consciousness. Thereupon the executioner drew away the bench from under his feet, and seizing a fork, thrust the same into a bundle of straw and held the latter to a pot with fire standing on the scaffold, until it caught fire,				→
1562	whereupon he applied it to the gunpowder. The blaze flashed up to his eyes but did not burn his hair. He lifted up his hands to heaven once more, after which he showed no further sign of life. "Thus did Heyndrick Eemkens offer up his sacrifice, as a valiant witness of the Lord, on the 10th of June, 1562, about between 10 and 11 o'clock A.M."b				→
1563			**Charles IX** promulgated the edict *De pacification* which led to further	In Poland, as the Gospel was bearing fruit under the reign of Sigismond, when his	The **Spanish Inquisition** burned alive many suspects of heresyc →
1563			atrocities by those of **La Saincte Ligue** [The holy league]c	son became king, several heretical teachers ruined within the church, being	At Tournay [Belgium], G. **Cornu**c, elder of a church, strangled →
1563			Rape and murder committed against **Huguenots** in the towns of: Le Maine,	**Stancarus** and an Italian named **Blandrata** (a Socinian like **Servetus**); then	and burned; W. **Oom**c and J. de **Wolf**c drowned in Anvers prison; →
1563			Tours, Chateau de Loir, Vendome, Blois, Bourgogne, Dijon, Languedoc, Provencec	the **Tartars** and **Moscovites** invaded Poland extirminating over 20,000 peoplec	N. de la **Tombe**c and the lame R. du **Mont**c burned alive in Tournay →
1563				At Halewijn, Flanders: 14 apprehended, one did not remain faithful: 6 burned alive in pairs to stakes: J. de **Swarte**b, and his son K.b, P. the shoemakerb, H. **Aerts**b, P.	→
1563				van den **Berg**b, and J.**Maes**b; several days later, K. de **Swarte**, wife of J., her remaining 3 sons, C.b, H.b, and M.b, and also **Herman**b were burned alive; a year	→
1563				later, two women who were arrested at the same time were imprisoned for 1 year, then burned alive: J. **Cabilhaus**b and K. **Steens**b	→
1563				At Ghent, Flanders: D. **Lamberts**b, C. van **Wetteren**b, A. de **Wale**b executed	Arrested at Somerdijk, tried and beheaded at Zierickzee, J. **Jans**b →

Reformed pastor from Paris, **La Roche-Chandieu** wrote, *History of the persecutions and martyrs of the church of Paris*; which was added to Crespin's 1570 edition

1564							
1564 Council of Trent Rendered Binding [on All Christians; and on all humanity]		Calvin (~55 yrs old) died	J. Mutonis[C], former Dominican turned pastor, hung for evangelizing in Provence (4 Feb), without trial	J. de Madoc[C], pastor, arrested in Lorraine, strangled in secret, and thrown into some bushes	Coverdale was named rector of St. Magnus' near the London Bridge	M. Robillard[C] arrested in Tournay, held prisoner 1½ years, burned alive at the marketplace	**Council of Trent** rendered binding upon all Catholics by **Pope Pius IV** (hence it was deemed absolutely binding on all baptized Christians, and theoretically binding on all humanity!); this council required absolute submission to the Pope and to all of Rome's decrees
1564		Crespin published 8th book of his martyrology				Also in Tournay, H. Destailleur[C] and J. Pic[C], arrested with a Geneva book and a letter from Anvers, burned alive at the marketplace	In Flandres, J. Catel[C], having taken his children to Germany, returned and was arrested in Lisle, where he was burned alive over a slow fire
1564						At Anvers, C. Smit[C], former Carmelite, Reformed pastor in Anvers, betrayed by a false seeker, tortured when questioned, a riot occurred at his burning, resulting in his being stabbed by the executioner	The fourth rule of **Pius IV's** *Index* (of prohibited books) stated, "Experience proves that if we allow the indiscriminate reading of the Bible in the vulgar tongue, it leads to temerity [rashness or boldness] among men more for evil than for good"[s]
1564						In Tournay, former Franciscan P. Millet[C], called "Horseman", married, studied as a minister, tormented and burned alive	
1564						At Venice: two Baptists arrested in Capo d'Istria were brought to Venice, F.	Following the decrees of the **Council of Trent** the **Cardinal A. Perrenot** established new bishops as inquisitors in the major cities of the Low Lands
1564	**Jan Gerrits Explained His Torture in a Letter**[b] "Thus, let everyone build up the house with lively stones, that it may become a glorious priesthood, and that they may offer up spiritual sacrifices, acceptable to God by Jesus Christ. 1 Pet 2:5. We may always be of good cheer in the Lord, for His power is so great with those who fear Him, that all death, hell, fire and sword, must yield to Him. All this cannot hinder those who are built upon Christ; for we can do all things through Him who makes us worthy, and through His love everything is overcome, and it casts out fear (1 John 4:18), as I can indeed say; for when I was brought into the king's hall, and stood there almost an hour,						

COLOR GUIDE: YELLOW=Roman Catholic areas; TAN=Bad years for Anabaptists; GOLD=Important events for Catholicism; ORANGE=Catholics "martyred"; RED=Evangelicals martyred; GRAY=Other martyred; Disclaimer: some dates may vary PINK=Marriage issues; PURPLE= Crusades or massacres; TURQUOISE=Martyrology info; BLUE=Part Protestant areas; AQUA=U.S. Const; LT GREEN=Disputed areas; LIME=Bible issues; GREEN=Major dates.

(Page 143)

Thomas P. Johnston
Geographic History
Page 144

Date	Germany-Austria-Scandinavia	Switzerland	France-Alsace	British Isles	Italy, Spain, Low Lands	
1564	before the lords came, and saw how everything was being put to readiness to torture me, I again and again thought in my mind: 'O Lord, unless Thou now succor me, I am utterly lost;' and I prayed Him to give me a mouth to speak to His praise and glory, and to close it against everything tending to blaspheme His holy name and that of my neighbor.				van der Sach[b] and A. Welsch[b], interrogated for 2 years; they were	At Armentiers: D. Kalvaert[b], arrested, brought to Rijssel,
1564	"While I thus spoke and they were getting ready to torture me, I felt neither fear nor apprehension; however, they handled me in a very severe and fierce manner, so that the president said: 'Why will you not tell the truth?' …"				finally drowned in 1564	returned and burned to ashes, thrown in River Leye
1564					At Ghent: S. de Graet[b] and his mother Sijntgen[b], martyred	At Armentiers: P. van Oosthove[b], apostacized once, rearrested, stood firm, strangled and burned
1564					At Ghent: P. van der Meulen[b] arrested and martyred	At Ghent: 4 women arrested: F. Ketels[b] and her mother Leentgen[b],
1564					At Doornick: female Maeyken Boosers[b] arrested and burned alive	and P.[b] and M. van Male[b], all martyred
1564					At Ghent: 2 sisters beheaded for their testimony: P.[b] and M. Maelbouts[b]	At Middelborgh, Zealand: W. Corneliss[b] put to death for the evangelical truth
1564					At The Hague: J. Gerrits[b], arrested and burned alive	At Middelborgh, Zealand: J. Matthijss[b] (he wrote a long letter to his wife
1564						explaining his arrest and imprisonment)
1565 A measure of peace in France,		Farel (~76 yrs old) died	Pierre de la Place wrote, *Commentary on the state of religion and the republic*	W. Allen secretly returned to England, where he conspired against the religious persuasions of	Former Reformed preacher turned inquisitor at Renay in Flanders, Titelman, arrested J. de Cruel[c], one who had at one time recanted, was sentenced to	J. De Grave[c] arrested for suspicion of heresy, and for not baptizing his child at the Catholic church,

1565							was strangled and burned in Flanders death, which he protested; he was beheaded in Renay
1566				[There was a measure of peace for the Reformed churches in France from 1565 to 1566]			**L. de Blekere**c, from Flanders, accused by his wife and mother-in-law, strangled, partially burned, and left hanging; buried by sympathizers who were then arrested	An illiterate man, 70 years old, saved in his later years,
1566								**J. Desreneaux**c, burned alive in Lisle
1566							Four men, **M. Bayart**c, **C. du Flot**c, **J. Datricourt**c, and **N. Tournemine**c, arrested for giving a	Following a request from 200 Bourgeois of the Lowlands, to moderate the law
1566 Spanish Inquisition in Low- lands ended 1566							pamphlet to someone open to the Gospel, burned alive in Lisle	called "Les placards" of the King of Spain, the law was rather
							J. Tuscaenc, 22 years old chose a feast day to enter a Church and take the hoste from the priest and trample it, his hand was cut off, he was burned alive, and his ashes were thrown in the river, at Audenarde	made more severe Agreements signed and **King Philip** put an end of the Spanish inquisition in the Lowlands
1566							**M. Bardelots**c imprisoned and hung in Flanders for preaching where it was not allowed	Further atrocities and sacking took place against the Reformed in Anvers
1567			**M. Tachard**c, minister from Montauban, hung in Toulouse			**Queen Mary** abdicated the throne; Parliament declared "Reformed Church" as the official church in Scotland	Pastors **G. de Bres**c, **P. de la Grange**c, and others arrested after the siege of Valenciennes, hung; when Guy was hung, he fell off the ladder, which led to a	Others martyred in Valenciennes: **M. Herlins**c (father and son), and **J. Mahiev**c, decapitated, as well as **M. de la Haye**c,

(Page 145)

COLOR GUIDE YELLOW=Roman Catholic areas; TAN=Bad years for Anabaptists; GOLD=Important events for Catholicism; RED=Evangelicals martyred; ORANGE=Catholics "martyred"; GRAY=Other martyred; Disclaimer: some dates may vary
PINK=Marriage issues; PURPLE= Crusades or massacres; TURQUOISE=Martyrology info; BLUE=Part Protestant areas; AQUA=U.S. Const; LT GREEN=Disputed areas; LIME=Bible issues; GREEN=Major dates.

Thomas P. Johnston — Geographic History — Page 146

Date	Germany-Austria-Scandinavia	Switzerland	France-Alsace	British Isles	Italy, Spain, Low Lands
1567				"An Act of the **Scottish Parliament** made it compulsory for every house-holder whose income was above a specific sum to buy a copy [of the **Geneva Bible**]"w2	stampede in which many were killed **P. de la Rue**c, and **F. Pattou**c
1567				**J. le Seur**c and **J. Catteu**c, former monks, tortured and hung in Cambray	Four drowned in Venice inquisition: **J. Guirlauda**c, **A.** (former priest)
1567				**Richard Fitz** founded the **Privy Church** as a separatist church in London; he was arrested and died in prisonm4	**N. du Puis**c tortured and hung in Artois under one of the new Bishops — **Ricetto**c, **F. Sega**c, and **F. Spinola**c
1567				**William Bowman** founded a church in Plumber's Hall, London, separating from the **Church of England**;	(Oct 3): in Rome: Martyrdom for heresy of **P. Carnesecchi**
1567				he was arrested and released when he agreed not to observe communion "in anie howse, or any	(former Secretary to **Pope Clement VII** and Apostolic Protonotary)b5
1567				other place, Contrarie to the state of religion nowe by publique authoritie established"m4	
1568				**W. Allen**, who later helped produce the Catholic **Douais-Rheims** version to compete against the **Geneva Bible**, had to flee England for his life for his treasonous designsw2	In Bruxelles: the Duke of Alve showed his new power by hanging Reformed noblemen and church leaders: **G**c. and **T**c. **de Battembourg** (two brothers), **P. Dendelot**c, **P.**
1568					In Bruxelles: Several days later were decapitated two Counts: of **Edmond**c and of **Horne**c, also **J. Le Grain** killed by the sword in Bruxelles
1568				**Archbishop of Canterbury**, **M. Parker** revised the **Great Bible** to compete with the growing	**Wingle**c, **M. Cock**c, **J. Formault**c, and others
1568				popularity of the **Geneva Bible**; hence the **Bishops' Bible** was publishedw2	In civil war of the **Prince of Orange**, several died in Liege for the Gospel: **C. de**

Year									
1568					Bishop Grindall of London complained in a letter to **Henry Bullinger**: "Some London citizens of the lowest order, together with four or five ministers, remarkable neither for their judgment nor learning, have openly separated from us; and sometimes in private homes, sometimes in fields, and occasionally even in ships, they have held their meetings and administered the sacraments. Besides this, they have ordained ministers, elders, and deacons, after their own way"m4	**Lesenne**c (a minister) and **M. Charles**c			
1568									
1568									
1569			**Crespin republished the English Geneva Bible** (privilege of John Bodley, 4 vols dated 1568, 1569, 1560) with the Psalms in typical "Geneva" verse	King's author **P. Hamon**c strangled in Paris	Six bourgeois decapitated by the **Duke of Alve** in Lembourg: decapitated: **H, Huesch**c and **G. Frekin**c; tongues branded, partially burned, and hung outside the city. **F. Nize**c, **T. Tolmont**c, and a third c, and burned alive: **J. van Aken**c; surgeon **M. Guillaume**c decapitated	In Tournay, **M. de Lanoy**c and **J. Le Grean**c burned alive with mouths strapped as do the Spaniards; **G. Touard**c, 80 years old, could not stand when preparing for the burning, was returned to prison		
1569				**N. Croquet**c, **P.**c and **R.**c **de Gastines** (father and son), strangled and hung in Paris				
1569									
1569					Confession regarding believer's baptism by the Anabaptist **J. de Roore**b while in a prison in Flanders	where he was drowned; **J. Sorret**c burned alive; **P. Cottree**lc tongue		
1569						pierced and burned alive		
1570			**Crespin** completed Book 8 of his books, *History of*	**Peace of Saint-Germain-en-Laye** put an end to the		Queen Elizabeth was excommunicated by Rome		
1570			*the True Witnesses to the Truth of the Gospel*	Third War of Religion on 8 August 1570		for favoring Protestantismw2		

COLOR GUIDE: **YELLOW**=Roman Catholic areas; **TAN**=Bad years for Anabaptists; **GOLD**=Important events for Catholicism; **ORANGE**=Catholics "martyred"; **RED**=Evangelicals martyred; **GRAY**=Other martyred; Disclaimer: some dates may vary
PINK=Marriage issues; **PURPLE**= Crusades or massacres; **TURQUOISE**=Martyrology info; **BLUE**=Part Protestant areas; **AQUA**=U.S. Const; **LT GREEN**=Disputed areas; **LIME**=Bible issues; **GREEN**=Major dates. (Page 147)

Thomas P. Johnston

Geographic History

Page 148

Date	Germany-Austria-Scandinavia	Switzerland	France-Alsace	British Isles	Italy, Spain, Low Lands
1571		"Viret dies near Orthez, and is buried at Nerac"v2	The Huguenot, Admiral Gaspard de Coligny, was readmitted into the king's council, Sept 1571		
1571					
1572 St. Bartho-lomew Massacre in Paris	A vow of safe passage was useless to a heretic, as the Catholic leader or ruler was absolved from fealty to a heretical ruler (see 1073, 1207, 1215, 1243, 1415), as well as absolved from all contracts with a heretic (1487)	Crespin died (12 April)	Despite a vow of safe passage for a royal wedding, approx. 100,000 Huguenots killed in Paris and surroundings on St. Bartholomew Day Massacre (24 Aug);	John Knox died (24 Nov)	Pope Gregory XIII minted a medallion in honor of the massacre in France, inscribed *Ugonottorum strages 1572*	J. Wouterss van Kuyck[b] arrested for being rebaptized
1572					[inscribed "Huguenots slaughtered 1572"]	Feb 5, in Delft: M. Janss[b] and J. Hendrickss[b] put to death with fire ↙
1572	Extract of sentence of **Maerten Janss**, corn porter, citizen of this city, and **Jan Hendrickss** of Swartewael, Steersman, put to death with fire:					
1572	"Whereas **Maerten Janss** of Swartewael, corn porter, citizen of the city of Delft, and **Jan Hendrickss** of Swartewael, steersman, prisoners, have confessed, without torture and iron bonds, to belong to the evil and reprobated sect of the Anabaptists, and consequently to have attended various forbidden and improper meetings; and also confess to be rebaptized, and to have withheld the holy sacrament of baptism from some of their infants: that they also hold very evil views concerning the mass, despising and utterly rejecting the holy sacrament of the altar, as also all other sacraments, services and ceremonies of the holy Roman Catholic Church, and, what is worse still persist and					
1572	obstinately adhere, to the aforesaid damned reprobated heresy, without in any wise repenting, or being willing to abandon it, notwithstanding all the good admonitions frequently and at divers times addressed to them by various good spiritual Catholic persons; all of which are enormous, wicked and scandalous matters, which for an example unto others ought not go unpunished; therefore, the judges of the city of Delft, according to the import of the					
1572	decrees issued by his royal majesty, have ordered and do order by these present, the aforesaid **Maerten Janss** and **Jan Hendrickss**, prisoners, to be led upon the scaffold erected in the marketplace of this city, and there to be tied to a stake and burned till death ensues, and their dead bodies then to be brought to the Gallows Hill and there placed at stakes. We furthermore declare all their property confiscated and forfeited for the benefit of his royal					
1572	majesty. We further condemn the aforesaid prisoners to the costs of their imprisonment and the expenses of their execution. Done the fifth of February, A.D. 1572, Delft Style." [Extracted from the first book of criminal sentences, fol. 195, preserved in the archives of the city of Delft, 23rd Aug 1659. Secretary of Delft][b]					

1575	Two thirds of the Czech (**Bohemian Brethren**) joined the **Lutheran Reformation** by accepting in 1575 a confession of faith inspired by the 1530 Augsburg Confession						
1575							
1591							
1591		"The Mennonites came from the areas of Canton Bern and Zurich, Switzerland. They were driven to inaccessible highlands and mountains to escape severe persecution In Switzerland. (for further information, see Mennonite Encyclopedia, Vol. I, under Bern.) Persecution consisted of various forms. Mennonites were either whipped, branded, banished, imprisoned, drowned (reserved for women), or sold as galley slaves. A special prison was erected for the Mennonites in the Emmenthal Valley of Canton Bern, Switzerland, called Trachsewald Castle, in 1591.[6] There were Anabaptist hunters who were paid $2,000 for each Anabaptist preacher, $1,000 for each deacon, $500 for each male, and $250 for each female.[7] **Felix Manz** was the first Anabaptist martyr [in 1527]."b6					
1591							
1591							

COLOR GUIDE   YELLOW=Roman Catholic areas; TAN=Bad years for Anabaptists; GOLD=Important events for Catholicism; ORANGE=Catholics "martyred"; RED=Evangelicals martyred; GRAY=Other martyred;   Disclaimer: some dates may vary
PINK=Marriage issues; PURPLE= Crusades or massacres; TURQUOISE=Martyrology info; BLUE=Part Protestant areas; AQUA=U.S. Const; LT GREEN=Disputed areas; LIME=Bible issues; GREEN=Major dates.   (Page 149)

Geographic History

Table of Notations for Sources

a = J.-H. Merle d'Aubigny, *Histoire de la Réformation du Seizième Siècle*, 4 vols (Paris: Firmin Didot Frères, 1867).

b = Thieleman J. van Braght, *The Bloody Theater or Martyrs Mirror of the Defenseless Christians Who Baptized Only Upon the Confession of Faith, and Who Suffered and Died for the Testimony of Jesus, Their Savior, From the Time of Christ to the Year A.D. 1660*, trans from the Dutch by Joseph Sohm, 2nd English edition (1660; 1837; 1886; Scottdale, PA: Herald Press, 2007).

b2 = E. H. Broadbent, *The Pilgrim Church* (1931; Grand Rapids: Gospel Folio, 1999).

b3 = Lorraine Boettner, *Roman Catholicism*, 5th ed. (Phillipsburg, NJ: Presbyterian and Reformed, 1962).

b4 = Jean-Marc Berthoud, *Calvin en France: Genève et le Déploiement de la Réforme au XVIe Siècle* (Lausanne: L'Age d'Homme, 1999).

b5 = John T. Betts, *A Glance at the Italian Inquisition: A Sketch of Pietro Carnesecchi: His Trial before the Supreme Court of the Papal Inquisition at Rome, and His Martyrdom in 1566* (London: Religious Tract Society, 1885).

b6 = Sandra Smith Bales, "The Swiss Mennonites of Moundridge Kansas," unpublished resource. Bales cited: footnote 6: Martin H. Schrag, *The European History of the Swiss Mennonites from Volhynia* (North Newton, KS: Mennonite Press, 1973), 16; footnote 7: William E, Juhnke, "A Study Guide of the Swiss Mennonites Who Came to Kansas in 1874 (Moundridge, Kansas; Swiss-German Cultural and Historical Assn., Inc., 1974), p. 2.

c = Jean Crespin, *Histoire des vrais tesmoins de la verite de l'evangile, qui de leur sang l'ont signée, depuis Jean Hus iusques autemps present* [*History of the True Witnesses to the Truth of the Gospel, Who with Their Blood Signed, from John Hus to the Present Time*] (Geneva: Crespin, 1570; Liège: Centre nationale de recherches d'histoire religieuse, 1964).

c2 = *Catholic Encyclopedia* (1913); available at: http://en.wikisource.org/wiki/Catholic_Encyclopedia_(1913) (online); accessed: 6 Dec 2011; Internet.

d = Bibliography of Jean Duvernoy (http://jean.duvernoy.free.fr/auteur/biblio_duvernoy_2002.pdf) [inquisitions were only listed in chronology if they had dates associated with them. However, once an inquisitor became established in a particular city, it was generally a perpetual office, whether or not records are extant].

d2 = Georgene Webber Davis, *The Inquisition at Albi, 1299-1300*, from Studies in History, Economics, and Law, No. 538 (New York: Columbia University, 1948).

d3 = Jean Duvernoy, "Les Cathares, les Vaudois, les Béguins," http://jean.duvernoy.free.fr/heresy/cathare.htm; accessed 4 July 2004.

d4 = Jean Duvernoy, *Le Catharisme: La Religion des Cathares* (Toulouse: Privat, 1976).

DS = Le Magistère de l'Église (Heinrich Denzinger et al.), *Symboles et définitions de la foi Catholique*, 38 ed. (Paris: Cerf, 1996); cited as DS with the section number.

f = John Foxe, *The Acts and Monuments of John Foxe*, 4th ed., edited by Josiah Pratt, in 8 vols (London: Religious Tract Society, n.d.).

g = Jean Gonnet and Amedeo Molnar, *Les Vaudois au Moyen Age* (Torino, Italy: Claudiana, 1974).

h = Léon-E. Halkin, "Table alphabétique des noms de personnes et de lieux du martyrologe de Jean Crespin" [Alphabetical table of the names of people and of places in the martyrology of Jean Crespin] (Liège: Centre national de recherches d'histoire religieuse, 1964).

h2 = Léon-E. Halkin, "Hagiography Protestant" [Protestant hagiography], in "Mélanges Paul Peeters, 2", *Analecta Bollandiana* (Bruxelles: Société des Bollandistes, 1950), 68:453-63.

h3 = Léon-E. Halkin, *Initiation à la Critique Historique* [An initiation to historical criticism] (Paris: Armand Colin, 1963).

j = James Hastings, ed., *Encyclopedia of Religion and Ethics* (1928).

l = Daniel Lortsch, *Histoire de la Bible en France* [History of the Bible in France] (Paris: Société biblique, 1910); accessed: 4 March 2005; from: http://www.bibliquest.org/Lortsch/Lortsch-Histoire_Bible_France-2.htm; Internet.

l2 = Henry Charles Lea, *A History of the Inquisition of the Middle Ages*, 3 vols (1887; New York: Russell, 1955).

l3 = Lewis Lupton, *The History of the Geneva Bible* (London: Fauconberg, 1966).

l4 = Kenneth Scott Latourette, *A History of the Expansion of Christianity*, 5 vols (Harper and Row, 1938, 1966; Grand Rapids: Zondervan, 1970).

m = J. C. Wenger, ed., *The Complete Writings of Menno Simons* (Scottdale, PN: Herald Press, 1956, 1984).

m2 = Samuel Morland, *History of the Evangelical Churches of the Valleys of Piedmont* (London, 1658; Gallatin, TN: Church History Research and Archives, 1982).

m3 = *Malleus Maleficarum* (written in 1486 by Dominican Inquisitors Heinrich Kramer and Jacob Sprenger under the German title *Hexenhammer*, was considered affirmed by Innocent VIII's Papal Bull *Summis Desiderantes Affectibus* [9 Dec 1484]); available from: http://www.malleusmaleficarum.org/mm00e.html; accessed: 21 May 2008; Internet.

m4 = H. Leon McBeth, *The Baptist Heritage: Four Centuries of Baptist Witness* (Nashville: Broadman, 1987).

m5 = R. I. Moore, *The Formation of a Persecuting Society* (Malden, MA: Blackwell, 1987, 1990).

m6 = Amedeo Molnar, "Czech Reformation and Mission," in *History's Lessons for Tomorrow's Mission: Milestones in the History of Missionary Thinking* (Geneva: World Student Christian Federation, 1960), 128-36.

m7 = William Monter, "Les exécutés pour hérésie par arrêt du Parlement de Paris (1523-1560)," *Bulletin de la Société de l'Histoire du Protestantisme Français*, 142 (1996).

n = Augustus Neander, *General History of the Christian Religion and Church*. Translated from German by Joseph Torrey. London : George Bell, 1881-1884, 9 vols.

o = Zoé Oldenbourg, "Chronological Table," in *The Massacre of Montségur*, Peter Green, trans (New York: Pantheon, 1962), 390-95; translation of *Le Bucher de Montségur* (Paris: Gallimard, 1959).

o2 = Jean Odol, "L'acte de naissance des échévés Cathares: La charte de niquinta, Saint-Félix, 1167" [the birthing act (or articles of incorporation) of the cathar bishoprics: the chart of Niquinta, Saint Felix, 1167]; from: http://www.couleur-lauragais.fr/pages/journaux/2005/cl69/histoire.html; accessed 21 Sept 2007.

o3 = Jean Odol, *Laurangais: Pays des Cathares et du Pastel* (Nice: Privat, 1995).

p = Franck Puaux, *Histoire de la Réformation Française* [History of the French Reformation], 6 vols (Paris: Michel Lévy, 1859-1862).

r = Matthieu LeLièvre, *Portraits et récits Huguenots* [Huguenot portraits and accounts], premiere série (Toulouse, Société des Livres Religieux, 1903).

r2 = Dennison, James T., Jr., *Reformed Confessions of the 16th and 17th Centuries in English Translation*, volume 1: 1523-1552 (Grand Rapids: Reformation Heritage, 2008).

s = *Histoire du Livre Saint en France* [History of the Holy Book in France], from: http://perso.wanadoo.fr/hlybk/bible/ france.htm; accessed 2 February 2005; Internet.

s2 = Jean Charles Léonard Simonde de Sismondi, *History of the Crusades against the Albigenses*, in the Thirteenth Century (London: Wightman and Cramp, 1826; New York: AMS, 1973).

s3 = Philip Schaff, ed., [*The Schaff-Herzog Encyclopedia of Religious Knowledge*] *A Religious Encyclopedia or Dictionary of Biblical, Historical, Doctrinal, and Practical Theology: Based on the Real-Encyklopädie of Herzog, Plitt, and Hauck*, 3rd Edition, 4 vols (New York: Funk and Wagnalls, 1891).

t = Thomas Armitage, *History of the Baptists*, revised and enlarged (New York: Bryan, Taylor, 1889).

v = Henry C. Vedder, *A Short History of the Baptists* (Philadelphia: American Baptist, 1907, 1926, etc.).

v2 = "Pierre Viret Timeline 1511-1571", available at: http://www.pierreviret.org/timeline.php; accessed 13 Aug 2013; Internet.

w = David Watson, "The Martyrology of Jean Crespin and the Early French Evangelical Movement, 1523-1555," Ph.D. dissertation, University of St. Andrews, 1997.

w2 = Paul D. Wegner, *The Journey from Texts to Translations: The Origin and Development of the Bible*. Grand Rapids: Baker, 1999.

w3 = J. A. Wylie, *The History of Protestantism*. 1878; London: Cassell, 1899.

y = Roy Lutz Winters, *Francis Lambert of Avignon (1487-1530): A Study in Reformation Origins* (Philadelphia: United Lutheran Publication House, 1938).

z = Monique Zerner, ed., *Inventer l'hérésie? Discours polémiques et pouvoirs avant l'inquisition* [Inventing heresy? Polemic discourses and powers before the inquisition], Collection du centre d'études médievales de Nice, vol. 2 (Paris: C.I.D., 1998).

z2 = Monique Zerner, *L'histoire de catharisme en discussion* [The history of Catharism in discussion] (Nice 2001).

www.ingramcontent.com/pod-product-compliance
Lightning Source LLC
Chambersburg PA
CBHW041510220426
43661CB00047B/1525